MW01101459

ROAD TRIP AROUND OZ IN 61 DAYS

DISCOVERING THE TREASURES OF AUSTRALIA

A travelogue by Christian S. Knoll

Join Chris, Susan and Tyler as they travel over 17,000 kilometers around the world's largest island. Explore the home to: the witch of King's Cross, the Law of the Tongue, one of the great wines of the 20th century, the world's largest Cornish Festival, Greg Almighty, Staircase to the Moon, Woolybutt, Vicious-Hairy-Mary, and some of the world's oldest continuous living cultures. During the journey, you will make connections and peel away layers of the onion that is Australia, discovering dark truths, treasures, and the lighter side of this magical place and its enduring people. This family adventure journey takes them and the reader to unexpected places. Enjoy!

Library and Archives Canada

Knoll, Christian S., 1957-

Road Trip Around Oz in 61 Days: Discovering the Treasures of Australia / Christian S. Knoll

Includes bibliographical information

ISBN: 978-1-7750934-2-8

1. Adventure Travel 2. Road Trips 3. Australia Travel 4. Australia Geography 5. Title

DISCLAIMER: The publisher and author do not represent or warrant that the information accessible via this book is legal, complete, or current. It is accurate to the best of the author's knowledge. This information is provided for educational purposes only. References are provided for informational purposes only and do not constitute endorsement of any websites or other sources.

Dedication

"We are all visitors to this time, this place. We are just passing through. Our purpose here is to observe, to learn, to grow, to love... and then we return home."

Indigenous Proverb

This book is dedicated to the People of Australia

We respectfully advise Indigenous and Torres Strait Islander people that this book contains images and writing of deceased Indigenous people.

Smoking Ceremony, Matagarup, Boorloo (Perth) (WA)

Author's Preface

What on earth compelled me to write this book? I do not consider myself an author. It is quite bold of me to expect that people will want to read it. Why then write it? That has been the burning question that got me out of bed in the middle of the night more than once. The first time, was when I came to the realization that although there were some travel and adventure books about Australia, none of them recounted in any detail, the trip that I was planning to undertake. The second time was when I realized that most of those who I told about the journey did not think that it was possible. Even some Australians, looked at me with that don't be daft expression, and said, "That's not possible mate. It'd take you two years to travel around the country". The third and most defining time was in Mount Isa, Queensland. We were into the sixth week of our trip in 2015, when I had an epiphany. The great mythology around the dangers in Australia, largely ignored by many Australians and almost every adventure seeking German backpacker, have been holding back the rest of the world from exploring this unique continent. Fear is a great agent of governments and media. Heighten the Threat Level and keep everyone hunkered down in their homes, glued to their screens, believing the Myth, rather than being in touch with Reality. This book is for those, such as young Daniel in Mount Isa who was so entirely enthralled with our trip and where we came from. With his geography book in hand Daniel uttered, "A land that has lions and bears" as he perused the map of Canada. And then very confidently said, "I'm not afraid of anything!" Fires, floods, cyclones, venomous spiders, snakes, jellyfish, sharks and big arsed crocs, indeed. Fear should never get in the way of a great adventure or a good story. Thank you, Daniel.

Basking saltwater crocodiles
Broome, Kimberley region (WA)

Table of Contents

Planning

"Without Leaps of Imagination, or Dreaming, we lose the Excitement of Possibilities. Dreaming, after all, is a form of Planning."

Gloria Steinem

As a young child in Toronto, apart from forays into Thorncliffe Park and the Don Valley with my sister and friends, my greatest adventures began by spinning my desk globe. Shutting my eyes and running my finger up and down the globe, till it stopped spinning, I then looked to see where my finger landed. I then imagined escaping the confines of my apartment to visit that country. The finger on the globe not only sparked journeys of my imagination, but also trips to different parts of the world, and so it did for this journey to Australia. This time I wanted a big trip and I used the palm of my hand. It came to rest on parts of Asia as well. Originally our Australian adventure was to be part of a much larger Asian tour encompassing China, Japan, Indonesia and New Zealand. During planning I could see that this trip was far different from travelling to Europe. Seeing five countries in five days was not going to happen. China and Japan were good choices because of proximity to our home, near Vancouver. Yet, it was the furthest point, the land down under, where everything seems odd, that drew my attention and had been beckoning for a long time.

As the finger firmly planted on Australia, the next question was where to visit? Go to Sydney and up the east coast as many of our friends had done. Susan has a very dear friend on the West Coast of Australia in Perth. Surely, it should be included in our trip. Asking around with anyone I knew who had travelled to Australia, all had flown to Sydney, and then flown to Brisbane and Cairns to visit the Great Barrier Reef. A few had travelled the route by car or recreational vehicle. I then asked Australians who I knew or met at conferences for recommendations of places to visit in Australia. Most of them were either Sydneysiders or Melbournians. In short order the places to visit and those not to bother visiting became clear as mud. One can only understand the founding of Canberra after going through this process, where neither recommended a visit to each other's city, and especially not to Canberra, the nation's capital. "There's nothing there, Mate!" This was a futile effort, as I slowly clued in, that although many of these Australians had travelled extensively in Europe and America, they had not travelled to other parts of Australia. Or perhaps they were hiding something? Thankfully, these days with the internet, one has access to all kinds of information. Australia has an excellent tourism website www.australia.com . As soon as I viewed the iconic destinations, that are parcelled out in 16 sections I realized, "Wow, we've got to see all of this. Look at how amazing Australia is. Why hasn't anyone from Australia told me about all these different places to visit?" In short order, it became obvious that a trip to see Australia could easily take two to three months and leave lots unseen.

The next dilemma with travelling in Australia, is getting around. Domestic airfare in Australia is relatively inexpensive. It starts to add up, as you count all the cities you want to see and the parts in between. The longer I stared at the map of Australia, the island continent, the more I thought, "I wonder if we can travel around the whole island?" Australia has a network of highways that make up the National Highway #1 that circumnavigates the entire continent. The total length of the highway is 14,500 kilometers, making it the longest national highway in the World. The national highway was cobbled together from existing state roads and effectively leads to the major cities and countless other important port cities and smaller towns throughout Australia. Well, why not a road trip? I have many fond memories of traveling across Canada, the US and Europe by automobile in my youth, and later with a young family. How difficult could a road trip around Australia be? Around Australia on Hwy 1 by George Farwell 1911 – 1976 that is listed as available in sixteen libraries in Australia, was far more difficult to order online than I first thought. I never did obtain a copy. I read a few unfinished travel blogs and heard from one Australian, who thought she knew of someone who might have made the trip. As I planned our journey, I sensed that it might be more unusual than the routine tourist vacation. I expressed my interest in the trip to a few friends, and many thought that it was not possible to go completely around Australia as the road conditions probably do not allow for that.

My father, sister and I used to kayak in some remote locations in Northern Ontario for weeks at a time. If there is anything I ever learned from my Dad, it was to plan and be prepared. No sooner was Dad home from one trip, and have all the gear cleaned up, that he already started planning the next kayak trip. My father ordered topographic maps and pored over those for months planning the route, determining exactly how long each leg of a trip took. He made sure that enough supplies and food fit into the boats to keep us alive and took care of every detail right up until departure day. I needed to be as diligent for this journey, as my father was for those camping trips. The online maps of Australia show that there are roads however, give no indication if the roads are paved or subject to flooding. The other issue is the distance between towns and fuel. The internet maps are poor for determining fuel and rest stops, so we invest in an Australia Touring Atlas for more details on road surfaces and services. After a long, careful look it appears that the roads will be drivable and that there will be adequate services for fuel, if not a place to sleep. There will be many days of travel between towns that are several hundred kilometers apart where no services of any kind will be available. (1)

The Northern Hemisphere refers to that half of the planet that is north of the equator, and the Southern Hemisphere refers to that half of the planet that is south of the equator. There are some significant differences between these two hemispheres. The seasons are opposite: when it is summer in the Northern Hemisphere it is winter in the Southern Hemisphere. 90% of the planet's population lives in the Northern Hemisphere on 68% of the planet's land mass. Combustion and the resulting pollution is higher in the Northern Hemisphere. The Polar Regions in the Southern Hemisphere are colder than the Polar Regions in the Northern Hemisphere. Hurricanes and tropical storms rotate in a counter clockwise rotation as does water going down a drain in the Southern Hemisphere, and these rotate clockwise in the Northern Hemisphere. (2) Australia is squarely in the Southern Hemisphere some 13,500 kilometers south west from Vancouver, Canada. It is 3,400 kilometers north of Antarctica at its most southerly point, and a mere 1,400 kilometers south of the equator at its most northern point. Australia is subject to strong winter storms and cold weather from Antarctica, and blistering heat and killer cyclones from the equator in summer months causing large scale fires or flooding, depending on your luck. I took the potential for flooded roads very seriously. I'm glad I did, as Highway 1 could also be called Floodway 1, based on the thousands of floodway signs encountered along its entire route.

The timing of our travel is important for a safe and enjoyable trip. Travel either in the Australian spring or fall is optimal for us. Our choice is the

Australian fall (our Canadian spring), as the average temperature is cool in the south and moderate in the north. Australian fall is also good for avoiding much of the rain associated with cyclones, and most of the mosquitoes, flies, snakes and jellyfish. At this point in planning it was already late April, and we concluded that it was best to delay our trip by a year. We had realized our travel would be during April, May or June if our son was joining the trip during his university semester break, and more planning was required for a safe and amazing journey.

Our first notion was to travel by recreational vehicle (RV), thinking it more economical and the best way to travel though Australia especially when in the more remote locations. I began investigating the different options available from the larger RV rental companies. An air-conditioned vehicle for our purposes, plus mileage charges, plus additional insurance required to cover the vehicle (that still had coverage exceptions), plus the cost of camp sites was adding up. When compared with the cost of a rental car and hotel rooms and considering our visits to numerous cities where RV travel and parking is awkward, the latter seemed to make more sense. At this point, I had not even considered that we had never driven a RV, nor on the other side of the road than we are used to and had no idea of the road conditions. Next, I investigated car rental, insurance and mileage policies to confirm whether those were an improvement. I then confirmed the availability of hotel accommodation in the more remote locations of Australia within reasonable driving distances. Car rental is generally more expensive in Australia than in North America. The car rental including mileage and full coverage insurance was more reasonable, yet only if you rented from a major airport location. So, an automobile was our ultimate choice for road travel around Australia. I imagine that the Australians reading this story are already grimacing and thinking, "He's out of his bloody mind!"

TIP:

If you plan to camp in more remote Outback National Parks, it is highly advisable that you rent a good four-wheel drive Ute with a snorkel and tow a rugged camping trailer as many of the off-track roads will destroy a conventional recreational vehicle.

With our Australia Touring Atlas in hand, I began mapping out our road trip. Should we drive clockwise or counter-clockwise around the continent? As our arrival will be in late April or early May, winter will begin setting in. As over time the average temperature will become uncomfortably cold in the south and more comfortable in the north, our decision is to land in Sydney and travel clockwise around the continent, primarily along the coast of Australia on Hwy 1, with a few deviations inland. I plotted our trip out to the major city centres, and to attractions along the way discovered during planning. I received advice that it was unsafe to drive at night because of the high chance of colliding with a variety of animals. There will only be ten hours of daylight each day during our journey. I must make sure that we can travel a good distance, and still have time to see the things of interest to us. The challenge will be to complete the journey comfortably within the three-month restriction on our travel visa.

TIP:

Electronic travel authorizations (ETAs) are required prior to travel to Australia unless you are from New Zealand or Australia. You can apply for these online at https://www.eta.immi.gov.au/ETAS3/etas (cost $20.00 AUS) at the time. ETAs are good for one year from the time you are approved, for 3 months of travel at a time. Approvals are usually rapid so long as your documents and payment are in order. Other forms of visas (such as student or temporary work) are available. Approval periods vary and may take months, so it is best to apply well in advance of your trip.

As a young bachelor, I had no problem throwing caution to the wind, travelling from town to town in whatever direction looked interesting at the time. Yet, when travelling with a family it is best to ensure that you have a place to stay, food to eat, something to do and if possible Wi-Fi. I put together a travel planner that detailed our planned destinations, the estimated distances and travel times. The planner included two or three potential places to stay in each town, the tentative nights of stay, two or three places to dine, things to do along the way or on arrival, historical average temperature and rainfall. Once that was prepared, a sales pitch to the family got them to sign off on the madness and ensure that something of interest to them was not missed.

Although the preparation seems to be overkill, it isn't, if you want to get the most out of such an extensive trip, without having to do all the planning while underway. It was simple to get started on the task, and after planning forty visits to different destinations in Australia, a year had gone by. I had just completed booking hotels; had a good idea about what to wear, the likelihood of which roads will be drivable, and the points of interest to us along the way. Just as the Boy Scouts, Be Prepared!

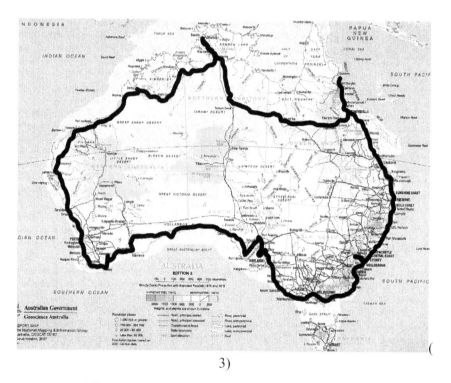

3)

The Route: Starts and finishes in Sydney (NSW)
17,780 kilometers clockwise around Australia

And so, the Journey Begins

We shall not cease from exploration
And the end of all our exploring
Will be to arrive where we started
And know the place for the first time.

T.S. Elliot

Sunday May 3: Vancouver, Canada, Day of departure Sunny 20°C

Although beginning many journeys with some anxiety, none compare to the anxiety and anticipation over the journey that we are about to embark on. I have checked and double checked our plans. Only two weeks ago, I read the fine print in our car rental agreement and discovered that the agency I hired from, will not allow the vehicle to travel in Western Australia or Northern Territory. I scramble reading through the fine print on half a dozen different rental car company agreements, until I find an agency that accommodates our trip as planned. Price be damned, I book it!

TIP:

Read the fine print agreement when renting a car or recreational vehicle in Australia, especially regarding travel restrictions and damage waivers.

The big question on everyone's mind. Why Australia and why for so long? It will be expensive. I have no answers just the need to go and see for myself. It is compelling, and it is going to happen just as imagined, or maybe not. The trip better work out as planned. Our rolling backpacks, previously used for our trip throughout Europe for a month one summer, are packed with clothing for both summer and fall weather conditions. I am pleased that we are managing to travel with a minimum of luggage. A taxi picks us up at seven pm and attempts to drop us off at the Greyhound bus station instead of the Sky Train station. Taking public transport to the airport, no sooner are we on the Sky Train, when the public-address system advises us that the train will not be able to get us to the airport, because of a malfunctioning switch. The train drops us off at a station with no cab stand, and our frantic search for some form of transportation to the airport begins. Things are going well wouldn't you say? And these tourists are heading into the Outback of Australia for a couple of months?

Eventually we flag down a cab on the street. After having worked up a sweat, lugging our luggage down the street, we cool down in the cab and relax, hoping that there will be no other hiccups. Checking in three hours in advance of our flight goes uncharacteristically smooth and security is a breeze as well. Hurry up and wait. Our flight with Air Canada is 15½ hours direct from Vancouver to Sydney Australia, Air Canada's longest non-stop flight. Just before leaving one of the Air Canada ground attendants (Suzanna) shouts out to me, "Hey neighbour!" and comes over to talk to us. I had never met her before in my life. She lives in our neighbourhood and sees my son Tyler, and I walking all the time. The chance encounter serves to remind us, that as big as the world is, it is still a small world. We are feeling at ease and looking forward to the long trip ahead.

The flight is very long and uneventful. If we had $24,000.00 to spare, the first-class sleeper seats are the ideal way to fly. Paying a little extra for emergency aisle seating, helped with leg room and comfort, although we are feeling somewhat guilty for taking these. There is a score of tall and brawny men on the plane, possibly cops or firefighters, flying home from a conference. Standing throughout most of the flight, they are clearly uncomfortable in their assigned seats. It will be our experience throughout our journey, to see many tall Australians. Must be from good stock or it is something in their water?

Otherwise our Boeing 777 is comfortable and between naps and the occasional movie the flight goes by quickly. The meals are typical for airline food. If starving one might consider eating them. Tyler, my lean and always hungry teenager skips the meal. Before landing, a very helpful flight attendant gives us helpful hints about dealing with jet lag and things to see while we are in Sydney. Her "Must dos" include the Botanical Garden, the Opera House and the afternoon tea tour in Sydney Harbour with the Captain Cook line, going to the Blue Mountains and the Hunter Valley. To avoid jet lag, the flight attendant advises us to carry on through the day, eat early, get to sleep early and then just have a normal day the following day. She also suggests that when we get back to Vancouver, to go home, sleep for four hours and then wake up to carry on through the day. Thank you, the advice was very helpful!

Australia

Area: 7,741, 220 km². Population: 24 million. Established as an independent state on January 1ˢᵗ, 1901.

The original inhabitants are Aboriginal Australians and Torres Strait Islanders. Australian society is diverse and after Canada, Australia is the second country in the world to adopt multiculturalism as an official policy. Most Australians descend from the people of the British Isles, with 25% of Australians descended from British convicts. The top ten largest immigrant populations in descending order have come from the UK, New Zealand, China, India, Philippines, Vietnam, Italy, South Africa, Malaysia and Germany. (4) Australia is a democracy and all Australians over the age of eighteen must vote in both federal and state elections. As a member of the Commonwealth, the Government structure is as Canada's, a constitutional monarchy. The head of state of the day is Her Majesty Queen Elizabeth II. The Prime Minister of the day is Tony Abbot, head of the Liberal Party, a classical liberal and conservative party. His and his party's policies mirror that of the Prime Minister of Canada of the day, Stephen Harper leader of the Conservative Party of Canada. Other parties in Australia include the Labor Party that is a center right de-facto socialist party, a center left Green Party and a collection of other minor parties, many that are conservative in outlook.

The world's sixth largest country in area, Australia is rich in agriculture, mineral and energy resources including natural gas, coal, gold, and iron ore. Australia's economy is primarily based on exports of these natural resources, with coal making up 29% of total global coal exports, making it the world's largest coal exporter. Most of these natural resources are shipped to Asia, with Australia's three largest trading partners being China, South Korea, and Japan. The climate of Australia is diverse with a tropical north, a temperate south and east, with the west and center being semi-arid or arid. Aside from a few mountain ranges and tropical rainforests in the north, overall the terrain is mainly flat ranging from desert to fertile plains. Australia consists of six states: Queensland, New South Wales, Victoria, South Australia, Western Australia, and Tasmania; and two territories: Australian Capital Territory and Northern Territory. Alongside these are a collection of external territories, most that are unpopulated.

The Indigenous population of Australia originally consisted of up to one million persons in more than 500 different nations. Colonialism destroyed many of these language/tribal groups, with most going extinct. The 110 surviving Australian Indigenous languages are largely in danger of being lost. In Tasmania, the full blooded Indigenous population was pushed to extinction, with mixed-race people known as Palawa, being the only survivors of Tasmania's Indigenous heritage. Indigenous culture in Australia, although widely varying is classified into two distinct groupings: Aboriginal Australians and Torres Strait Islanders. Indigenous Australians are custodians of one of the oldest continuous living civilizations in the world, dating back over 60,000 years. It is unknown who Aboriginal Australians descend from, although it is believed that there may be a connection to the Dravidians of Southern India owing to similar physical and cultural characteristics. Torres Strait Islanders are a Melanesian people more closely related to the people of Papua New Guinea and Vanuatu. (5) (6)

Indigenous culture in Australia is structured into family groups or tribes. Tribal leadership is assigned to a council of elders who as judges, are given the sole right to interpret and make decisions on matters of law and custom. Elders are also the sole transmitters of the oral history and religion of Indigenous people. Because of that and hostile relations between whites and Indigenous people, there is only slim knowledge of Indigenous history and how the various people in Australia came to arrive on the continent. As our Rough Guides travel guide puts it, "there's a long way to go before black and white are truly on equal terms in Australia". (7) Despite a bloody history, most Australians are friendly and helpful, and once you get to know them, you are charmed by their eccentric, yet fun personalities. Overall the Australian continent is a mysterious, exciting, and at times challenging landscape inhabited by some of the most fascinating flora, fauna, and people to grace the Earth.

New South Wales (NSW)

Area: 809,444 km². Population: 7,500,600. Established as a Colony on January 26, 1788.

The first state of Australia, New South Wales (NSW) is the birthplace of Australia as we know it today. Many Indigenous peoples including the Eora of the Sydney area and the Bundjalung people of the northern coasts inhabited NSW before Europeans arrived. The discovery of NSW was first made by Captain James Cook when he observed the coastline from his ship in 1770. British settlement began with the First Fleet including convicts led by Captain Arthur Philip. The promise of a better life turned out to be false, as disease and other issues hampered the colony at Botany Bay. Chaos and poor management under Governor William Bligh (famous for the Mutiny on the Bounty) led to his overthrow. Eventually order was restored by Lieutenant Colonel Lachlan Macquarie who reformed the colony and gave convicts more rights and the opportunity to reform their lives and become freemen. Under his rule New South Wales moved from being a penal colony to a free settlement.

As the move towards federation of Australia began, a rivalry between Victoria and NSW developed as both states desired that their own capitals, Melbourne and Sydney, become the Australian capital. To end the long feud, it was decided that a new capital city be developed in modern day Canberra in Australian Capital Territory (ACT). Over time New South Wales developed as a center of industry with Sydney itself experiencing enormous growth after the 2000 Summer Olympics. NSW's most famous area is its legendary coastal strip that can be cool and temperate on its southernmost point yet subtropical in the north of the state near the Queensland border. There are the mountainous areas of the Great Dividing Range including the highest mountain in all of Australia, Mount Kosciuszko in the Snowy Mountains. Agricultural plains cover more ground than the other populated regions, and the sparsely populated Western plains make up two thirds of the state's area.

As the country's first state, NSW is home to some of Australia's most important cultural institutions including the Museum of Contemporary Art in Sydney, the Sydney Symphony Orchestra, the Australian Museum, and the famous Sydney Opera House. Sydney is the home of NSW's vibrant culture. A harbor town turned vibrant cosmopolitan metropolis, Sydney is one of the world's major financial and cultural centers. The city is known for its hot summers and mild winters, and for having the largest natural harbor in the world. Sydney's beaches such as Bondi are legendary. Although Melbourne has a cemented reputation as a multicultural city, Sydney proves itself as a noteworthy rival. With large Chinese, Lebanese, Greek, and Indian communities, Sydney is home to a large variety of ethnic foods that are excellent and exquisite. Outside of Sydney are towns including the Hunter River Valley coal exporting harbor of Newcastle, and the seaside town of Wollongong in the Illawarra region. New South Wales is a perfect starting point for any Australian journey and as an introductory state to those unfamiliar with the Australian lifestyle and culture. (8)

The Three Sisters and the Jamison Valley (NSW)

Sydney (NSW)

Area: 12,145km². Population: 4.3 million. Founded on January 26, 1788. Traditional Lands of the Eora People consisting of 29 family groups. The first European colony founded in Australia. A convict colony that still carries the name of "Sin City". Capital of NSW and home headquarters to sixty percent of Australia's top 100 companies. Generates 25% of Australia's total economic activity through finance, manufacturing and Sydney sea port. A notable person born in Sydney is actor Hugh Jackman. Most known for and a Must-See attraction is the Sydney Opera house.

Tuesday, May 5. Sunny 20°C

Our flight arrives in Sydney at 8:30am. During our trip to Australia an entire day has been lost. We are assured not to fret, as the day will be returned to us on our journey home. Being a day ahead of everyone else back home is a strange, yet empowering sensation, as though we have gained an advantage. Our first surprise on arrival in Australia, is the mandatory spray down with a pesticide inside the aircraft for five minutes.

YOU SHOULD KNOW:

Australia is very conscious of foreign pathogens and insects. Disinsection is somewhat controversial as some see the chemical procedure as invasive however, passengers have no choice other than being returned home. Air operators are obligated to inform employees and passengers that disinsection will take place. (9) The message is delivered, just before the entire cabin is sprayed via the air system. Pyrethrins are used as disinsecting agents. Although usually made by industrial means, Pyrethrins are naturally occurring in the Chrysanthemum flower and were derived from these in China, as early as 1000 BC. Pyrethrins are very effective in targeting insects yet are relatively harmless to mammals. Australia has rich and diverse agriculture, and the insecticide plays an important role in protecting it.

We grin and bear it and are all too happy to get off the plane and join the line ups to get through customs. Customs clearance goes very smoothly as does the rental car pickup, although the desk agent wants to save us money by changing the contract. There is only one minor hitch in that change. We will lose the unlimited mileage option which will cost us much more in the long run on the trip around Australia. Fortunately, I am not too tired to let that slip by, and I ask the agent to just print the contract as it was originally booked online.

TIP:

When renting a vehicle in Australia ensure that it has an E-Toll Tag installed. These devices debit your credit card instantly for any toll roads and save you time, aggravation and money in dealing with toll payments and administrative fines for late payments. The one tag serves toll roads in all states.

Figuring out right hand steering and left-hand driving in our Toyota sedan is more challenging than I had imagined. Thankfully, I am not driving a full sized Recreational Vehicle (RV). It is a real challenge cutting corners and staying in my lane during morning rush hour traffic into the city centre. Susan has a look of terror on her face the whole time and keeps reminding me that I am about to scrape the left side of the car into walls or other vehicles. I am constantly hitting the windshield wiper selector instead of the turn signals, adding to the chaos. We make it to the hotel and are happy to park the vehicle for a few days, not at all sure, about driving it again. So far, we have driven about twenty kilometers with only 17,000 kilometers more to go. It is not looking that promising. Fortunately, our hotel is well situated in Potts Point near Kings Cross. The harbour bridge, opera house, botanical garden and many restaurants are all within walking distance and transit is nearby. The hotel can accommodate our early check-in. So, things are looking up.

Our room has a great view, and despite the temptation to lie down and fall asleep we head off to lunch as Tyler who did not eat dinner or breakfast on the plane, is now absolutely famished. Wandering through the local neighbourhood to get our bearings, we eventually find our way to the Botanical Gardens and harbour. The temperature is very comfortable. Obvious to us almost instantly are the exotic sounds and sights of Australia's birdlife, be it the magpies, or a great variety of small songbirds, lorikeets, parrots and cockatoos. There is no doubt. We have arrived down under, in the land called Oz.

View of the Botanical Garden, the Harbour Bridge and the Opera House
Sydney (NSW)

Enjoying a very satisfying lunch at an Italian restaurant down near the naval base, we watch the sailors and ships of the Royal Australian Navy, whose funnels are tattooed with the red kangaroo emblem. Following lunch, we walk over to the Botanical Gardens and are accosted by sulphur crested cockatoos. This is a marvelous introduction to Australian wildlife. Some of the creatures here are apparently not shy at all about meeting you face to face. The cockatoos are extremely loud, screeching and brashly swooping down out of the trees just over our heads. If you happen to have some food in your hands, well then, you become a landing station, and all which that entails including tousled hair and shattered ear drums. While wandering through the gardens admiring the large Fig trees and Palms we take pictures along the ocean-carved sandstone shoreline opposite the Opera House and then stroll over to the Opera House. The Opera House is a design marvel and is one of the world's unique architectural structures.

The Sydney Opera House is one of the world's most identifiable buildings, and the performing arts center is an icon of both Sydney and Australia. The opera house located on Bennelong Point in Sydney Harbor, is overlooked by the world-famous Sydney Harbor Bridge.

Construction of the Opera House was inspired in the late 1940s, when Sir Eugene Goossens, the Director of the NSW State Conservatorium of Music, lobbied for an appropriate venue for large-scale productions. Sir Goossens successfully insisted on making Bennelong point the sight of construction. He however, would not see its construction, as Sir Goossens left Australia in disgrace after being charged by police with scandalous conduct for his pornographic relationship with the Witch of Kings Cross, Rosaleen Norton. (10)

After a design contest with 220 final entries, it was decided in 1957, that Danish architect Jorn Utzon's famous design would be used. The NSW government and the design team had tense relations during design and construction. The government demanded continual revisions, unhappy with the costs and work involved in the construction of the building. The government only furthered tensions by demanding an early start to construction, even though the design team had not fully completed the design yet. Much of the delay involved the complexity of constructing the large sculpted roof shells and their vaulted concrete ribs that were precast and held together by steel tendons. The innovation along with the meticulous care that went into creating and manufacturing the over one million glazed ceramic tiles that cover the roof were genius however, added to the cost and time delays.

Once the Liberal Party came to power in NSW, there was even more criticism as the leader of the party of the day Sir Robert Askin, had been a vocal critic before the construction of the Opera House had even been approved. The new Minister of Public Works Sir Davis Hughes also directed a lot of animosity towards Utzon and refused to pay him, causing Utzon to resign. Despite petitions and protests by leading Australian architects Utzon was not rehired to finish the interior of the building. The government appointed new architects, Hall Todd and Littlemore who blew the budget out even more, from $18.4 million to a total cost of $102 million.

Despite its tempestuous origin and history of conflict, the spectacular building was finally completed and formally opened by Queen Elizabeth II on October 20, 1973. Although many believe the building to be a single venue as we did, this is a misconception. The building contains multiple performance venues making it one of the busiest performance art venues in the world with 3,000 events attended each year by two million persons. The four primary resident companies are: Opera Australia, The Australian Ballet, Sydney Theatre Company, and Sydney Symphony Orchestra. As one of the world's top fifty tourist attractions, the Opera House receives more than eight million visitors a year, with 300,000 persons annually participating in its guided tours. On June 28, 2007, the Opera House became a UNESCO World Heritage Site. (11)

Viewing the Opera House with sailboats in Sydney Harbour as a backdrop, its true inspiration is undeniable. The Opera House up close is much more immense than one thinks. From a height and distance, it becomes clear that it is several venues. Close-up pictures reveal the detail and intricate pattern of the medium-sheen soft white ceramic tiles that reflect both artificial and sun light so well. After taking several pictures, we make our way into the central business district and then walk back to our hotel via a long and convoluted path. We are beginning to crash from jet lag and are getting cranky. We eat a quick meal in the hotel and head up to our room and pass out in our beds.

Wednesday, May 6. Sunny 24°C

After a good night's sleep, I decide that I am going to keep a journal and make my first entry of the prior day's activities. We enjoy a perfect little breakfast at Libraries, a coffee-shop whose walls are lined with bookcases in bohemian Potts Point, a beautiful and relaxing breakfast spot. We then walk to the Botanical Gardens viewing the various gardens and art displays. One of the textile artists asks us about our home and our plans while in Australia. Although she is somewhat dubious about our making it around Australia in our planned time frame, the artist does recommend investing in some cans of tire puncture repair sealant. A little later another artist asks about our visit and is even more blunt, "There's no way you'll make it around Australia – that'd take at least three years". Hmm! Some doubts are forming in my mind, and we still have not driven more than twenty kilometers.

Sulphur Crested Cockatoo dining on Cypress nuts, Botanical Garden
Sydney (NSW)

From the Botanical Garden, we saunter through one of the older Sydney districts known as "the Rocks" and climb our way up along the stairways to the Harbour Bridge and walk out to mid-span, taking some great pictures of Sydney Harbour, the city itself and of course the Opera House. Being quite high enough for our liking, there is also the option of climbing to the top of the support towers. For real adventure and $158.00 to $363.00 depending on the time of day, one may climb to the very top of the bridge arch. The weather is sunny for great viewing and quite windy. We forgo the bridge arch walk. Some might call us chicken. Not so. We just have other plans for the day.

Returning down to the harbour, we stop in at the Museum of Contemporary Art and take an hour to view some of the great Indigenous Art in their collection. A young Australian guide shows us a pole with an intricate dot and line painting of a celestial map on it. The guide tells us that she learned nothing about Indigenous people while going to school in Australia and says what a shame that so much culture has been lost. I feel the same way, as my generation learned very little about the First Nation Canadians except in their service to the French and the British colonists. There is a story here, just below the surface, that does not require any real digging. With a long journey ahead of us there will be much to discover.

We have booked tickets for this afternoon, and board the Captain Cook coffee cruise around Sydney Harbour, the largest natural harbour in the world. It is a lovely afternoon, not too cool, so long as you stay out of the wind. The tour takes us past the naval yard, homes of the rich and famous, scenic Taronga zoo, and a sailing yacht race. Sydney Harbour is a bustling port that serves cruise ships, the navy, container ships, bulk ships and tankers alike, and yet boasts 600 species of fish in the harbour. It is also home to 19 of the top 25 wealthiest neighbourhoods in Australia and many of the homes with their large plate glass windows remind us of the humble coastal properties in West Vancouver. The onboard coffee and snacks are tasty, and our tour guide knows her stuff, though most of it goes in one of my ears and out the other. I am jet-lagged. We chat with a gentleman who snaps a photo for us. He owns properties in Los Angeles and Sydney and splits his time between both cities. While Susan is busy chatting with him, I keep wondering: "What's he doing on the Captain Cook Coffee Cruise? CIA, con-artist, maybe he is Captain Cook? Whatever!". The gentleman is nice enough to share some insights and tips with us. His impression is that Sydney is a young LA. LA is dying a slow death regarding energy and water supply. He feels Sydney will be in the same position unless it prepares properly. He tells us about the bizarre hail storm that happened in Sydney prior to our arrival in late April. It knocked out power and collapsed some local warehouses.

As our tour finishes near the opera house and harbor bridge all of us are knackered. To top it off, we have not learned a thing from our experience the previous day, and suffer through another long, frustrating walk home, accentuated by jet lag. It is decided to avoid this in the future, as transit is right next to our hotel and it is time to start using it. After a short rest, we set out for a beautiful dinner at Bay Bau Vietnamese restaurant. The family run dining spot, that comes highly rated, has a great crispy duck that is delicious. We are in the Bohemian part of town with a mix of everything from upscale boutiques and restaurants to massage parlours and strip clubs. My stereotypical view of the Australian white male has been shattered. Gay pride is high in the neighbourhood and Australia is indeed diverse.

The high fashion in Sydney was pointed out by our flight attendant and it truly is intriguing and noticeable. Expensive loose fitting casual wraps. Women commonly wear dresses to the office, accessorized with expensive and stylish shoes. It is obvious that people dress for success in Sydney which is very different from our dressed down casual look in Vancouver. Our first impressions of the people, is that they are very friendly and willing to help when asked. Australians are also down to earth. They seem to be good at quips, sarcastic comments to someone else quietly, yet just loud enough to be heard, whether it is a racist comment about a passerby, or a pimp intimidating his girl in public.

Thursday, May 7. Sunny 22°C

Another beautiful day. Prince Harry will be making a public appearance at the Sydney Opera House and we are headed in the opposite direction to Bondi Beach. As it turns out, Harry enjoyed Bondi earlier in the morning. Our goal today is to hike from Bondi to Coogee Beach and take in the sights. The public transit taking us seven kilometers to Bondi Beach is clean and efficient. One train ride and a single bus connection from our hotel and we arrive in 45 minutes. Seeing it, we now understand why the one-kilometer strip of beach known as Bondi is world famous, attracting two million visitors annually. The sand is pristine and the aquamarine water crashing into the beach is mesmerising. The street side reminds me of Venice Beach with its American surfer kitsch catering to the young, free and cashless. The strip contains all the essentials McDonalds, Hungry Jack better known in America as Burger King, lots of little bars, cafes and board shops.

At the beginning of our hike today Susan requires assistance from the famous Bondi lifeguards. Susan wittingly wears shoes that cause blisters on her feet, just so she can be surrounded by some brawny Australian lifesavers and get some special attention. These lifeguards play a critical role in keeping the beach safe and have been known to save as many as 300 persons in one day, as on "Black Sunday" in 1938 when 35,000 persons were on the beach and three rogue waves rolled in sweeping hundreds of persons out to sea. (12) One plaster later and Susan is good to go.

World-famous Bondi Beach, Sydney (NSW)

The half day walk to Coogee Beach along the cliff side of the South Pacific Ocean is just breathtaking. There is a lot to take in, aside from the many avid surfers. The hike is very popular, and the path takes us past many unusual formations carved into the sandstone cliffs by the sea. There are numerous beautiful homes along the way, and a cemetery with a view to die for. There is an abundance of beautiful plants and flowers, some just clinging to life from the bare sandstone. Along the way we see some unusual sights for us, that are probably just a typical day in Australia. A man is swimming by himself, a good hundred metres offshore, well out of bounds from any shark-net protected beach. The guy must eat sharks for breakfast. Another is tempting the waves crashing against the rocks while rock fishing, completely untethered. At any moment we expect to see him sucked into the sea, until all of us tire of watching the nonsense, and continue with our hike.

The crystal-clear emerald waters are a transparent canvass over a crustacean painted rock backdrop, amidst the swirling seafoam from waves crashing on shore. It is simply a magical day. We take pause and some pictures at the Bali bombing memorial at Coogee, that commemorates the 202 lives lost in 2002, to a terrorist bomber, 88 of whom were Australians. At Coogee, we eventually locate a bus line that takes us relatively close to Kings Cross and then walk the rest of the way back to our hotel. This evening's dinner is Japanese at Oshinuri with sushi rolls for the boys. It is the first time that Ty tries eel in the big dragon roll, while Susan enjoys the tempura. It is another great meal from a highly-rated restaurant that is relatively inexpensive, for Australia. Our plan is to take advantage of ethnic food restaurants, when and where available.

YOU SHOULD KNOW:

If you are coming from the North America prepare yourself for sticker shock when dining out in Australia. Although there is typically no tipping in Australia, there are few mid-range priced dining experiences when compared to North America. It is either Hungry Jacks, or you are paying for a meal often costing as much as, or more than your hotel room. The Canadian dollar was on par with the Australian dollar at the time. One may equate most meal pricing in Australia with that in Western Europe. Australia is one of two countries in the world, where the minimum fair living wage ($16.78 in 2015) is determined by an industrial relations tribunal.

TIP:

Groceries are relatively reasonable, if not less expensive compared to home. Preparing your own meals is a very desirable option, especially on a long trip, so plan for accommodation with kitchens. Many restaurants in Australia are BYOB, and some that are noted as such will not have any liquor for sale. You may bring your own wine and pay a corkage fee that is usually reasonable.

Fri May 8. Sunny 18°C

After our taste of Sydney, leaving is sad. Nonetheless, all of us are excited about the road trip ahead, have been anticipating it and are anxious to get on with it. The first challenge is getting ourselves out of Sydney through rush hour traffic without any major incidents. With over forty years of driving experience, I am still trying to get the hang of keeping the car centered in the lane. We finally make it to the main highway to Canberra with only one near miss, on one of our lane merges. We are satisfied with that result and are feeling better about driving here.

TIP:

If you are not renting a vehicle with a navigator, make sure to bring one along with you. Our navigator was worth its weight in gold, especially since it measured our speed compared to the posted highway speed. Navigators are very useful in a country where you are ticketed by photo radar when driving over the speed limit.

The trip to Canberra, 289 kilometers via the Hume Highway is on one of the few four lane highways. It is a great way to ease into the car and highway travel while adjusting to right hand steering and left lane driving. The scenery along the way looks the same as California in the summer, golden grasses punctuated by green trees, although the trees here are mainly Eucalypts. We see lots of cattle and sheep wandering amongst pastureland and dried out lake beds. The only Australian wild mammals viewed so far, are dead wombats and one dead kangaroo, on the side of the road. These gruesome sights help to reinforce the policy as outlined in our car rental agreement, drive by daylight only. Approaching Canberra, we leave New South Wales and enter Australian Capital Territory.

Australian Capital Territory (ACT)
Area: 2,358 km². Population: 385,600. Founded in 1911.

The ACT is a federal territory carved out from within the state of New South Wales and is home to its most populous city and the capital of Australia, Canberra. The same as Washington D.C., in both function and layout, Canberra is very much a politician's town. Home to multiple Australian national museums and the impressive old and new parliaments of Australia, Canberra is a planned city. Surrounded by agricultural land of ACT, in a temperate climate, Canberra is not the most ideal Australian tourist destination. As unassuming as it may appear, the capital city, provides great perspective of modern Australia's history.

ACT and Canberra were created as an idea when Australia was federated in 1901. The state of NSW transferred the land to the commonwealth as a territory for the federal government in 1911. The capital's construction commenced in 1913. There are many excellent and informative museums in Canberra. The touching and somber Australian War Memorial along with being an informative museum of Australia's military endeavors, provides a look at the role of ANZACs in shaping Australia's national identity. The National Gallery of Australia houses an impressive amount of Aboriginal Australian and Torres Strait Islander art that is worth the trip to Canberra alone. (13)

The Old Parliament of Australia provides a look at the governance of early Australian politics and is home to the Australian Museum of Democracy. Outside the Old Parliament is the Aboriginal Tent Embassy, the world's longest running protest camp that has been active since Australia Day, January 26th, 1972. (14) It is a great place to visit if you want to learn more about Indigenous Australian issues, from their point of view. The New Parliament of Australia has fascinating architecture and is a perfect viewpoint of Australia's own national mall. It provides a good introduction to modern Australian politics as well. Canberra as a town itself, is not particularly exciting and struggles to find a distinct image. It does not have the flair of Melbourne or Sydney, or the charm of Adelaide, Brisbane, or Darwin. Rather, it is Australia's government town, presenting the national perspective and fine informative value for tourists through its many museums and public buildings.

Australian War Memorial, Canberra (ACT)

Canberra (ACT)

Area: 814 km². Population: 381,488. Founded on March 12, 1913. Traditional lands of the Ngunnawal people. Capital of Australia and home to the Old and New Parliaments, National War Memorial, National Gallery, National Museum, National Zoo, National Library and National University. Government is the largest employer. A notable person born in Canberra is actress Mia Wasikowska. Most known for its Parliament Houses. A Must-See attraction is the National Gallery Indigenous art collection.

Arriving in the outskirts of Canberra, we shop for some essential items for our road trip: a cooler, water, icepacks and a twenty-liter petrol can. Although it is somewhat premature, it will not be long until we will be driving long stretches of highway where both water and petrol will be in short supply. We have taken the hint from the many other vehicles on the road, that are carrying both, either on the roof or at the back of the vehicle.

Driving in Canberra, reminds me of driving in Washington DC, although significantly less congested. The locals drive fast here. It is challenging to get around and into the proper lanes, as the major arteries are laid out the same as spokes on a wheel. There are lots of roundabouts and a combination of divided roads and one ways. We experience another near miss with oncoming traffic, as I have misjudged the turn into a divided road. The driver of the other vehicle is probably cursing under his breath, "Wish the damn tourists would learn to drive". That near miss was much too close for comfort.

TIP:

Keep a marker on the dash (I used a sticky note) reminding you to drive on correct side of the road and get your passengers to remind you as well. This is especially helpful early in the trip, though I kept the marker on the dash for the entirety of the trip.

When Federation was being debated in late 19th Century Australia, there was a strong debate between Sydney and Melbourne over which city would be the nation's capital. These were the two largest cities in the country and had developed a rivalry in their quest for prominence. As a compromise in 1908, the site that is now Canberra, in between the two cities was established as the capital. It was to be designed as a planned city in the mold of Washington D.C. or Brasilia. An international contest decided the design, with the accepted blueprints coming from two Chicago architects, Walter Burley Griffin and Marion Mahoney Griffin. Construction commenced in 1913, following the Griffin's plan using geometric motifs such as circles, hexagons, and triangles, centering on axes aligned with significant topographical landmarks in Canberra.

The city's design was inspired by the garden-city movement that believed in planned communities surrounded by greenbelts. The abundance of so much natural vegetation led to the city being nicknamed the "bush capital". The city's growth and development was stifled by both World Wars and the Great Depression. After WWII development increased with patronage from Prime Minister Robert Menzies and the formation of the National Capital Development Commission. Although self-governing under the ACT, to this day the Commonwealth retains some influence through the National Capital Authority. (13)

We check into our apartment at the East Hotel, not far from Capital Hill and then drive over to the Australian War Memorial. The War Memorial is a beautiful and fitting tribute to Australia's fallen soldiers, with a spectacular view along an avenue as wide and long as the national mall in Washington, DC looking across both the old and new capital buildings. For a small country of 24 million persons, Australians have fought in a lot of wars. Australia has a long tradition of being involved in wars abroad. These wars are usually started by nations Australia is in a close alliance with. Australian military units were first deployed by the British in New Zealand in 1860 during the wars against the Indigenous people of New Zealand, the Maori. Australian soldiers and sailors did not experience much fighting during their deployments in New Zealand. It is estimated that fewer than 20 soldiers were killed in action there. Australian colonial troops were used later in Sudan in the Mahdist War and in South Africa during the Second Boer War. The Boer War is notable, as during that war the six separate units made up of soldiers from the different Australian states federated into one united Australian Army by the time hostilities ended in 1901. Australian sailors later participated in quelling the Boxer Rebellion in China. (15)

The war that marked Australia's independence was WWI. As a dominion of the British Empire, upon the UK's entry, Australia was automatically at war with the Central Powers. The Australian Imperial Force was formed and began their efforts by seizing German New Guinea in a relatively bloodless invasion. The battle that marked Australia and New Zealand's history forever, was the Battle of Gallipoli in 1915. An ambitious plan concocted by Winston Churchill to open a second front in the Dardanelles, it involved the first large scale amphibious landing in history on the Gallipoli Peninsula in Turkey. The invasion was a disaster, as high cliffs allowed Turkish guns to rain down heavy fire on Australian and New Zealand Army Corps (ANZAC) troops. Australian troops were slaughtered by Turkish guns for 8 months. By the time Allied troops were evacuated after the campaign's failure, 8,700 Australians had perished. After this, Australian infantry soldiers were sent to fight on the Western Front while the light horse assisted with fighting in Egypt and Palestine. By WWI's end, 60,000 Australians had been killed. The development of an Australian identity is largely considered an outgrowth of this war, and ANZAC Day is a major holiday in Australia. (16)

After WWI Australia helped briefly in the Allied Intervention during the Russian Civil War before engaging in World War II. Initially Australian troops assisted in fighting against the Germans in North Africa and Italy. With the outbreak of war in the Pacific and the bombing of Darwin, Australia withdrew from the war in Europe. Australia realized the Japanese were a far greater threat to their nation's security and with Britain in no position to help them, Australia turned to the US for support. Working with the Americans, the Australians helped liberate much of the South West Pacific including a bloody battle with the Japanese at the Kokoda Track in Papua New Guinea. Eventually with the Japanese defeated, Australia made a pivot to making the US its primary ally in security. 27,000 Australians died in WWII. The war resulted in a larger peacetime security force and industrial base.

Post-WWII Australia assisted in the struggle against communism in Asia. In the 1950s, Australian forces joined the UN coalition during the Korean War where 340 Australians were killed. Australian soldiers also maintained a presence in Malaysia during the 1940s, 50s, and 60s. Australian forces helped defeat communist guerillas during the Malayan Emergency and assisted in the defence of the newly independent Malaysia in the face of Indonesian invasion. Australia also got involved in the controversial war in Vietnam. Although Australia entered the war with patriotic fervor, protests erupted over time, as Australians did not understand the purpose of the war. 521 Australians were killed, in what many felt was a pointless war.

After Vietnam, Australia avoided conflict until the Gulf War erupted in 1991, and Australia joined the coalition to liberate Kuwait. Australia also assisted in the UN mission in Somalia in 1993. Australia has helped in the defence of the newly independent East Timor from pro-Indonesian militias in 1999. Post 9/11 Australia got involved in both the Iraq and Afghanistan Wars. 41 Australians died in Afghanistan and three in Iraq. Australia continues to be involved in the mission against ISIS in Syria and Iraq. War is considered by many to be the single greatest shared experience between white Australian males. The ANZAC spirit is an important part of Australian identity, and the ANZAC traits of courage, mate-ship, larrikinism, humour, and ingenuity, are heavily ingrained as definitions of Aussie character. Gallipoli was a pointless waste of human life, and it undeniably had a role in creating the modern independent Australian nation. (15)

View overlooking the Australian Parliament buildings, Canberra (ACT)

The history of these conflicts is graphically detailed at the War Memorial. The chapel and the archway memorial walls smothered in poppies, with the names of the fallen read off by school children, is a mesmerizing experience. It is the witch-like screeching of the sulphur-crested cockatoos menacing smaller galah cockatoos out on the front lawn, that brings us around, on our departure from the memorial. The air temperature is cooling down fast on our drive to the hotel. Our dining choice this evening is at the hotel, delicious rotisserie pork and lamb before retiring for the evening.

Saturday, May 9. Windy, Partly Sunny 15°C

We have breakfast in our room, and then go out to purchase tire puncture repair kits, do some banking and get some items at the pharmacy before returning to the hotel. After deciding to walk to the National Gallery, it becomes evident that almost no one in this town walks. The receptionist at the front desk thinks it might take us an hour and be five kilometers away. It turns out to be closer to half that distance. During our stroll along scenic Lake Burley Griffin, the central artificial lake named for its designer, we encounter the beautiful black swans of Australia. These birds are as regal and stunning as their white counterparts. Having no idea of their existence, we did indeed, experience what is known as a *Black Swan Event*. Black swans are nomadic within Australia, though rarely seen in central and northern Australia. In an Aboriginal tale, the white swans lost their feathers during an attack by eagle-hawk and were feathered by the crows who felt sorry for them. Black swans play an important symbolic role in Australian heraldry and culture, in distinct contrast to the white swans of the Northern Hemisphere and are central in the Australian coat of arms.

Approaching the National Gallery from the lake, we stroll up through the sculpture gardens containing modern works, as well as some pieces by Auguste Rodin. In the National Gallery, our time and attention is focused on the vast Indigenous art collection. Most of the art is 20th century and is very thought provoking in its style, design and use of colours. Much of the artwork is a line or dot style of painting either on bark, canvas or on poles. The art depicts land forms, rivers, animals of Australia, both from this world and the spirit world, and stars in the night sky.

The modern Indigenous art is even more thought provoking, and cuts straight to the chase about racism in Australia. The print *Austracism* (2003) by Vernon Ah Kee, is a piece that incorporates multiple statements that begin with, "I'm not racist" and finish with, "…if only Aboriginal people could learn to live like us". The print, R*acebook* (2012) by Raymond Zada, is that of a *facebook* logo, only with an r instead of an f, and incorporates multiple lines of hate speech directed at Indigenous people, taken directly from Facebook, and is underscored with the thumbs down "too many people like this". The oil on canvass, *Treasure Island* (2005) by Daniel Boyd, is an enlightening painting for the uninitiated in Indigenous culture. It maps out Australia, not by state boundaries but by the traditional lands of its first people.

Australian Black Swans on Lake Burley Griffin near the National Gallery, Canberra (ACT)

The Aboriginal Memorial is off to one side in the main rotunda and consists of 200 painted hollow log coffins from the human beings (Yolngu) of central Arnhem Land in Northern Territory. It was created between 1987- 88, by 43 Aboriginal artists from Ramingining and commemorates the Indigenous people who lost their lives defending their land since colonial occupation began in 1788. The different styles of painting on the logs vary by clan and the designs are inherited. These are the artist's copyright of the imagery and are the same as those painted on bodies during burial rights. None of these mortuary logs, that are naturally hollowed out by termites, have carried the bones of deceased people from Central Arnhem Land, as is their usual intended purpose. The installation is a war memorial and testament to the resilience of Indigenous people and is on public display for us and future generations. A single visit to the monument does not do it justice. There is so much to see and take in, as you travel along the Glyde River estuary and absorb the different painting styles, designs and images. (17)

Aboriginal Memorial, National Gallery of Australia, Canberra (ACT)

Spending half the day in the Gallery, we have lunch there, before walking a kilometer past the High Court of Australia to the Old Parliament Building. The area appears similar in geometry, length and breadth as the national mall in Washington, DC. That is where the similarity ends. There is an Indigenous protest camp out in front of the Old Parliament Building, with large tents, a campfire, flags and a large banner demanding Sovereignty. It looks temporary, and not understanding its significance or permanence we carry on without stopping in. The Old Parliament is the only building where an entry fee of $5.00 is required. It is a relatively plain building with a Senate and a House of Representatives built in the 20th century during a period when Australia's economy was primarily agricultural. Canberra in 1880, had a population of 200 persons and 300,000 sheep. It was decided on as a location for the nation's capital, strictly because it was the only place that both Sydney and Melbourne could agree on. The Old Parliament building is home to the Australian Museum of Democracy, and houses a large collection of political cartoons, that are completely lost on us, yet judging by the laughter, are clearly entertaining to visiting Australians.

We hike another kilometer farther to the New Parliament building. The building is an impressive modern structure, that looks as if it is built into a hillside. It has a beautiful interior with modern marble columns, floors and stairways. Many of the main hall panels and floors are finished in beautiful Australian tropical hardwoods. There is a spectacular view from the top of the building out towards all vistas and especially towards the war memorial. Some maple tree leaves are changing colour to brilliant red in the inner courtyard. A tour guide points out that the trees are from America. Borrowing from my short experience with the Australian art of quipping, I quip, "these are Canadian trees.' The guide quips back, "of course Mate, everything is made in Canada." That gets a resounding laugh from everyone on the tour. That will teach me to try to quip with an Aussie.

The weather is windy and cooling down during the walk back to our hotel. Not making restaurant reservations on the evening before Mother's Day is a definite mistake on my part. After being turned away at two restaurants we finally get into an Italian restaurant, although out on the patio under a tent. It is bone-chilling cold and windy, reminding us of late fall in Canada. Fortunately, the gas heaters keep us warm. Dining on pasta with Ty having dessert the bill comes in at $150.00. Underwhelming and overpriced.

Sunday, May 10 (Mother's Day). Overcast and very windy 12°C, feels like 2°C

I have thought about it all night, and Tyler and I discuss it in the morning. We have missed something and somehow know that leaving Canberra without stopping in to the Indigenous protest camp is a missed opportunity. After breakfast and packing up, we check out and drive to the Old Parliament Building to visit the Indigenous protest camp. Knowing nothing in advance about its significance as a national icon for Indigenous political rights and struggle Tyler and I meet with Raxley Foley, Vince and a dog who stroll out to stoke the fire. We are welcomed and sit by the fire on a very windy day with dust, wood chips, leaves, and smoke swirling around consuming our bodies and clothing. Man, are we getting smoked in. The fire is the Sacred Fire for Peace and Justice, maintained by the guardians of the Sacred Fire who live at the Tent Embassy. It is bitterly cold, and most of the guardians are tucked into their sleeping bags inside the tents, trying to stay warm. Tyler introduces himself as a writer from the Simon Fraser University student paper "The Peak" and begins to peel the onion that is Australia.

We have an hour-long chat, listening mainly, about Indigenous life in Australia and learning about the long struggle Indigenous people face in gaining equality and an end to racism. From Tyler's notes, Raxley explains, "how the sovereignty movement of Indigenous Australians is taking on a republican nature, in that they want to determine their own future through self-determination as highlighted under the UN Covenant on Civil and Political Rights. He explains that there are higher rates of removals of Aboriginal children from their homes now, than there were during the time of the Stolen Generation. He says that there are plenty of responsible guardians in Aboriginal communities including grandmothers, who could help if parents are irresponsible, yet the federal government ignores them. Indigenous people consider themselves a national treasure, that have been and still are being abused. The camp is the longest running protest camp in the world and has been planted on the front lawn of the Australian parliament for the last 43 years since its foundation in 1972. Police may not enter the Embassy without permission. The Embassy is courteous and is willing to make space for other festivals and protests in support of other Australian minorities. Raxley reveals to us that his father Gary, helped design the original Australian Aboriginal flag and that it was originally flown upside-down as a symbol of the oppression of Aboriginal Australians. The current Aboriginal flag is very distinctive with a black stripe for the people, red stripe for the earth and is centered with a yellow circle for the sun.

Raxley shares with us that Indigenous people from the eastern Australian states are bringing a convoy of support in the coming weeks with solar panels and water purifiers. After sharing that our journey will take us to Western Australia, we learn that it is the harshest state towards Indigenous people, with many being incarcerated in privatized prisons. We learn that there is no actual treaty with Indigenous Australians, merely a watered-down version of native title with no access to mineral or fishing rights. Even the so called left wing parties such as the Labour Party, compromise for mining interests with corporations against any progressive dialogue with Indigenous people. In Raxleys words, 'there is a collective amnesia towards Australia's rich Indigenous heritage.'"

Indigenous Australian cultures are some of the most distinctive and oldest cultures on the planet. Dating back at least 60,000 years, Indigenous Australian society is ancient in its fabric, and exemplary in its sustainability. Witnesses to megafauna, volcanic activity, earthquakes and climate change, Indigenous Australians adapted to an Ice Age that arrived approximately 20,000 years ago and lasted for 5,000 years. Average temperatures fell by 10°C, rainfall decreased by half and high winds were more numerous forming large sand dunes in the center of the continent. At one time, sea levels were 100 meters lower than today, and Tasmania and Papua New Guinea were joined with the mainland. (18)

Most Indigenous Australians lived as hunter-gatherers living as an integral part of the land, rather than off the land. Many Indigenous Australians were nomadic, others semi-nomadic, and some had permanent settlements with signs of land management for food. They maintained traditional territories and migrated between these for trade and cultural purposes. The greatest population density of Indigenous Australians was in the southern and eastern regions of the continent, especially around the Murray River valley. Fire-stick farming allowed Indigenous Australians to master their environment and caused the extinction of Australian megafauna, that survives only in Dreamtime stories. Although Indigenous Australians were limited in the range of foods available, they had an almost extrasensory knowledge of what was edible and where it could be found. Women foraged for yams, edible roots, nectars, honey, fruits, berries, seeds, vegetables, and insects. Men hunted kangaroo, emu, birds, possums, lizards, and snakes. Indigenous hunters were excellent trackers and stalkers and used mud and camouflage disguises to conceal themselves when making kills. Fishing was done by hand or using the crushed leaves of poisonous plants to stupefy fish, spears, nets, or traps depending on the area. Dugong, turtle, and large fish were harpooned from canoes. Hunting was often done in a cooperative manner between men and sometimes animals, with a clear division of labor.

Before the British arrived in Australia it was estimated that between 750,000 to one million persons using stone age knowledge and technology thrived in Australia. Indigenous Australians lived in up to 600 distinct clan groups or nations around the continent, many with distinctive cultures and beliefs. Post-colonization, Indigenous populations were absorbed into Australian society, losing their heritage and cultural traditions, although in the Great Sandy Desert tradition persisted for much longer owing to a lack of European settlement and interest. The mode of life for Indigenous cultures differed from region to region. Torres Strait Islanders were agriculturalists, whereas most Aboriginal Australians were hunter-gatherers. Indigenous Australians living along the coasts and rivers fished, and other Indigenous peoples relied on the dingo as companion animals to assist in hunting. The only animal domesticated by mainland Indigenous people was the dingo, although Torres Strait Islanders also domesticated pigs. In Victoria, there is evidence of Aboriginal eel farming near the Murray River. The main hunting tools of Indigenous Australians were spears and boomerangs.

Although Torres Strait Islanders lived in villages, on the mainland most communities were semi-nomadic moving over a defined territory following food sources and returning to the same area in a regular cycle. Aboriginal Australians have experienced great climactic changes and are masters of adapting to their environment, migrating only when necessary. Fire allowed Indigenous Australians to greatly control their environment. Control of fire encouraged the growth of edible plants and fodder for prey, reduced the risk of brushfires, made travel easier, eliminated pests, was used in ceremonies, war, and to clean up the country. Indigenous oral history not only provides evidence of a continuity of culture, it corroborates changes in the Australian climate. Sea level rise, megafauna, comets, and changes in shorelines are all recorded in Aboriginal oral records. It is believed that between 3000 BCE and 1000 BCE that the hunter-gatherer lifestyle of Indigenous Australians intensified with increased environmental manipulation, population growth, trade, and social structures.

Indigenous communities have a very complex and intricate kinship structure. These place strict rules on marriage as men are required to marry women of a specific moiety. This was done to reinforce goodwill between clans and to prevent inbreeding. It is still in practice in some communities to this day. Although Indigenous Australian tradition has been harmed by colonialism, to call it dead is a mistake. Even in cities, aspects of it exist within the Indigenous people.

As in the Americas, diseases brought over by Europeans such as influenza and smallpox ravaged Indigenous populations after the establishment of New South Wales in 1788. The settlers took the view that Indigenous people were nomadic hunter-gatherers who did not value the land and had no concept of land ownership. The settlers felt free to occupy the land and allow their animals to graze on it. The land was vital to Indigenous people. Not only for food and water. It also had great spiritual and cultural significance to Australia's Indigenous people. Proximity to settlers also brought venereal diseases, alcohol, opium, and tobacco. This led to the substance abuse problems that still plague Indigenous people in Australia today. It is estimated that ninety percent of the Indigenous population of Australia died out between 1788 and 1901 diminishing to 93,000 and hit its low point of 75,000 by 1954.

The Palawah, the Indigenous people of Tasmania, faced extermination owing to a vicious campaign by settlers known as the Black War. By 1872, the last pure-blooded Tasmanian Aboriginal Truganini had died however, mixed blood Tasmanian Aboriginals still live and carry on Tasmanian Aboriginal culture. On the mainland things progressed in a similarly disastrous manner. In 1838, eight Aboriginal persons were murdered in the Myall Creek Massacre and white convict settlers responsible for the crime were hanged, marking the first time that white settlers had been punished for the crime of killing Aboriginal people. Indigenous people did resist against British settlement. A prominent example being Yagan, a Noongar warrior who fought the British and later had his head sent back to England after being killed. Efforts of resistance were unsuccessful owing to the increasing numbers of settlers arriving while the Indigenous population declined because of disease. There were a few examples of British and Indigenous cooperation, such as Bennelong who helped mediate between the British and Eora people. Indigenous people also assisted in European expeditions and worked as stock hands and labourers, both paid and unpaid.

No treaty was made with Indigenous Australians, unlike those made by the British Crown in New Zealand and Canada. The land was considered Terra Nullius by the new settlers, essentially that it was empty, prior to British colonization. That was not challenged until Torres Strait Islander Eddie Mabo made a case against the Queensland government on behalf of the Mer people. On June 3, 1967, the High Court of Australia agreed with Mabo abandoning Terra Nullius and acknowledging the pre-existing rights of Indigenous Australians. That said, the ruling did not confer land or sea rights to Indigenous people, and definitely not on any lands taken and owned by colonizers whether settlers or mining conglomerates.

In WW II Indigenous Australians served and came back to a country that did not appreciate their sacrifice. Indigenous Australians were finally given the federal right to vote in 1967, and the first Indigenous Australian Neville Bonner joined the Senate in 1971, making him the first Indigenous elected official. An issue that impacted Indigenous Australians greatly was the Stolen Generations, the taking of children by the government. These children were raised outside of their traditional cultures losing their languages, customs and traditional education. Many of these children were traumatized by their experiences and abused by their state guardians. These children have since lost any connection to their traditional culture and are often plagued by alcoholism and mental illness in the aftermath. The main issues facing Indigenous people today is their over-representation in the prison system, lack of education, poor health conditions, unemployment, substance abuse, and a lack of land rights.

Indigenous Australian religion is often referred to as Dreaming or Dreamtime by most of Australian society. For Indigenous Australians, the Dreaming are not mere fables, these are doctrines, traditions, laws, history, and geography for Australia's first people. The Dreaming stories are transmitted orally and have been passed down for generations. It is through these song lines that more than 60,000 years of history has been transmitted down the generations. The name Dreamtime was misinterpreted from the indigenous word "altyerrenge" that is used by the Arrernte people of Central Australia. It translates to "see and understand the law". (19)

Indigenous Australians believe the Earth and heavens always existed, and for them the Dreaming is a period in which the Ancestor Spirits shaped the world as we know it. For Indigenous Australians, these ancestor spirits are the creative force in their world, not deities. Although Indigenous Australians believe in deities these are not worshipped in the same ways, as in other parts of the world. These ancestor beings created the Earth's features and their journeys across the Earth's landscape are referred to as song lines or Dreaming tracks. Some Dreaming are linked with animals such as a honey-ant or kangaroo. The people living in those lands have a deep connection to those creatures and see themselves as their descendants and as Indigenous culture heroes. Sacred sites such as waterholes, caves, mountains and rock formations are regarded as places where the ancestor beings returned to the Earth and have a rich spiritual significance to Indigenous Australians.

Dreamtime is different from the European concept of time in that Indigenous Australians believe that the spirits of the Dreamtime are linked to the present and assist in determining the future. There are various creation spirits based on the mythos of the Aboriginal and Torres Strait Islander people. The rainbow serpent is a very common one. The sky is believed to be the home of the ancestral spirits and to some Indigenous peoples it is also where souls go after death. Stars and constellations are important to Indigenous people as these are used to navigate the land. Stories on the formation of the stars may differ between nations however, there is a common theme of the Milky Way being a celestial river or stream. Although today Dreamtime stories are treated as children's stories by many Australians, for Indigenous people these stories are used to impart many values, laws, responsibilities, and cultural knowledge on their people. These stories use sophisticated metaphors to impart subtle details. Because Indigenous knowledge is recorded orally, some stories may only be told by people of certain status within the clan. Those not initiated to specific levels may not hear certain stories, and some stories are dictated as men's business, and others as women's business. Because Indigenous people are so in touch with their environment there is an emphasis placed on respect towards nature and other people. Principles of reciprocity, respect for Elders, respect for the distinct roles of women and men, and respect for the environment are very important to Indigenous Australians. (5) (20) (6) (21)

The National Gallery and our enlightening fireside chat on this cold and windy day, not only penetrated our clothing with dust and smoke, but also our hearts and minds with seeds of knowledge that inspire us during our journey and discovery of Australia. We say our goodbyes and leave the capital region making our way towards Eden 350 kilometers away on the south-eastern corner of Australia with lots to think about and discuss. It is very windy. The Eucalypts are bending in the wind with their long branches whipping around wildly back and forth between the sky and the ground. There is lots of loose flying bark, dust and debris blowing across the highway. The trip is through rolling hills and pasture lands, reminding us of Montana. The two-lane highway then takes us to elevated forests along the New South Wales coastline. The winding roads are steep with little to no shoulder in places. My first thought about this stretch of road is that it is not designed by American civil engineers. It is a great road for compact sports cars. I am so glad that we did not rent a large recreational vehicle, as it would likely have several dents in its left side, by now.

Not far from Eden, descending a hill with cars close behind us in a turn, a road train comes barreling down into the turn from the opposite direction, and has crossed the centre line. I am not interested in becoming a hood ornament. Susan looks on in sheer terror as I take the car to the far left on a very narrow gravel shoulder. Our vehicle spits gravel back at the cars behind us, as the truck whisks by centimetres away to our right with horns blasting from all vehicles. That was near-miss number three. This time not our fault, and absolutely the most dangerous and scary of all. Third times a charm, so we hope that this is the last of dangerous road encounters. Barely underway, I sense that we may not expect many more lives out of this old cat. Arriving in Eden at four in the afternoon, a looming Antarctic cold front storm sweeps in across the Tasman Sea.

Eden (NSW)

Population: 3,600. Founded in 1843. Traditional lands of the Thaua people of the Yuin Nation. Tourism, whale watching, and fishing are the primary industries and the port of Eden is the largest fishing port in NSW. A notable whale from Eden is the orca, Old Tom. Most known for and Must-See attraction is Eden's Killer Whale Museum.

Eden is an old coastal whaling town that now lives off fishing and tourism. Dining at the Great Southern Hotel we line up to order our surf and turf dinner and pick up our drinks from the pub side of the hotel. The dinner is the largest and best value meal that we have enjoyed in Australia to date. The bed sure feels good after a long day, although the room smells strongly of smoke from our jackets infused by the Sacred Fire for Peace and Justice.

Monday, May 11. Sunny 17°C

We start our day down at the commercial fishing and oyster harvesting wharf at Snug Cove in Eden and have a good breakfast at the Wharf Side café. We then walk around the wharf, taking pictures with a plaque commemorating the mapping of Twofold Bay by Lt. Mathew Flinders October 10, 1798. We watch as pelicans surf in the winds overhead, landing with great dexterity on the lamp standards. From there we drive a short distance over to the Killer Whale Museum which is listed as a top attraction in town. Although there are few living whales that still visit Eden, the museum that was established in 1938 is a great place to learn about some very unique whaling events in history, that happened right here in Twofold Bay.

As recorded in the Guinness Book of World Records, the largest marine animal ever killed by a hand harpoon was a blue whale, killed by Archer Davidson, in Twofold Bay in 1910. It measured 29.56 meters (97 feet) in length. Even more surprising is that the killer whales (orcas) in Twofold Bay worked alongside men for many generations in Indigenous history, to hunt baleen whales, of which right whales were the most popular. The Indigenous people of the area saw the orca as an ancestor spirit of theirs and held great reverence and respect for the orcas. The relationship was imparted on the European whalers of Eden who eventually held this Indigenous practice in high regard. The killer whales worked as three separate hunter packs with independent tasks. One pack drove the right whales into the Bay. Another pack sealed off the Bay and the third pack drove the whales towards the whalers near shore. After harpooning the whales, the human whalers rewarded the killer whales with the lips and tongues of their prey. A tongue could weigh as much as four tonnes. This agreement was named the Law of the Tongue by whalers.

The most famous of these orcas in recent history was Old Tom. Old Tom signaled whalers by leaping out of the water and often assisted whalers by holding harpoon lines to slow down escaping whales and towed boats to their prey. Old Tom was a large orca measuring 22 feet and weighing six tonnes, who developed a close working relationship with humans, demonstrating the great bonds man may have with nature, when reciprocity and respect are shown. On September 17, 1930, Old Tom was found dead in Twofold Bay. The skeleton was preserved by local whalers and Old Tom was put on display in the original Eden museum in 1931, just as orcas and other whales stopped coming in shore.

We learn another peculiar piece of whaling history at the museum. In the 1890's, freshly killed whales were used as a cure for rheumatism. Naked patients inserted themselves in cavities cut into the sides of whales when their body temperatures were at 40°C. The museum has a lot of other informative displays about whaling, sharks, Indigenous whalers, water craft, and Indigenous trading routes. In addition, there is a beautiful view and scopes for viewing whales when offshore. Australia is now an anti-whaling nation and both right whales and orcas are beginning to re-establish themselves on the Southern Coast and appear off Eden from time to time. This small and modest museum, is much more than it seems, presenting a fascinating piece of maritime history in this charming coastal community.

Tyler and Susan at Snug Cove Fishing Port in Twofold Bay
Eden (NSW)

The town annually celebrates the return of humpback, sperm and some right whales. It has also recently seen the return of orca pods. It has been a great visit, and after speaking with a very helpful museum attendant, we are enlightened about the exaggerated dangers of Australian wildlife. I must say that this removes a great deal of the confusion for us. Our minds have been preoccupied with the various dangerous animals, especially the venomous creatures, over one hundred species of snakes, and a great variety of spiders and jellyfish that may possibly kill you here in Australia. I have been driving around with the image firmly implanted in my mind from Bill Bryson's book *In a Sunburned Country* of the poor fellow who has a deadly tiger snake strike out from behind the dashboard of his car and bite him in the groin. (22) We have been very careful on exiting and entering the car, not to mention checking our shoes daily for spiders. We have also been very conscious not to wear open toed shoes and meanwhile all the locals are walking around in thongs (flip-flops) or in bare feet. There is clearly a disconnect, so we lighten up a bit.

TIP:

If you see signs about dangerous wildlife, read them and follow the instructions. Otherwise be observant and relax.

From Eden, driving 240 kilometers to Lakes Entrance through windy and rainy conditions we have begun our journey west along the southern coastline of Australia. Crossing the border into the state of Victoria, on two lane highway that takes us through Eucalypt forests, some show evidence of previous wildfire. It is easy to visualize how quickly fire may travel through the dry underbrush when it is whipped around by these winds. The bark on the larger Eucalypts is scorched part way up the trunk, although overall many of the larger trees have survived unscathed. Everything else on the ground has been incinerated, other than the new green growth sprouting through the char layer. The highway provides a fire break in some areas and in others the fire completely ignores man's intervention. Discussing it, all of us prefer not to witness a fire first hand, especially when miles from civilization. Eventually, we arrive in cool, sunny and beautiful Lakes Entrance.

Evidence of a significant forest fire on route to Lakes Entrance (VIC)

Victoria (VIC)
Area: 237,629 km². Population: 5,821,300. Founded in 1851.

Victoria is known as the Garden state and is considered the home of sophistication and multiculturalism in Australia. Settlement began in 1803, with the land being incorporated as part of NSW's Port Philip district in the 1830s. In 1851, it was made a separate colony by the British crown. The land, taken from its original Indigenous Koori inhabitants, became home to arguably Australia's largest metropolis, Melbourne. Settlers were drawn to Victoria initially, by the gold rushes in the area. The wealth from mining strikes eventually led the colony to self-government in 1855.

Victoria is considered a liberal state, second only to South Australia regarding progressive attitude. Victoria's capital, Melbourne is known for its sophisticated café culture, and is also the birthplace to multiple Australian artistic endeavors in film, literature and painting. It is a multicultural city and is home to large immigrant populations from Europe, Asia, and the Middle East. To understand the scope of this, Melbourne has the third largest Greek descendant population after Athens and Thessaloniki. Melbourne's tram system and public transit is impressive. Melbourne is home to the Melbourne Cricket Ground (MCG), known as the hallowed ground of Australian sports, specifically Aussie Rules Football (Footy) and Cricket. Melbourne's restaurants are excellent, with plenty of variety and lots of ethnic foods from around the world, thanks to its large immigrant population. It is an exciting city. You feel its very essence and energy as you walk the streets.

The landscape of Victoria is diverse for its small size. From the snowy Victorian Alps, to wet and temperate Gippsland in the southeast and the plains in the west. The state has an extensive river system with the Murray River being its most prominent. Of the mainland states, Victoria is the coldest and the wettest because of its southern location. Victoria's other prominent attraction is the Great Ocean Road. It is a spectacular ocean side drive that is home to the monolithic limestone stacks known as The Twelve Apostles. Victoria's beaches are vast and gorgeous, with excellent views out on to the open ocean. One should not miss the great views offered by the Great Ocean Road. Simply put, Victoria is amazing and absolutely worth a visit while in Australia. (23)

Outlook over Lakes Entrance (VIC)

Temperate rainforest, Great Ocean Road (VIC)

Lakes Entrance (VIC)

Population: 4,569. Founded: Feb 5, 1870 as Cunninghame and renamed on January 1, 1915. Traditional lands of the Kurnai people. Tourist resort and fishing port that is also popular for camping. A notable person born in Lakes Entrance is Pro football coach Aaron Symons with Dempo – Indian I league. Most known for and a Must-See attraction is Ninety Mile Beach.

Lakes Entrance is at sea level and the highway is flooded in spots, on our arrival. Fortunately, our vehicle can still get by and into town. We check into the hotel at just after 3pm and get the heat going in the room as it has cooled down substantially. I get some tips on places to eat from the acting hotel manager who happens to be looking after things for his kids, while he is visiting from Darwin. I tell him about our trip around Australia. He shows me some great pictures of scenery from Darwin and a large saltwater crocodile who snuck up on him while cleaning fish during a fishing expedition. He suggests that we are going to love our trip up north and is the first person to give me some sense that our road trip is possible. He suggests fishing on a charter when in the north. I am quite certain that we will pass on that activity. Those close-up pictures of the Saltie just helped to seal that deal for me.

We drive into town to do some shopping and restock the cooler with beverages and breakfast foods. On our return it is already dusk, so we decide to walk to the restaurant. Dinner is pricey seafood, in what appears to be a good restaurant. In all fairness, the place is understaffed on a Monday night and is one of the few places that is open. We probably should have gone to the local fish and chips place, by the looks of how busy it is. All of us are off to bed early, in anticipation of our journey to Melbourne.

Tuesday, May 12. Partly Sunny 14°C

It is hard to believe that a week has already gone by here in Australia. It is even more difficult to imagine what lays ahead of us despite our thorough trip itinerary. Heading west along the A1 Princes Highway towards Melbourne, 290 kilometers away, our trusty GPS navigator veers us off our coastal route. It sends us on a more direct overland route early into our trip. Susan realizes the change and gets us back on track, via the road to Yarram where we happen upon the massive Loy Yang power plant and coal mine. It is extremely windy and difficult to stand without being blown over while viewing the stunning and immense 800-hectare site. Brown Coal (lignite) is mined by four bucket wheel dredges 24 hours a day, seven days a week and is conveyed directly from the mine to two power plants Loy Yang A and Loy Yang B. I snap a few pictures of the complex that produces thirty million tonnes of coal annually, providing Victoria with 47% of its electricity requirements. Although the flue gases look clean enough, it is estimated that the combined power plants emit 28 million Tonnes of greenhouse gases (GHG) each year. (24)

Australia's climate ranges from temperate and desert over most of the country to tropic in the north. This mineral resource rich country relies heavily on electricity for cooling, water desalination, pumping and distribution; as well as for its heavy industries, some that are very energy intensive, such as mining, gas and aluminum. Australia has over 27,000 kilometers of mainly state owned and operated transmission lines delivering over 200 Terawatts (TW) of electricity per year at an average price of 29cents/kwh, one of the highest prices in the world. (25) (26) In 2015, 73% of electricity in Australia was produced from coal and 13% from natural gas. (27) Australia is the fifteenth largest emitter of greenhouse gases in the world with total GHG emissions in 2013 of 538.4 million tonnes or fifteen tonnes per person. (28) Seven percent of electricity is generated from hydro and the remaining seven percent from other renewable energy sources primarily wind and solar. (27) Australia has installed over one million solar panels that deliver two percent of the electricity. 21,000 Australians work in renewable energy although 2014 saw the lowest investment in renewable energy since 2003. (28) The Abbott government has not been supportive of renewable energy generation. This is not surprising, coming from a Prime Minister who is a well documented as being dismissive of climate change. When Abbott's government came into power, it axed Australia's "job killing carbon tax", gaining an instant ally in Canada's then Prime Minister, Stephen Harper. (29)

Loy Yang coal-fired power station, La Trobe Valley (VIC)

The Indigenous people of Australia have survived significant climate change adapting to sea level changes and ice ages in Australia since their appearance on the continent. The last glacial maximum was approximately 20,000 years ago. Indigenous people of that time had to adapt to a drop in average temperature of 10°C, mass animal extinctions, expanding desertification, and a fall in sea level of 100 meters resulting in land bridging of the main continent with Tasmania and Papua New Guinea. It is suspected that up to eighty percent of the population at that time, had to relocate to more suitable environments on the continent. (18)

As advised by news reports, Queensland is in the midst, of what has been declared since March of 2014, the most severe and widespread drought ever in recorded history. Forty percent of the same region experienced widespread flooding affecting ninety towns and 200,000 persons between December 2010 and January 2011. The drought that has been triggered by below average wet summers for the last three years, has initiated a $350 million aid package in 2015 to farmers in NSW and Queensland. The cycle of floods and droughts is likely to get worse in the short term, over the next 50 to 300 years as green house gases accumulate in the atmosphere. It will have significant bearing on 85% of Australia's population that lives, works, and plays on the coastline of Australia. The government of Australia has estimated that a rise in sea level over one meter is plausible by 2100. It will put at risk up to $63 billion of residential buildings, up to $87 billion of commercial and light industrial buildings, and up to 35,000 kilometers of road and rail valued at up to $67 billion. (30)

The number of hot days is forecast to increase, and annual rainfall is forecast to decline, affecting water availability. It will reduce the general health of the human population especially the elderly, increase animal extinctions and reduce crop and range animal productivity. (31) We witness conservation efforts made here that we have not seen back in Canada. Water restrictions are in place for most communities during our visit, and many of the hotels request that showers be limited to three minutes. Each electric wall socket has a plug load on and off switch. Heat pumps are the primary cooling and heating device in most of the buildings during our visit.

Australian standard electric socket AS-3112 Voltage 220-240

TIP:

You will need a travel adapter for US and Canadian electric appliances. You may need a step-down transformer if your appliance does not say Input 100-240V 50/60HZ indicating that it can handle multiple voltages.

Conditions are very rough. Cold winds and a dark foreboding storm sweeping in from the Antarctic is blowing everything around including our little car. Out here on the rural highways there are a preponderance of four-wheel drive Land Rovers and Toyotas better known as off-road Utes. Many are fully equipped with long whip antennae for UHF CB radios, over the hood nested fishing rods, bull bars, winches, extra gas and water cans, solar panels, sleepers, coolers and tool kits. We are feeling very inadequate in our two-wheel drive Toyota Camry, for our outing into the Australian Outback.

Our trusty Canadian moose mascot - ODB

Melbourne (VIC)

Area: 9,990 km². Population: 4,442,919. Founded on August 30th, 1835 by free settlers. Traditional lands of the Kulin Nation comprising the Wurundjeri, Bunurong, Taungurong, Dja Dja Wurrung, and Wathaurong people. Melbourne is the capital of Victoria and is rated for the fifth year in a row as the most livable city in the world. Entertainment, tourism, education, research & development, sport and finance are key economic drivers. A notable person born in Melbourne is conservationist Steve Irwin. A Must-See attraction is the Queen Victoria market.

The cityscape is a blend of old and new Melbourne (VIC)

Arriving in Melbourne city at around four pm, we are fortunate in having avoided any of the notorious hook turns. Hook turns are present on the downtown tramline intersections. You must line up on the left adjacent to crossing passengers to execute your right turn when it is clear to do so. These turns are unique to Melbourne and are confusing for us foreigners. We check into the Radisson at Flagstaff Gardens, a nice hotel that used to be the headquarters for the Victoria State Police. The rooftop gym and spa provide a beautiful view of the neon lit city at night. Our dining experience this evening is at a reasonably priced and busy Italian restaurant near Victoria market. Simply delicious.

Wednesday, May 13. Showers 11°C

We take a cab early in the morning to the Melbourne Convention Centre. Our cabbie gives us the rundown on how the famous Melbourne hook turn works making it sound a lot easier, than it looks. He then makes it abundantly clear that Melbourne is far superior to Sydney, as Melbourne hosts more sports, entertainment and is more culturally diverse and accepting of people from other countries. People from 143 different nations make their home in Melbourne. Want the goods on anything? Just ask a cabbie. Dress appears to be less fashionable here than in Sydney. It seems more down to earth, mind you most people are bundling up because of the cool weather.

We have a quick coffee and muffin and then attend the Solar 2015 conference. The morning is spent visiting booths viewing the latest in solar collection and storage equipment. Evidently the sizeable show is only 1/50th the size of the Solar show last month in Shanghai. There is not much on display of solar integration into building products, an innovation I was hoping to see more of. Our most profound lesson of the day is at the booth for Yingli Solar, one of the worlds largest suppliers of solar panels. We learn that China built ten Gigawatts (GW) of solar capacity last year and are building eighteen Gigawatts of solar collection infrastructure in 2015. That is almost equivalent to the power (22.5 GW) from the world's largest dam Three Gorges, that took 27 years to build. The main driver for adding solar capacity so rapidly is the heavy air pollution in China. Unseen greenhouse gases steadily accumulating and changing global climate are not as effective at motivating behaviour change, as the heavy clouds of toxic gases from burning coal. The toxic gases kill hundreds of thousands of China's citizens prematurely each year and are a compelling reason for shifting the worlds largest consumer off fossil fuels. I ponder the shock and impacts that China's new policy will have on the global fossil fuel industry and society in general.

We go to a very busy restaurant near the Convention Centre, The Merrywell for lunch and have some great burgers & drinks. After lunch, we take the free City Centre Tram line tour of Melbourne and then visit one of the great libraries of the world, The State Library of Victoria. The six story Victorian building houses many different exhibition halls including a history of Melbourne, and many historically significant rare books and works of art. Its center piece is the spectacular octagonal La Trobe Reading Room that holds over one million books and up to 600 readers. Most of our afternoon is used, taking our time browsing throughout the various library exhibits.

The library is the custodian of the armour, the Jerilderie Letter, and the death mask belonging to the infamous bushranger Ned Kelly. The bushranger was essentially the Australian version of the outlaws of the American Old West. The name originates from escaped convicts who had the survival skills to live in the bush and avoid pursuit by the authorities. By the 1820s, the term's meaning changed to refer to the outlaws of colonial Australia who made their living as robbers based out of the bush. Most of these bushrangers were the colonial born sons of convicts. Many were of Irish Catholic background. By 1840, fifty thousand "Irish rebels" had been transported to Australia.

The most famous bushranger of all was Ned Kelly, whose death marks the end of the era for bushrangers in Australia. Born in Victoria, in December 1854, Ned Kelly was the third of eight children born to an Irish convict and an Australian mother of Irish descent. Kelly was left to become the man of the house at age twelve, when his father died after a six-month stint in prison. The Kelly family downtrodden by brutal poverty, were victims of police persecution and land encroachment from cattle grazers. His first arrest was at age fourteen, for stealing ten shillings. Ned was later charged for armed robbery for holding the horse of bushranger Harry Power, although those charges were dismissed for lack of evidence. He was eventually convicted of stealing horses and was imprisoned for three years. After being indicted for the attempted murder of a police officer in 1878, Kelly fled to the bush with his brother Dan and the rest of the Kelly gang members, Joe Byrne and Steve Hart. His mother Ellen, was sentenced to three years hard labour for aiding and abetting the escape of her sons and assaulting Constable Fitzpatrick. Ned reached full outlaw status when alongside his brother Dan and two associates, they fatally shot three policemen. During his crime spree, Ned and his gang committed two major armed robberies and murdered a police informant. (32)

The La Trobe Reading Room, The State Library of Victoria
Melbourne (VIC)

In his manifesto, the 56-page Jerilderie Letter, Ned Kelly outlined the debilitating poverty he and many innocents suffered, and denounced the police, Victoria, and the British Empire for his fate. His closing words tell much about the man, "I give fair warning to all those who has reason to fear me to sell out and give £10 out of every hundred towards the widow and orphan fund and do not attempt to reside in Victoria but as short a time as possible after reading this notice, neglect this and abide by the consequences, which shall be worse than the rust in the wheat in Victoria or the druth of a dry season to the grasshoppers in New South Wales I do not wish to give the order full force without giving timely warning but I am a widows son outlawed and my orders must be obeyed." (33)

When an attempted ambush of a police train failed, Ned Kelly and his gang dressed in their homemade suits of steel armor got into a notorious shootout at Glenrowan with Victoria Police on June 28, 1880. Ned's entire gang were shot to death. Ned was shot in both legs and captured.

While in gaol he wrote a long letter to authorities about discrimination against poor Irish settlers. On November 11, 1880, Ned Kelly, age 25, was hanged by the neck in Melbourne Gaol. His reported last words were "such is life". (32) He has since, become a Robin Hood-like folk hero in the eyes of many Australians. Ned Kelly resonates with many Australians who feel downtrodden by government and police and is seen by some as "Australia's Che Guevara". Outlaw or freedom fighter, it does not matter how you view the man, Ned Kelly is without a doubt, an Australian icon. After enjoying dinner at Rice Paper Scissors a great Asian Fusion Restaurant on Liverpool Street in the Central Business District, we walk back to our hotel through town, window shopping along the way.

The fare free City Circle Tram, Melbourne (VIC)

Thursday, May 14. Rain/Cloudy 10°C

This morning is overcast and cool on our walk over to the Queen Victoria market. We run into Mona, a charming and well-dressed Ethiopian self-made business woman who is looking for the law courts and asks us for directions. After getting into a discussion, us being Canadian and her able to speak French, a common bond developed, despite our limited French. Mona invites us to a restaurant that she owns for this evening. We graciously decline and in retrospect that was probably a mistake. It was lovely to meet you Mona. Thank you for making us feel at home in your adopted country. We have a very reasonable bacon and eggs breakfast at a corner restaurant, Josey's near the market. The Queen Victoria market, the largest open-air market in the Southern Hemisphere, operates 5 days a week and has an enormous selection of high quality fruits, vegetables and soft goods at reasonable prices. Today is the first and not last time that we take note of the exceptional size, quality and range of fruits and vegetables grown in Australia. Apples, oranges, lemons, mangoes, bananas, grapes, apples and a myriad of green vegetables as well as a wide assortment of stunning flowers, many that I have never seen before. We pick up fruit, T-shirts, clothing for Susan & Tyler, and souvenirs including my Australian made genuine kangaroo leather desert hat.

Queen Victoria Market, Melbourne (VIC)

After our market visit and enjoying lunch in our hotel room, we travel by tram to visit the Koorie Heritage Trust to learn about the local Indigenous history and culture. Koorie or Koori refers to the Indigenous people of New South Wales and Victoria. Entering the ground floor foyer, we are met by works of modern art made from barbed wire, bedsprings, fence wire some combined with boomerang and fire-stick.

The centrepiece within the multi-story building is a simulated scar tree of a River Red Gum that still stands at Ebenezer. Scar trees are found throughout Victoria often along rivers. These trees have had sections of wood removed from them to make canoes, temporary shelters, containers and shields. The deep respect for the tree, allowing it to live, removing only what is needed to sustain the community, reveals the true understanding and veneration of nature by indigenous peoples. In the forests of our West Coast of Canada there is evidence of similar forestry practices by indigenous nations dating back several hundred years.

A plaque dedicates the resting place of the skeletal remains of aboriginal people who are the representatives of the 38 tribes whose traditional lands reside in the state of Victoria each listed on the plaque that has the Aboriginal flag as its center piece. Below it is the following inscription:

"RISE FROM THIS GRAVE

RELEASE YOUR ANGER AND PAIN

AS YOU SOAR WITH THE WINDS

BACK TO YOUR HOMELANDS

THERE FIND PEACE WITH OUR

SPIRITUAL MOTHER THE LAND

BEFORE DRIFTING OFF INTO THE

"DREAMTIME""

This is sobering, along with exhibits of news reports of deaths of Indigenous peoples during incarceration, and an exhibit questioning, "if Aboriginal people had become British subjects, why didn't the law, so concerned with property, protect their property rights?" Thankfully, before leaving we are inspired by the words from the following exhibit poster:

"Working Together

Koorie clans in Victoria have always had a diverse range of languages, spiritual beliefs and practices, social structures and art. These old ways have been handed down to us from our ancestors and today we incorporate them with influences from other Aboriginal communities from around Australia and the world. Our unique identity as Koorie people is shaped through a blend of these old traditions and the new through local and world wide contemporary influences.

It is through an understanding of our history, and culture that the wider community can begin to understand our people as we are today. This exhibition is a celebration of our survival. We have a lot to celebrate with the survival of not only our people, but also the world's oldest continuous culture that is still alive and continues to be practised today."

Better informed, our sightseeing continues with visits to St. Paul's and St. Patrick's Cathedrals. We then stop into the tourist information centre near the grand Victorian Flinders Street Railway Station, for maps and information about our upcoming road trip. Melbourne's architecture stands out even on a dreary day. It is a stunning blend of well preserved Victorian structures with bold and colourful modern buildings. Exhausted by our full day of sightseeing, we go back to our hotel to plan and pack for our upcoming journey.

Daryl, our hotel concierge recommends a Spanish food restaurant in Warburton lane. The laneways and alleys of Melbourne are packed with great bars and restaurants throughout the downtown. Many of the lanes are unmarked, and it is challenging to locate our restaurant even by GPS, thanks to the kind assistance of a passing Melbournian. I get the foreboding sense that we are heading into Diagon alley, although our destination is well worth the search. Portello Rosso serves up great mussels, crispy pork belly with almond and garlic puree and an outstanding mixed meat-seafood paella. The evening is an enjoyable and memorable experience. Good call Daryl.

YOU SHOULD KNOW:

Our experience as pedestrians in Australia including at crosswalks is that most cars assume the right of way, with the only exception being at traffic lights, even though the law says otherwise. Australian pedestrians on the other hand got upset with us when we yielded our vehicle to them at crosswalks, waving at us to move along, ensuring that the road was cleared of all vehicles before crossing. In Australia do as the Australians do, and take care when crossing any road. The same rule applies to sidewalks as roads, keep to the left of oncoming pedestrians.

Friday, May 15. Partly Sunny 14°C

This morning begins with an early breakfast at Josey's in the market, and after checking out of the hotel, our vehicle is on the road by 8:30am. Our destination today is Warrnambool, 350 kilometers away via Apollo Bay on the Great Ocean Road. Despite heavy traffic, exiting Melbourne goes smoothly and it is not long till we find ourselves on the Great Ocean Road. The road is very scenic and reminds us of Highway 1 in California. It cuts into the coastline with winding roads and great views of the Ocean, perfect for sports cars and motorcycles. Speeds are well enforced with visible and invisible photo radar along the highway system and most drivers keep below the limit or only slightly over it.

Two of the Twelve Apostles at Port Campbell National Park (VIC)

The Great Ocean Road is stunning and the crown jewels along the way are the Twelve Apostles, giant limestone pillars that have been cut out of the cliffs of the Victoria Coastline. These cliffs and beaches are relatively fragile and subject to erosion. Over a period of 6,000 years the coastline has receded by over two kilometers. The amazing scenery with the beautiful and powerful Southern Ocean pounding the shores provides a surfer's heaven for miles. Along with a smattering of VW buses and the usual beach 4x4 vehicles there are also many Utes travelling along this stretch of highway that are specifically designed to carry surf boards. These stylish surf cars are essentially raised back Holden station wagons or El Camino Holden Utes.

Chris and Tyler at Port Campbell National Park (VIC) | Susan Bryant

GM Holden Ltd. or Holden as it is commonly known, is Australia's first domestic automobile manufacturer. Although the first major car maker was the Ford Motor Company of Australia, Holden was the first domestic designer to mass produce Australian automobiles. Headquartered in Port Melbourne, Victoria, the company was founded in the year 1856 in South Australia as a saddle maker. The company named after its founder James Alexander Holden, began evolving with Edward Holden the grandson of the founder. He joined the company in 1905 and was interested in automobiles. In 1908, the business moved towards minor car repairs and upholstery, beginning its entrance into the automotive field. By 1919, Holden began building car bodies and opening factories. (34)

With the Great Depression in 1931, came a downturn in production and the company was purchased by General Motors. Holden is responsible for GM vehicle operations in the Australasia region and distributes other car brands such as Chevrolet. On November 29, 1948, the then prime minister of Australia Ben Chifley, unveiled the first all-Australian car, the Holden FX. The selling price was $733 including tax, the equivalent of two years of wages for the average Australian worker at that time. Holden was defined by the release of the FJ in 1953. With two tone paint and chrome trimmings, glamorized and Americanized, Holden FJ was a car designed for Australian conditions that did not break down as often as English or American cars.

Today all Australian built Holden vehicles are made at the factory in Elizabeth, South Australia with the engines being built at Port Melbourne. Holden has tried to enter international markets to make itself a more profitable company. Since the 1950s, Holden's exports have fluctuated. In 2002, Holden contributed over one billion dollars to Australia's balance of trade. (34) In 2013, Holden announced that local manufacturing will cease by 2017. Holden has experienced losses with the strong Australian dollar and a reduction in government grants. Although the design center in Port Melbourne and the Lang Lang proving-ground will remain in Australia, Holden is dying a slow death as Australia's car maker. Beyond 2017, it is expected that Holden will consist of a national sales company, a parts distribution center, and a global design studio. Holden's fate will ultimately be defined by the Detroit auto industry's own success. (35)

Having seen a plethora of bird life to date, the only mammals encountered so far have been road-killed: kangaroos, wallabies, wombats and smaller animals. At the main viewing point of the Twelve Apostles, a busload of tourists, are so overcome by seeing a live mammal, that they are feeding a small brown rat and crowding in to snap photos of it. The tourists think it is a field-mouse or small marsupial. It all seems rather desperate, yet somewhat understandable. We stop at shipwreck point and photograph a beautiful arch cut into one of the Apostles and then at Bay of Islands, another viewing point not to be missed. This is usually the return point, if not sooner, for any of the tour buses that have come from Melbourne.

London Arch at Port Campbell National Park (VIC)

Travelling on westward it is not long till we are tempted to stop in at Allansford Cheese Factory and Museum. Recently purchased by Saputo, a Canadian Cheese & Dairy Products company, the dairy is surrounded by miles and miles of dairy farms with lush pasture lands dotted with dairy cows. We go through the museum and then to a wonderful tasting of fabulous cheeses including Colby, Cheddars of different ages and flavours including pepper, garlic and chili cheeses. Unable to leave without purchasing an international award winning extra old Cheddar (Warrnambool Vintage) and mocha milk shakes, the cheese factory is a delightful stop on the way to Warrnambool and is highly recommended by us.

Warrnambool (VIC)

Population: 33,948. Founded in 1850. Traditional lands of the Gunditjmara people known for eel aquaculture. Tourism and agriculture, primarily dairy and dairy processing are the main economic drivers in the community. A notable person born in Warrnambool is comedian Dave Hughes. Warrnambool is most known for the world's first successful trial using maremma sheep dogs to guard a threatened species: the little penguin. Must-See attraction is Tower Hill wildlife reserve.

Arriving in Warrnambool and checking into our hotel, the innkeeper is very helpful in suggesting some things to do and directs us out to a local park, Tower Hill for viewing of wildlife. 5:30 pm, dusk is the best time for viewing. We decide to head straight to Tower Hill before it gets too dark. It is about ten kilometers out of town and as it turns out is inside an inactive volcano. Entering the park by descending a roadway down the crater wall into a Jurassic-like park, after driving cautiously for no more than three minutes, we see grey kangaroos and emus roaming throughout the park. After parking our vehicle and walking a short distance it is not long before the local wildlife comes in close to examine us.

Eerie close encounter of the Emu kind Warrnambool (VIC)

Our first face to face encounter with a wild Emu is quite chilling, as the creature is close to my size and is making a weird clicking sound as it approaches us with no fear. It seems larger than life, more dinosaur than bird through my camera lens and vivid imagination. Backing off and giving the Emus wide berth, we are enthralled to see Joeys grazing from the comfort of mom's pouch and grey kangaroos bouncing through the bush, with the greatest of ease. Being our first encounter with live kangaroos, it is a thriller. Spending 45 minutes wandering around searching for the elusive koala we eventually spot one high up in a Eucalypt, with the help of some German visitors. Returning to town before it gets too dark, we dine at an Italian restaurant before retiring after a complete and satisfying day. The weather is cold, with the night time temperature going as low as 5°C.

Saturday, May 16. Overcast 15°C

It is cold and windy as we depart from our hotel at 9:30am for a warm scrambled eggs breakfast and lattes at the Wharf in Warrnambool. We are treated to a sight we have never seen before. A horse is being exercised out in the ocean, led around by trainers in a row boat. After breakfast, we drive to the other side of the wharf facing the ocean and go for a short hike to view the local penguin colony on Middle Island.

Little (Fairy) Penguins on Middle Island, Warrnambool (VIC)

We had not associated Australia with penguins. Because of its location, in the southern hemisphere, in relative proximity to the penguin mecca of Antarctica, Australia does have small and fragile communities of little penguins. The smallest species of penguin, the little penguins, also known as fairy penguins are the only penguins that live along the southern coast of Australia mainly on offshore islands. One of these islands is Middle Island, just off the coast of Warrnambool, and within sight of shore.

Italian Maremma sheepdogs were assigned in an environmental trial to protect the little penguins from foxes, stray dogs, cats and rats. The little penguin population of Middle Island was reduced to less than ten birds in 2005. The introduction of the sheepdogs in 2006, managed to save what was left of the breeding colony. Middle Island was closed to the public. The penguin population has steadily increased to over 140 Penguins today. The daffodils are blooming with winter just around the corner. Only in Oz.

After an interesting morning, we depart and drive west to Robe, 215 kilometers away through pasture lands filled with dairy cows and sheep, with the odd kangaroo sighting along the way. We stop at Codrington Wind Farm, the first large scale private sector wind farm in Australia. With capacity of eighteen MW it has been operating since July 2001. While taking pictures, it is easy to notice the harmony of the giant wind turbines turning in the breeze, as the cows graze peacefully in the foreground. Renewable energy not only appears to be a better fit with the natural surroundings, it also sounds and feels that it is. We munch on apples and yogurt for lunch at a public park across from the Coach House in Dartmoor. The public toilet is assigned to either squatters or squirters eliminating any gender confusion. After a short rest break, we make our way toward the South Australia border.

Grazing grey kangaroos, Warrnambool (VIC)

Codrington Wind Farm (VIC)

South Australia (SA)
Area: 1,043,514 km². Population: 1,682,600. Founded in 1834.

Although less notable than other states in Australia, South Australia is unique in both origin and attitude. Unlike many of the states in Australia that were founded as penal colonies, South Australia was founded as a free settlement by the British. The official settlement itself was proclaimed on December 28, 1836, at the Old Gum Tree under the direction of Governor John Hindmarsh. The British first established settlements on Kangaroo Island, before settling the area that became the city of Adelaide. As a free settlement, the British attracted immigrants with the promise of civil liberties and religious tolerance. Unlike other states, South Australia was not founded under Terra Nullius and The Letter of Patent attached to the South Australia Act acknowledged the state as traditionally Aboriginal land. Unfortunately, the South Australia Company authorities and squatters largely ignored the policy.

South Australia has traditionally been a progressive state, drafting one of the British Empire's most democratic constitutions providing universal male suffrage from the beginning. In 1861, South Australia granted restricted women's suffrage and in 1895, universal women's suffrage making it second only to New Zealand in the world. It was also the first place in the world where women had the dual right to vote and to stand for election. This progressive attitude dominates South Australian politics that tend to be more centrist or left wing, with the Labour Party usually being elected into office.

South Australia is known as both "the wine state" and "the festival state". South Australian wineries are known for their quality wines. The Barossa Valley is one of the largest wine regions in South Australia and is a major producer of fine Australian wines. South Australia is also home to numerous cultural festivals including the Fringe Festival and the German Schutzenfest. South Australia's landscape is a mix of desert in the north, temperate coast in the south, and plains in the west. Adelaide is the capital of South Australia and is a multicultural and dynamic city. It is almost a smaller version of Melbourne. Culinary offerings in Adelaide are diverse and delicious, with plenty of great Greek, Italian, and Spanish restaurants. The South Australia Museum is home to a remarkable collection of Indigenous Australian artifacts and is absolutely worth a visit. Outside of Adelaide is Australia's oldest surviving German settlement, the village of Hahndorf, that is also a significant tourist trap. South Australia also offers the stunning beaches and landscape of Kangaroo Island, and the wasteland mining town of Coober Pedy that is famous as a filming location for the *Mad Max* movies. South Australia is a lovely and underrated state that is absolutely worth a visit for its fine wine, great cuisine and relaxed atmosphere. (36)

Known for its lobster, Robe (SA)

Robe (SA)

Population: 1,246. Founded in 1847. Traditional lands of the Buandig people. One of the oldest towns in South Australia, the seaside resort and fishing port has seen busier days during the gold rush. Robe's namesake is Governor Fredrick Holt Robe one of South Australia's most unpopular Governors. Most known for and Must-See attraction is the 17-kilometer, Long Beach.

On our arrival in Robe we check into our hotel and spend the latter part of the afternoon catching up online and doing laundry. Enjoying a wonderful dinner at Sails, Susan has the Calamari while Tyler and I dine on kangaroo steak and roasted beets. The kangaroo tastes the same as venison, yet less gamey and tenderer and makes for an excellent meal. Today, we crossed our first time-zone in Australia and have gained half an hour. Our time adjustments seem peculiar and take getting used to. Flying west to Australia we lost a day. Now that we are driving west in Australia, we are gaining time. Only in Oz.

Sunday, May 17. Sunny 15-21°C

We depart from our hotel after breakfast and stop in to take pictures with Robes famous lobster before heading west for Adelaide, 337 kilometers along the Princes Highway via Salt Creek. We stop in at the General Store in Salt Creek for coffee and a washroom break. And yes, the place looks the same as it sounds. It is a stereotypical Ozarks-style fisherman's & hunter's pit-stop, with lots of Deer and Elk heads on the wall, origin unknown. It is a great place to pick up bait, lures and roadkill jerky. The highway has changed from rolling, narrow two-lane English-style road with hedgerows and curves on the tops of rises, to flat and straight two-lane highway with shoulders. There is good clearance of brush on either side of the road and a 110 km/h speed limit allowing us to make good time.

We stop in Tailem Bend on the Murray River for a picnic lunch and then poke around inside the town rail museum for twenty minutes and chat with the curator. Our journey continues to Hahndorf, a former German settlement in the suburbs of Adelaide that has since been converted into a bustling tourist trap. The town is crowded with tour buses and cars overwhelming the local streets, with everyone seeking some authentic retail therapy. The only thing remotely German, is the fellow playing the accordion in his Lederhosen. A gallery is selling authentic Indigenous art and didgeridoos at premium prices. The didgeridoos range in price from $550.00 to $700.00 and the paintings are considerably more. Spending less than an hour poking around we get out alive, spending only $2.50 on what appears to be an authentic pepperoni stick. I pop it into the glovebox to keep as an emergency ration if our vehicle breaks down in the middle of the desert.

Main Street of Hahndorf (SA)

Adelaide (SA)

Area: 3,257 km². Population: 1,304,601. Founded on December 28, 1836. Traditional lands of the Kaurna people. The capital of South Australia is also rated as one of the world's most livable cities. Government, financial sector, health care, auto manufacturing, high tech electronics and defense industries are key economic drivers for the port city. A notable Adelaidean is brewer Thomas Cooper, founder of Coopers (1862), the largest Australian owned brewery. Most known for its food and wine culture. A Must-See attraction is The Australian Wine Centre.

Arriving at the Playford Hotel in downtown Adelaide at 3:30 pm, we unload our gear, and take a few hours to relax and get adjusted to our new surroundings. After dining on a decent $100.00 Hamburger dinner at the Bread and Bone wood grill, we walk back to our hotel the long way and get to bed early. Our hotel is located close to the rail station/casino and there are a lot of drunks wandering the streets.

Monday, May 18 (Victoria Day, Canada). Cloudy 12-20°C

After breakfasting near the hotel, we do some window shopping for opals at Rundle Mall. Stopping in at Haigh's chocolates to buy some dark chocolate covered Macadamia nuts, we then purchase some West Coast Eagles Football tickets for our stay in Perth. We are very lucky to get the last three seats together available for the game in two weeks from now. We are so pleased as we have been told that this will be a great unforgettable experience. It took quite some time to arrange the tickets and we thank you. I did not understand the difficulty of making these arrangements till some time later, when it was explained to me that most tickets belong to club members and do not necessarily come up for sale that often.

Shopping Mecca, The Rundle Mall, Adelaide (SA)

We then shop for a book for Tyler and go for lunch at Subway. After lunch, we visit Adelaide Botanic Gardens, and work our way through these impressive gardens over to the National Wine Centre of Australia. We view the various exhibits that explain the different wines and growing regions in Australia. Then I get down to the serious business of sampling 7 different whites and reds from a selection of over 120 wines available from the different wine growing regions throughout Australia. The dispensing system is advanced. I am supplied with a card linked to my credit card, to insert and choose between three different serving sizes (taste, ½ glass, full glass), for each of the various wines ranging in vintage, quality and price with a 25ml taste of Penfolds Grange going for $35.00.

I pull down a fresh wine glass each time, insert the card for my selected wine and it is automatically dispensed. First, I taste a 2014 Hentley Farms Viognier from the Barossa Valley, a tricky to cultivate white wine variety with a pronounced stone fruit flavour that does not appeal to me. I then taste a delicious 2013 Ministry of Clouds Chardonnay from Tasmania. I am not too impressed with the 2013 Pinot Noir from Yabby Lake Victoria. A 2006 E & E Black Pepper Shiraz Barossa Valley is very good and on the heavy side as is the 2010 St. Hugo Shiraz from Barossa Valley. A Coonawarra Estate Cabernet is so delicious that I forget to note the year. My favourite of the day, is the Gewurtztraminer, Delatite 2013 from Dead Man's Hill that is by far the tastiest. In all fairness, a bottle of each of these wines, paired with the appropriate meal enhances any dining experience.

The more expensive full bodied Australian reds are very good, yet oaky and heavy. I am sure that these are an acquired taste, over time. Price does not necessarily guarantee a great sip of wine, and fortunately many of the less expensive wines sampled throughout our trip are quite tasty. Australia consumes forty percent of the wine it produces, almost thirty liters per capita annually. It is the fourth largest exporter of wine in the world, with vineyards in all states. With about 130 varieties in commercial use in Australia, it is better known for its Chardonnay, Sauvignon Blanc, Shiraz, Merlot and Cabernet Sauvignon. The most famous Australian wine is the iconic Penfolds Grange. The 1955 vintage has won more than fifty gold medals. Australia is a must-see destination for connoisseurs of fine wines. Cellar doors are usually open for tasting year-round at many fine wineries throughout the various wine regions of Australia, from the Hunter Valley in NSW to the Barossa Valley in SA and all the way to the Margaret River in south Western Australia. (37)

The beauty of the National Wine Centre is that I do not have to drive to it. I may sample wines from many different vintners in one location. I fully enjoy the wines and then carry on with our tour on foot. We venture over to the immense Palm House that has a unique three-dimensional sculpture made from sheet glass at its entrance and then over to the aquatic plants centre that houses giant tropical lily pads. As the Botanic Gardens are over fifty hectares in size it is a challenge to get them in entirely. It is surprising how many flowers and trees are in bloom now, including daffodils while at the same time fruits such as lemons, oranges and olives are ripening on the trees. With winter approaching, it all just seems counterintuitive for us Canadians. We walk back via Adelaide University and then rest before going out for dinner at Udaberri Pintxos Y Vino. Dinner is extraordinary, octopus, Portobello mushrooms with egg yolk, and rib eye steak finished off with cheesecake. All is excellent and reasonable at $102. The restaurant has an outstanding relaxed atmosphere with great music and Susan learns a new recipe for a watermelon and cucumber salad. Our bar tender gives us a few quick tips about beaches to visit and how to survive night driving across the

Nullarbor   Plain   if   necessary.   Thankfully,   it   wasn't.

TIP:

If forced by unforeseen circumstances to drive at night, "tuck in behind a road train and watch the roos fly off into the night". I'm not sure how effective the above approach is if you are driving in a car with low clearance. We never tested it. Driving during the daytime we often saw a great number of animal carcasses in the middle of the roadway that we could avoid hitting, by go around them.

Tuesday, May 19. Rain/Partly Sunny 10-18°C

We have a bacon and eggs breakfast near our hotel and then walk over to Adelaide Central Market to buy some lunch and things for tomorrow's breakfast. Afterwards our daytrip takes us over to the South Australian Museum to immerse ourselves in the world's largest collection of Australian Indigenous artifacts and stories. The remainder of our morning is spent going through the various exhibits and watching historic movies of Indigenous peoples. The collection is vast with boomerangs, spears, shields and digging tools. Topics cover medicine, dreaming and the law, ceremonies, fire and its use, and many other important aspects of Indigenous life. Our one criticism of the gallery is the low level of light, that makes it difficult to view many of the exhibits. After lunch at the museum we finish off the afternoon in the South Australian Gallery. We go back to our room for a rest and later go out to dinner at Pizzarea Melt, where we dine on salad, gnocchi, duck and cherry calzone and a Turk pizza with lamb and yoghurt before retiring to pack and ready for our long journey to Wallaroo.

Australian humour at its finest, Adelaide (SA)

Wednesday, May 20. Rain/Partly Sunny 8-14°C

We are up at 8:30 am and have breakfast in the room before checking out and leaving for our journey northwest and then south along the Yorke Peninsula. Our first stop is 150 km away in Ardrossan with its spectacular red cliffs looking out across the Gulf St. Vincent towards Adelaide. Ardrossan is a deep-water port that ships grain, dolomite and salt. It is famous for the home factory of the *stump jump plough.* This

Australian invention was designed specifically to plough difficult terrain containing numerous roots and rocks without damaging the plough.

The spectacular red cliffs of Ardrossan, (SA)

After lunching seaside with the seagulls, we drive on to Moonta, the home of Moonta Mines where rich copper ore was mined between 1862 and 1923. It was one of the largest towns in South Australia with a population of 12,000 in 1875, quadruple of what it is today. After viewing some of the mine buildings and the mine itself, our drive takes us to Kadina and then eventually to Wallaroo the long way, completing 230 kilometers for the day. The area is known as the Copper Triangle and was settled by Cornish miners in the late 1800s who mined the rich copper deposits. It is home to the world's largest Cornish Festival, Kernwek Lowender (Cornish Happiness) that is celebrated in May of every odd numbered year, over a period of seven days and draws up to 30,000 participants. Our timing is perfect although, as we are not Cornish, our family does not partake in the festivities or the drinking of Swanky beer. Susan does however, pick up a recipe for Cornish Pasties.

Wallaroo (SA)

Population: 3,053. Founded in 1851. Traditional lands of the Narangga people. Named after the Aboriginal name wadlu waru (wallaby urine). (38) The largest port on the Yorke Peninsula between 1865 and 1923 when copper production ceased. Still ships many agricultural products including barley that grows particularly well on the peninsula as it is surrounded by ocean climate. Most known for being one of South Australia's more popular seaside resorts. Must see the beach at sunset.

We check into our motel and snoop around town to find somewhere good to eat, making dinner reservations with Coopers Ale House at the Casino Apartments. The meal of seafood, schnitzel and vegetables is good and filling. Then off to bed in our cinder block room that has a heat pump that pumps no heat. I am learning the hard way about checking the room before checking in. I guess that is where the name comes from. I have travelled enough and am old enough to know that you get what you pay for, and tonight we do.

The anchor of Australian towns, the hotel/pub, Port Broughton (SA)

Thursday, May 21. Rain/Partly Sunny 7-14°C

Up and out of town by 7:30, we stop for a good breakfast in Port Broughton. Driving on and buying lunch in Port Augusta, we picnic at the road side. Our drive takes us past the lush Flinders Mountain range on our right with the Ocean and a large water pipeline to our left. Entering desert scrubland on our approach to Whyalla some 275 kilometers along the Lincoln Highway, we spot a large flock of white Cockatoos skimming through a low spot in the terrain. I am amazed that these social and versatile birds seem to know no bounds regarding habitat. As it turns out, the Morgan-Whyalla pipeline that was built between 1940 and 1943 is historically significant and necessary for the survival of Whyalla. The 359-kilometer pipeline provides freshwater from the Murray River not only for the townspeople of Whyalla. It provided the water necessary for steel making by Broken Hill Proprietary Company (BHP) that had been commissioned by the Australian government to supply the steel for shipbuilding for WWII.

The Whyalla Visitor Centre and Maritime Museum
Whyalla (SA)

Whyalla (SA)

Population: 20,088. Founded in 1920. Traditional lands of the Banggarla people. The third largest city in South Australia known for its shipbuilding history, its integrated steel works Arrium (One Steel), and hematite ore export port with eleven million tonnes annual capacity. A notable person born in Whyalla is New York Times bestselling science fiction author Sean Williams. Most known as Steel City. Must-see attraction: if you enjoy industrial tours, the steel plant tour is a good one.

Driving into town, we stop in at the tourist info centre and do a tour of the HMAS Whyalla an Australian WWII minesweeper and the marine museum. The HMAS Whyalla originally named Glenelg was the first ship built at the Whyalla shipyards. The Bathurst class corvette launched in May 1941, and served a range of purposes including minesweeping, antisubmarine and escort duty. The ship received three battle honours "Pacific 1942-45", "New Guinea 1942-44" and "Okinawa 1945". The museum does a great job of describing the Pacific naval campaigns during World War II. A colourful display catches our attention regarding the Indigenous people of Whyalla area who were known to sing to sharks and dolphins at Fitzgerald Bay and Lowly Point to drive fish into their traps. The story is not unique to Whyalla. We saw similar stories about South Pacific Islanders using singing with sharks and dolphins at the South Australian Museum and hear similar stories again from Arnhem Land. It reminds us of the incredible relationship between Old Tom and the whalers in Eden. These are all examples of highly sophisticated symbiotic relationships between humans and creatures of the sea.

We will return in the morning to take the bus tour of the operation at One Steel in Whyalla. We gas up in town at a reasonable $1.17/liter and fill our spare Jerry can as well. We check into our hotel and take a break to handle some administrative issues. Dinner is seaside at the Water's Edge Restaurant. It is expensive. I savour the seafood, while Susan enjoys "Big Donk" - a pork rib chop and Ty settles for a massive burger. The Shiraz is the best I've had so far. It could be that I am just acquiring a taste for it.

Friday, May 22. Sunny 8-15°C

We wake up at 7:00 am, shower, pack, have breakfast at the hotel and are off to the Whyalla One Steel tour. The Whyalla Steelworks is the largest steelworks in Australia with 1700 employees and 1200 contractors in 2011. It was first opened in 1941 by Broken Hill Proprietary Ltd (BHP) to supply pig iron to its other steel plants. BHP spun off the mines and steel works as One Steel in 2000, and in 2012 it became Arrium after acquiring Molycorp in Chile and Alta Steel in Canada. The tour takes us around the sprawling 1000-hectare steel plant by bus. The Arrium mines supply approximately twelve million tonnes per annum (2013-2014) of Hematite ore. Shipping to the coast by rail, most of the ore is exported to China after transferring from smaller ore vessels to larger Cape-size vessels offshore. 1.8 million Tonnes per annum of lower grade Magnetite is transported in a slurry, 62 kilometers by pipeline. It is converted to Hematite in their own processing plant and is used to produce ninety different grades of heavy steel for the domestic market. The plant produces universal beams and columns, parallel flange channels, angle iron, as well as all the rail and sleeper sections for Australian Railway. A good portion of the semi-finished steel goes on for further processing at Newcastle (NSW) to produce grinding rods and balls for the mining industry in Asia and Africa. (39) Our tour continues past the wharf, the reed beds that are used for water treatment, the blast furnace, rolling mills, steel making and casting plants. The highlight of our tour is the opening of the coking oven and the pouring of molten coke into a train right in front of our bus.

The tour is our introduction to Australian Industry, a world powerhouse, especially in the mineral resource sector. Australia is the world's largest exporter of iron ore for making steel. Most of the iron ore exported is high quality hematite ore. A great portion of the ore is mined in the Pilbara region that we will be visiting in June. The roots of the industry are in this region. BHP started mining lead, zinc and silver in Broken Hill, in 1885, eventually merging with Billiton whose tin mining dates to 1851, in Indonesia. Today BHP Billiton headquartered in Melbourne and London, is a leading supplier of commodities globally. (40) Another global giant with large iron ore mining operations in Australia is Rio Tinto, with its headquarters in London and management office in Melbourne. The company whose roots go back to mining copper in Spain, in 1873, also has roots in Broken Hill, going back to 1905, as Zinc

Corp. (41) These companies as well as others, are prominent during our trip as major employers in several communities we visit, and have been important in both the development of modern Australia, and the displacement of Indigenous peoples from their traditional lands. Proximity to the major industrial manufacturing and consumer centres of Asia gives Australia a significant advantage over competitors in the shipment of coal, iron ore, bauxite, gold, uranium, titanium, petroleum, gas and rare earths direct to market.

Whyalla is also world famous for its Australian Giant Cuttlefish spawning grounds out at Stony Point. Saving our diving for the Great Barrier Reef, we skip the trip to Stony Point and at 11:30am make our way to Port Lincoln 267 km via the Lincoln Hwy. Our lunch is a seaside picnic in Cowell, home to the nearby Cowell Jade Province, a ten-square kilometer area containing over 100 nephrite jade outcrops. It is one of the worlds largest known reserves, most of which is leased by Gemstone Corporation of Australia Ltd. Nephrite Jade is the official native stone of China where it is known as the Stone of Heaven. It may range in colour from white to green to black depending on the iron ore content. It is tough having been used in knife blades and axe heads. Fine grained premium black Cowell nephrite jade takes on a mirror polish and is considered the most valuable. Recorded production from the Cowell Jade Province between 1982 and 2013 is 479 tonnes. (42) Our home province of British Columbia, Canada has approximately 70% of the worlds known deposits of Nephrite Jade and produced over 400 tonnes last year, with most of it exported to China. (43) We arrive in Port Lincoln at 3:30 pm after a smooth drive from Cowell.

Port Lincoln (SA)

Population: 14,088. Founded in 1839. Traditional lands of the Nawu people. Claiming to be the seafood capital of Australia, it is reputed to have more millionaires per capita than any other Australian city. Tourism, grain handling, beef, wool, lambs, aquaculture (tuna, oysters, kingfish, abalone, oysters and mussels) and fish processing. A notable person from Port Lincoln is former tuna fisherman Dinko "Dean" Lukin, a weightlifter and Super Heavyweight Gold Medalist at the 1984 Summer Olympic Games in Los Angeles, USA. Most known for its seafood. Must-See attractions: For the adventurous, shark cage diving. For the less adventurous, swimming with tuna.

Convenient Drive-through liquor stores are a popular destination, Port Lincoln (SA)

Enjoying an afternoon coffee, before checking into our hotel we then walk along the beach. We visit the tourist information center and go shopping before retiring to rest and review email. We have dinner at Del Giorno Italian Seafood restaurant and it is excellent. Susan has the King George Whiting while Tyler and I have tuna. The tuna is raised in local sea pens. You can swim with it and then potentially dine on it, all in the same day. Port Lincoln also hosts swimming with sea lions and shark cage diving. The town is subdued, as one of its local youths lost his leg to a shark last week while out surfing.

Being quite aware of the dangerous animals in Australia, it was a real concern for us while planning our trip. Some time ago actor Sam Worthington while on the *Late Show with David Letterman* discussed the many dangers in Australia specifically from poisonous animals causing many North Americans to think twice about travelling to Australia. (44) We are well forewarned about all the poisonous spiders, snakes and jellyfish; as well as those creatures with sharp teeth and jaws, the sharks and crocodiles. We diligently shake out our closed toe shoes and are extra observant while walking outdoors. What we tend to see, is lots of local people walking around in sandals or barefoot, and some swimming or surfing far from shore even at dusk.

Fortunately, we have yet to see any dangerous creatures. Apparently, the poisonous snakes here in the south are all sleeping as the weather at night is dropping down to five degrees Celsius. Most of the menus in Australia especially in small towns are high in cholesterol and low on vegetable content. It is not surprising that the largest threats to life in Australia, are cardiovascular disease and stroke followed by dementia and Alzheimer's disease. Deaths caused by terrifying and poisonous creatures are so low down on the list, that these do not show up in mortality statistics. (45) As it is quite cool and none of us is particularly fond of swimming with tuna or sharks at night, we retire early preparing for our long drive next day.

National Highway or National Floodway?

Saturday, May 23. Sunny 8-16°C

We wake up early and depart from our hotel by eight in the morning, heading for our destination Ceduna, 400 kilometers along the Flinders Highway. Stopping for coffee and a muffin in Elliston, we are given a good tip about a scenic cliff side drive overlooking Anxious Bay. The views out to the offshore islands are spectacular, and as rolling waves crash inshore it is easy to understand its attraction to surfers. There are some art works and unique memorials honouring a local surfer who as it was told to us by one of the locals, was taken in one swallow by a great white shark with a six-foot dorsal fin.

The most fearsome fish known to humanity, the great white shark (Carcharodon carcharius) has a well-known reputation, thanks largely to the Steven Spielberg film *Jaws*, and the Discovery Channel's *Special Shark Week*. The great white shark has no known predators other than killer whales and humans. It preys on fish, turtles, seabirds and most marine mammals preferring seals for their fat and protein content. It has the most recorded attacks on humans of any shark species. Since 1580, there have been 314 confirmed unprovoked attacks globally by great white sharks, eighty have proven fatal (46). Great white sharks may measure up to six meters and weigh up to 3000 kilograms. They are estimated to live over seventy years making them one of the world's longest-lived fish. Great white sharks can swim up to 56 km/h when accelerating and have a variety of specialized adaptations allowing them to catch prey successfully. The good news is that because of our bony structures, humans are not their preferred prey. (47)

Great white sharks are listed by the IUCN as a vulnerable species owing to global overfishing. Although not the target of fishermen, if caught great white sharks are often stripped of their flesh, and fraudulently sold as smooth-hound shark. In Australia, great white sharks are protected under the Environmental Protection and Biodiversity Conservation Act. With national protection, there are much harsher punishments on illegal fishing and trading of white sharks with penalties up to $100,000 and two years in jail. (48) Not all sharks are protected, and there is a commercial fishery for blacktip sharks, gummy sharks, dusky sharks, sandbar sharks and school sharks that are classed as overfished. (49)

Australia has had the largest amount of shark related fatalities in the world, at 234 fatalities in total since 1791. White sharks, tiger sharks and bull sharks account for most of the incidents and 99% of fatalities. (50) The number of shark related incidents have increased from 6.5 prior to 2000 to fifteen per year in the last decade. There is no evidence to indicate that there are more sharks in the water. There are more people enjoying water activities on 11,900 Australian beaches and 35,000 kilometres of coastline. Surfing and swimming related shark attack incidents are the highest. It is important to keep in mind that over the last twenty years in Australia, annual fatalities because of shark attack have averaged just over one person, while fatalities because of drowning have averaged 87 persons. (51)

When enjoying the oceans in Australia you may easily avoid shark encounters by following some basic guidelines. Staying close to a beach and in the range of a lifeguard within a zone protected by shark safety netting is good assurance of avoiding a shark attack. Going out of bounds on your own at dusk, is more likely to result in one of the infamous death scenes from Jaws. Yet out of bounds, is the realm that cannot be denied, to the young and adventurous. We eat lunch on an intricately tiled picnic table, on a solitary cliff overlooking a terrific surf coming in from the Southern Ocean. The table is dedicated, in loving memory to Jevan

Wright 7-10-82 to 25-9-2000. The words commemorating Jevan, fired into inlaid tiles in the table, set a perfect tone to the moment and the scene.

"The search is the driving force...

For any restless souls who dream

Perfect waves hitting an uncharted reef ...

The eerie white silence of an untracked powder bowl...

The magic thrill of discovery...

The gripping rush....

Pure freedom where nothing else matters....

He joined the search".

Jevan Wright Memorial Picnic Table at Anxious Bay (SA)

It is experiences such as today's, resulting either from planned or chance actions where we encounter the unusual, informative, breathtaking or sometimes life altering, that causes great discussion in the car afterwards. Our road trip involves moments of silence in the vehicle, but not too often. If we are not actively taking in scenery or events and discussing them, then we are listening to pre-recorded music or books all conveniently stored on a portable USB flash drive. Although we drive hundreds of kilometers through tedious landscape on the road trip, there is never a dull moment in the car. The stretches of stunning and wonderful landscapes far exceed those that are tedious.

Driving north the terrain changes to scrub land mingled with dried out inland lakes. In spots, sand dunes strike inland, off the ocean. These are bleach white, contrasting against the chalky golden land and the crystal clear blue ocean. Susan finishes the final leg of today's trip with her first go at right hand, left side of the road driving. I for the first time, experience Susan's terrifying perspective as the passenger. We are travelling very close to the narrow shoulder on the left, at 110km/h. One slip and it is all over. Now that I have experienced the passenger's perspective I vow to myself, to do a supremely better job of hugging the centre line of the road as the journey continues. Our arrival in Ceduna is at three in the afternoon.

Ceduna (SA)

Population: 2,289. Founded in 1898. Traditional lands of the Wirangu people. Ceduna is known as the gateway to the Nullarbor Plain with almost a quarter of a million vehicles per year travelling through town. Aside from tourism its economy relies on oyster aquaculture, and its deep-sea port for shipments of grain, gypsum and salt. A notable person born in Ceduna is aerobatic pilot Chris Sperou, winner of thirteen Australian aerobatic championships and named the "The Legend of Outdoor Transport". Most known for its scenic beach and fishing. Must-see attraction: Ceduna Jetty is a great place to go for a walk and enjoy the sunset.

After checking into our hotel, we tour the town and make reservations for dinner at the Foreshore Hotel. Dinner is great, rack of lamb, prawns and pork belly are all delicious, if not a little rushed. Retiring to our room early to get some solid sleep is good, as we have a long day of travel and sightseeing ahead of us tomorrow.

Sunday, May 24. Rain/Partly Sunny 11-17°C

Departing the hotel at 8:30am our destination for the day is 500 kilometers west along the coastal Eyre Highway. It rained earlier in the morning and with water accumulating on the road, we have the good fortune of a daytime sighting of a wombat drinking from puddles. The reddish-brown creature that looks similar as a hairy pig, is quite cute. Being warned well in advance, that hitting one on the road is similar as driving into solid iron, we cautiously slow down. Entering the Nullarbor Plain, takes us from a treed scrubland to a treeless plain filled with succulents, heathers and other low-lying plants. Traveling through Yalta lands and coming to Head of Bight, we go out to view whales. There is a small chance of viewing right whales returning to their breeding and calving grounds, although it is still early in the season. Walking out to the viewing point, the weather is improving, and we are very lucky to spot one whale.

Right Whale calving grounds, Head of Bight
Great Australian Bight (SA)

Lunch is at Head of Bight, prior to leaving for the rest of our journey. Entering the wildlife refuge Nullarbor National Park, road signs warn us of possible encounters with kangaroo, wombats and feral camels here in the heart of the Nullarbor Plain, 200,000 square kilometers of flat and treeless limestone. Indigenous legend tells us that we are in the epicentre where *Baiame* (the Great Spirit) and *Yhi* (Goddess of Light, Warmth and Love) came down to earth from space to bring light and creation to the whole world. (52) I take pictures of the miracle of creation. Tiny green succulents with bright red flowers emerge ever so delicately from a hard, sun baked mineral soil that holds no promise of life, and yet here it is. The plain stretches as far as one can see, as does the road, and then 500 meters off to our left, it drops off a sheer cliff, 80 meters into the Southern Ocean.

The miracle of creation, Nullarbor Plain (SA)

Entering Bordertown and crossing into Western Australia at the Quarantine checkpoint we are searched for fruit and vegetables. The ladies doing the search are in no rush. There is no steady stream of traffic coming through these parts, so the inspectors try to make the most of our stop. They are quite inquisitive about us and our journey and are clearly wanting to chat. Unfortunately for them, choosing to chat with me rather than Susan is a mistake. Unlike her husband, Susan would be more than willing to oblige. After a thorough search of our vehicle and limited chit chat, we are off again and arrive in Eucla.

Western Australia (WA)

Area: 2,645,615 km². Population: 2,565,600. Founded on May 2, 1829.

The largest of the Australian states, Western Australia is sparsely populated. The first European visitor was the Dutch explorer Dirk Hartog, who visited the coastline in 1616. In 1623, British sailors crashed and briefly inhabited the Tryal Rocks area, before sailing on to Jakarta. In 1826, a convict supported military garrison was founded in Frederickstown, what is now modern-day Albany, and in 1829 the Swan River Colony was founded in what is now modern-day Perth. In 1831, the first inland settlement was founded in York. Western Australia finally achieved responsible government in October 1890. It was federated along with the other states in 1901, albeit with much resistance, and there is still a secessionist movement in the state today. (7)

Western Australia's population is mostly concentrated in the south-west corner from Albany up and around to Bunbury and the capital city of Perth where two million of Western Australia's inhabitants reside. The southwestern corner around Perth is Mediterranean in climate, although most of the state is arid and hot with desert farther inland. The north of the state is tropical. Economically, Western Australia is largely a mining state, shipping 46% of Australia's total exports. Gas and iron ore are two of Western Australia's primary exports to Asian markets. Many Western Australians are employed in the sector that has caused controversy with many Indigenous peoples, displacing them from their traditional lands.

Perth itself, is a jewel of a city. It reminds us of Vancouver in some respects. It is more low-key and not quite as exciting or vibrant as other major cities in Australia. Nonetheless, it is independent and confident in its stature as both the business administrative and capital city of Western Australia. It's remoteness from the rest of Australia seems to suit it just fine. The Fremantle suburb is home to the famous Fremantle Prison. It provides important perspective into Australia's history as a penal colony. Aboriginal communities in WA are poor and despite discrimination laws, there is visible segregation between white and Indigenous inhabitants in numerous communities throughout the state.

The north of WA is home to the blood red ochre Pilbara, The Great Sandy Desert and the rugged frontier scenery of the Kimberley. It is also home to gorgeous Cable Beach in Broome, its world-famous pearls, and an amazing saltwater crocodile sanctuary. WA is often ignored by visitors, because of its remoteness and vast distances between communities. The traveler that gives it an honest look does not go unrewarded. Western Australia provides many unforgettable moments, providing both subtle and great insights into life, history and the economy of not only Australia, but the world. These insights are refreshing and at times brutally honest and are important for understanding the attitude and condition of the nation, and civilization in general.

Kilometers from anywhere, Eucla (WA)

Eucla (WA)

Population: 368. Founded in the 1870s. Traditional lands of the Mirning people. Eucla is the largest stopping point on the Nullarbor Plain between Ceduna and Norseman. It provides a rest stop for gas and accommodation with mining and agriculture providing other sources of employment in the local economy. Eucla is most known for its former Telegraph Station that served as a significant repeater station for the Overland Telegraph line between Albany and Adelaide converting International Morse Code to American Morse Code for South Australia and Victoria. Most famous person in Eucla: The Nullarbor Nymph a half-naked blond woman who ran wild with the kangaroos as first reported by kangaroo shooters in 1971. The hoax resulted in sculptures, a movie and an installation at the National Gallery. Must-see attraction: The world's longest golf course, Nullarbor Links is an eighteen-hole, par 72 course that spans 1,365 kilometers.

Our reservation is for a rather basic, yet necessary hotel room at this desert roadhouse in the middle of nowhere. Having gone through another time zone gaining 45 minutes, we somehow sense that we have gone back in time. With no real sights to see or anywhere to go, our option is retiring to our room to be entertained by a colour/black and white TV with rabbit ears and two working channels. We have a hearty Schnitzel dinner. I go with the Pork Schnitzel covered in bacon and eggs over a plate of fries otherwise known as *The Australian.* Another delicious coronary disease dinner.

TIP:

Despite the beautiful selection of fruits and vegetables available in Australia, if you want these as part of your meal, you usually must order these as a side dish in most restaurants.

Monday, May 25. Partly Sunny 11-18°C

Today our journey continues west along the Eyre Highway for another 338 kilometers. It is uneventful except for navigating around over one hundred kangaroo road fatalities, that are being picked over by ravens and wedge-tailed eagles. These great eagles are amongst the largest in the world. Although great hunters, these birds are well known for finding, stealing and guarding carrion possessively. Travelling in the Outback we become very familiar with these apex predators that were a symbol of the Royal Australian Air Force, before being replaced by their dinner, the red kangaroo. Although wedge-tailed eagles are great solitary flyers we commonly see them in roadside gatherings of six to twelve birds, and from time to time over fifty birds gathering when the winds and thermals bring them together for a sailing party. There are no sights of any significance today, and crossing another 45minute time zone arriving in Caiguna, we check into our motel at the BP Gas Roadhouse.

View of dunes stretching inland from the Southern Ocean,

Eyre Highway (WA)

Caiguna (WA)

Population: 30. Founded in 1962. Traditional lands of the Mirning people. Caiguna Roadhouse is a 24-hour rest stop for gas, food and accommodation that was established for travelers just prior to the Commonwealth Games in Perth. A notable person who was murdered near Caiguna is the freed convict and explorer John Baxter who was travelling with explorer Edward John Eyre across the Nullarbor Plain. Must-see attraction: Caiguna Blowhole, four-wheel drive vehicle highly recommended.

There is not much to do here. Caiguna is a staging area for us, offering the essentials for life, and allowing us to rest for the next leg of our journey to Esperance, over 500 kilometers away. We investigate the road to Caiguna blowhole and after careful consideration decide not to take a chance with the car. The John Baxter memorial is even farther away on as rough a road. Ten minutes are spent looking at some artifacts in the local the museum before settling down to watch some 1970-80s TV shows from the US, Charlies Angels and Starsky & Hutch. Dinner is at five pm. The steak is quite good, but Tyler has a lot of trouble downing his burger. He has a well-deserved phobia about dining at petrol stations. We have no trouble falling asleep waking at six am, to warm showers and a hearty breakfast before heading back into the Outback.

It is remarkable that Caiguna Roadhouse even exists. It is in the middle of nowhere and everything must be trucked in over a very long distance. Milk comes in frozen and is stored on premises with a great many other things. The water is pumped in and the roadhouse has its own desalination plant. Judging by the "Don't Ask for Water" sign, the roadhouse does not offer water to passing motorhomes. It does provide all the necessary basics including a hot shower to those that stay and pay for it. Fortunately, our room reservation was made almost a month in advance and is honoured. A road construction crew has purchased all the remaining rooms. Other travellers wanting accommodation are turned away, and as soon as we vacate our room the following morning, it is snapped up.

Highway 1 complete with moving road hazards, Caiguna (WA)

Tuesday, May 26. Partly Sunny 12-19°C

Today our journey takes us 570 kilometers to Esperance via the Eyre and Coolgardie/Esperance Hwy. We enter 90 Mile Straight, the longest straight stretch of highway in Australia, that runs between the roadhouse communities of Caiguna and Balladonia. It, as many other stretches of Highway 1 is ideally suited in serving dual purposes, as a highway and as a landing strip for the Royal Flying Doctor Service (RFDS). The highway is signed and marked on the pavement with piano key striping in landing zones.

Royal Flying Doctor Service (RFDS) of Australia is one of the world's largest aeromedical services. The Flying Doctors Service is a non-profit organization providing emergency and primary health care services to those living in Australia's most rural and remote areas. The organization was founded by Presbyterian Reverend John Flynn who worked in the remote areas of Victoria. He originally tried establishing hospitals out in the bush. Lt. Clifford Peel, a WWI combat pilot gave Rev. Flynn the idea of using planes to reach remote areas as Peel had seen missionary doctors do in the battlefields of France. Peel died in the war, without knowing his immense contribution to Australian society. Flynn also realized that with advances in radio he could communicate with missions and stations in remote areas as well.

By 1928, Flynn had enough funds to start his experiment. With the aid of Qantas airlines, the first flight was launched on May 17th of that year. The Flying Doctors became the first comprehensive air ambulance service in the world. Over time the service relied less on donations, obtained funding from the Commonwealth and hired their own pilots. Today the Flying Doctors provide several services including emergency response, emergency evacuation, tele-health, primary health care clinics, consultation and support for rural and remote doctors, inter-hospital transfer of patients, and education. RFDS is structured as seven different legal, independent charitable organizations serving the different regions of Australia. 35 airbases support a combined fleet of 66 aircraft that include: Beechcraft Super King Airs, Cessna 208 Caravans, Hawker 800s, and Pilatus PC 12s and 4WD ground support vehicles. The service has Pilatus PC24 jets on order for 2017-18 that will halve the time on some of the longer routes.

The Flying Doctors have an important legacy of service and care to those living in Australia's most remote communities. As a humanitarian non-profit, their service is appreciated by many Australians who otherwise would not have proper access to health care. To understand their importance, on an average day the Flying Doctors travel 72,870 km by air, perform 203 landings, have 750 patient contacts, transport 112 patients, and conduct 243 telehealth sessions. Up to one quarter of RFDS medical evacuations are for city travelers who get into trouble on their Outback adventure. (53) Our family is determined not to become part of this statistic.

Exiting the Nullarbor Plain on the approach to Norseman, we meet the junction with the highway going north to Coolgardie. During the gold rush of the 1890s, Coolgardie was the third largest community in Eastern Goldfields region of Western Australia and at its peak in 1898, it had 15,000 inhabitants and 700 mining companies listed on the London stock exchange. (54) The town is now a mining ghost and tourist town. Instead of heading north to Coolgardie, we continue south along Highway 1 to Esperance.

Our lunch layover is with ten cops from the Western Australia Police whose shiny Holden interceptors surround the BP gas station in Norseman. Cops nearby, the friendly manager of the BP gas station introduces himself as we eat lunch by loudly declaring "I'm a racist....

I'm part English…. I'm part Irish…I'm part convict" and then what we are not expecting to hear, "and part Aboriginal", followed by the punch line, "I hate everybody equally." That is so Australia. It goes without saying that many white Australian men are tall and even at middle-age are well built as if on steroids, projecting a tough Ozzie exterior, the same toughness as the land. The police and the manager must all be working out at the same gym and fighting at the same bar. Tyler struggles opening the twist cap on his Ginger beer. The self-declared racist grabs the bottle trying to open it for him with all his might, and then unsuccessfully with his new jackknife. After giving up, he comps Tyler a new bottle of Ginger beer. Tough exterior, all heart inside. We will not forget. Ta.

Traveling through the roundabout in the centre of town, we stop to take pictures of the Norsemen camels. Camel teams were a common sight in Norseman in the early 1900s and played a large role in the transportation of household goods, wool and mining equipment into the Goldfields-Esperance region. The width of the main street of Norseman was dictated by the turning circle of a camel team which usually consisted of five pairs of camels hitched to a wagon. The camels could travel long distances without water. The largest wagon trains consisted of seventy camels and were managed by four Afghan handlers. At least 15,000 camels from Arabia, Afghanistan, and India along with their handlers were introduced into Australia between 1870 and 1900. As camels were replaced by modern transportation in the 1930s many handlers released their camels into the wild. Australia is home to the only remaining population of wild dromedary camels in the world. In 2008, it was estimated that too many feral Dromedary and Bactrian camels in Australia were having a negative impact on indigenous plant and animal species, livestock fencing and water infrastructure over an area of 660,000 square kilometers. The Australian Feral Camel Management Project was established in 2009 and concluded in 2013. It is estimated that the camel population had been reduced primarily through helicopter culling of 160,00 camels to the current estimated population of 300,000 camels. (55) Live Australian camels are exported to Saudi Arabia, Brunei, Malaysia and the United Emirates where the meat is considered a delicacy. The camels are also exported to racing and tourist venues throughout the world.

The Camels commemorating their part in the history of Norseman (WA)

There are a variety of feral and other pest animals that were introduced to Australia that have no other known predators and are damaging the natural ecology and native species. These include over 200 million cane toads, over 200 million European rabbits, over 23 million feral pigs, over seven million red foxes, over five million donkeys, over two million goats, over 300,000 Brumby (wild horses), over 150,000 water buffalo, and feral cats that are the most widespread and invasive of all species. The Australian Department of Environment works with states to provide assessments, develop plans, and fund key management strategies that usually employ private contractors to manage invasive plants and animals using the most effective and humane methods, ranging from biological & chemical control to trapping or shooting. (56) Although these measures seem harsh, it is important to know that invasive plant and animal species are a direct threat to Australia's biodiversity. Most of the estimated 570,000 species of plants and animals in Australia are found nowhere else on earth.

Travelling south towards the Southern Ocean, the terrain is changing from desert scrubland to greener pastures and larger trees. The trip goes smoothly with just one difficult pass of a massive oversized mining truck. After sighting our first dingo today, marching right down the middle of the highway, we arrive in Esperance at 3pm and check into our unit at the Captain Huon Motor Hotel.

The port of Esperance (WA)

The local vegetation shows off its fall display of brilliant colour
Esperance (WA)

Esperance (WA)

Population: 9,919. Founded in 1896. Traditional lands of the Wudjari people. Esperance (Hope) was named after the French vessel captained by Jean-Michel Huon de Kermadec on making first landfall in 1792. Tourism, agriculture and fishing are its main industries and the port can handle Cape-class vessels (up to 180,000Tonnes) for export of iron ore and grain. Esperance's notable family are its founding brothers: Andrew, Charles, James and William Dempster who leased 123,000 hectares of land to raise sheep and built the first jetty to ship sheep to market in Adelaide. Not so famous for the heaviest wave in Oz: Cyclops. Must-See attraction: Lucky Beach, Cape LeGrande National Park.

Our unit has its own parking space and is spacious with a kitchen and laundry. We make the most of the opportunity to get a few loads of laundry in. Tyler is very satisfied, with a nice rack of lamb for dinner. The seafood is "underwhelming", to put it in Susan's words. No beer or liquor at this restaurant, yet it has a corkage policy. It is a Bring Your Own Bottle restaurant, a common occurrence throughout Oz. There are days in Oz, that I would prefer Bring Your Own Dinner, as some of the underwhelming meal prices are through the roof. We get to sleep early, as the plan is for a full day outing to Cape Le Grande National Park.

Wednesday, May 27. Partly Sunny 10-17°C.

We leave for Mandooboornup, Cape Le Grande National Park after breakfast. The park is thirty kilometers east of Esperance on the coast and has the reputation for having the most beautiful beach in Australia. Along the way, we see some emus calmly parading through a pasture. Entering the park boundary, after paying our fee in the self-deposit envelope we make our way to Frenchman Peak. Frenchman Peak is notable for the wonderful view of the park, especially for those that journey up to the peak. It also has an impressive eye cave near the peak. A park sign informs us that the cave was carved into the granite over forty million years ago by a sea that was at least 250 metres higher than the current sea level.

From one perspective, the cave looks the same as the eye in an eagle's head, no doubt the inspiration behind the Walich (Eagle) Dreaming for this area. As the Dreaming story goes the rocks offshore are two Indigenous children who were warned not to steal eagle's eggs and stole them any way. Eagle picked them up and dropped them into the sea and did not allow them to return despite their numerous attempts. We take some pictures and then work our way down to Lucky beach.

The approach to beautiful Lucky Beach
Cape Le Grande National Park (WA)

The sensation approaching Lucky Beach is the same as the sensation approaching Crater Lake in Oregon. Nothing prepares you for the stunning intensity of the landscape, on a sunny day. All of us are awestruck by the brightness of the pure white sand against the backdrop of a turquoise ocean. We take in the view from the distance, and then drive down to the beach, park the car and walk the virtually empty beach. It is easy to see why many travel enthusiasts maintain that Lucky Beach is the most beautiful beach in Australia. Walking along the beach, taking in the breeze and the birds, we look for stray kangaroos and then lunch at a picnic table with one of the best views in the whole world.

The plant life as in most other places in Australia, is diverse and new to us. There are two plants that stand out for us today. One is a pincushion hakea with flowers that look the same as round red pincushions filled with white pins. The other is a yucca-like shrub that has a large two-meter spike poking out through the middle that is covered in tiny cream-coloured flowers, encrusted with honey bees. After lunch, we work our way back slowly stopping in to look at the natural boulder formations at Whistling Rock near Thistle Cove. It looks as though the boulders migrated here from Easter Island.

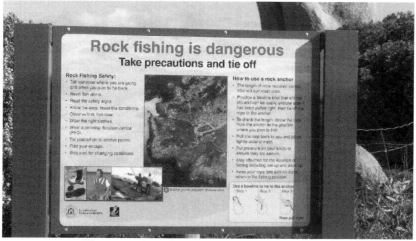

Clear warning signs are all too often ignored
Cape Le Grande National Park (WA)

Whistling Rock is a picturesque and popular spot with rock fisherman. Ocean fishing from rock outcrops is a popular pastime in Australia. It is also quite dangerous, taking many lives each year. On more than one occasion, in different locations throughout Australia, we see sport fishermen challenging incoming waves from the ocean, completely unharnessed and without life jackets. Today is a relatively calm day and there is no one in sight, other than warning signs requesting fisherman to tether and wear a life jacket. Little do we know, that tomorrow a rock fisherman will be swept out to sea from this exact location, never to be seen again. As with all warning signs in Australia, if you choose to ignore them, don't be surprised by what bites you. We drive down to Le Grand beach where the wind is driving in a high tide. A four-wheel drive vehicle from Sydney pulls out on to the beach for the scenic 22-kilometer drive down to Wylie Bay. I am glad that our vehicle is not four-wheel drive. If it was, I sense that at this very moment, I could easily be tempted into getting us into a situation that I might not be able to get us out of.

On our way back to our hotel, we skip visiting the re-creation of Stonehenge and head into town to buy groceries for a seafood pasta dinner. Susan surpasses most of the restaurants in Australia with a delicious meal that comes in under $50.00 for the three of us. Esperance itself is a truly beautiful seaside community with a long fishing jetty, a great waterfront park with covered picnic tables and all the necessary amenities for beach-side living. A sculpted whale tail framed with Jarrah (Eucalyptus marginata) wood and steel, with beautiful stain glass inlay shows off its beauty, as the sunset cascades through its coloured glass. The beautiful sculpture by Cindy Poole and Jason Woolridge, was inspired by the graceful display of a southern right whale fluke as a whale came in close to shore to rest one winter.

As relaxed as Esperance sounds, it is the place for those seeking adventure as well. Two hours offshore is Cyclops, the heaviest wave in Oz, and possibly the world. Owing to its remoteness and difficulty, Cyclops is Australia's most notorious, least surfed wave. The reef wave is not for the faint of heart. Kamikaze or experts only. If it doesn't crush your bones or tear you up, and the sharks don't get you, then you've had a G' Day Mate. As the Ozzies tell it, "To surf this wave you just need real big balls and to be crazy." (57)   Our qualifications for this experience are dubious, so we skip it.

Thursday, May 28. Rain/Cloudy 10-18°C

We depart at 8:30am for Albany, 480 kilometers west along the South Coast Highway. Today's journey will take us through the Fitzgerald Biodiversity Reserve, a UNESCO World Heritage Site with over 1800 species of native flowering plants. Prior to entering the Fitzgerald, we stop in Ravensthorpe for coffee. The café owner recognizes our accent and is one of the few Aussies who does not say: "You must be from America". He has worked in the film industry in Vancouver and spots our accents immediately. While sipping on our lattes he recounts an experience working with David Duchovny on a commercial shoot in Vancouver that was relocated to LA for $350,000.00 because of rainy weather. It seems that David had trouble getting along with everyone, and is missed in Australia, as much as he is in Vancouver.

Australia is home to an estimated 570,000 species of higher plants and animals. 84% of the plants, 83% of the mammals and 45% of the birds are only found in Australia. It is classed as one of 17 megadiverse countries by Conservation International. Many of these species have been threatened by the activities of man, and Australia in conjunction with the states and local communities are identifying areas at threat and restoring them. (58) The Fitzgerald Biodiversity Reserve was designated a Biosphere Reserve by UNESCO in 1978, because of its high biological diversity. It is home to over 2,500 vascular flora species, 100 of those grow no where else in the world. It is also home to 29 mammal species, 51 reptile species, fourteen amphibian species and 209 bird species. These include a number we keep our eye out for, including the threatened Carnaby's black cockatoo, the dibbler, and malleefowl, and some we prefer not to see, such as the southern death adder and the carpet python. (59)

incushion Hakea (Hakea laurina), Fitzgerald Biosphere Reserve (WA)

Along the way, I stop to take pictures of a variety of different shrubs and flowers that I have never seen before. The plants include a number from the Genus Acacia, better known as wattles that not only have beautiful displays but are also very fragrant depending on the species. There is such a variety of plants from the other Genus including Banksia, Callistemon, Melaleuca, Hakea, that frankly I give up trying to identify the specific species and just keep snapping photos. It is obvious that a great variety of the flowers here appear in spikes or pincushions doing their best to be noticed, either as a pollination strategy or to attract victims to their dew traps. The plants here are highly adapted to retain moisture and some species tap moisture from the roots of other grasses and plants. The leaves are waxy, have reduced surface area and are angled to reduce their exposure to sunlight. Many, such as the wattles, also fix atmospheric nitrogen in their root nodules.

Exiting the Fitzgerald, we stop in the shire of Jerramungup for lunch. On the advice of two friendly local ambulance drivers, we divert from our route, and take the scenic road through Stirling Range National Park. Along the way, we see warning signs for malleefowl. These ground dwelling birds look the same as bush chickens and are difficult to spot in the wild. Malleefowl lay their eggs in large compost mounds covered with sand, keeping the eggs at a constant 33°C temperature. Once the eggs are laid, the mother has nothing more to do with them or with the chicks after hatching. Malleefowl are considered a vulnerable species on the IUCN Red List suffering from predation by red fox and habitat loss. We stop in at the Yongergnow Malleefowl Centre in Ongerup and do get to see a stuffed malleefowl.

We depart the centre heading west/south-west eventually coming to a sign for Bluff Knoll. Taking the side road up to Bluff Knoll we take pictures of the lush forested mountains and vista below. It is one of the few places in Western Australia where it may snow. Signage reminds us that while in the Stirling Mountain Range we are in a sacred place to the Noongar people. Koi Kyenunu-ruff means mist moving around the mountains and that is exactly what is happening right now. Bular Mial (Bluff Knoll) means many eyes and is home to a powerful ancestral being who is feared and dangerous.

The Knolls visit Bluff Knoll (Bular Mial)
Stirling Mountain Range (WA)

A steady mist brings fragrant flowers into bloom in all their splendour. Bluff Knoll is home to 80 plant species found nowhere else on the planet. Numbats and Dibblers have been reintroduced into the area. It is astonishing at how lush Australia has been so far. All of us pictured most of Australia as a vast desert. Yet, there is substantial plant life even in the driest areas visited, thus far. Sure, there have some sand dunes along the way. To date, we have yet to see lands barren of any plant life.

Departing Bluff Knoll, we encounter our first live wildlife for the day, large numbers of bright colourful budgerigar and lorikeets. These lively birds are playing chicken with the car, swooping in low and close to the vehicle. I back off on the accelerator as I am concerned about hitting the birds. Getting closer to our destination and merging with a mining highway that has active trucking on it, we pass a three-trailer road train once. We follow the rest of the road trains thereafter, as the passing speed and distance required to pass is significant and the roads are tight. These trucks don't slow down at all and the trailers sway back and forth, especially on a breezy day. It must be unnerving to pass a four-trailer road train and I am reluctant to try that. We roll into Albany at the tail end of the day.

Red Tingle Tree, Valley of the Giants
Walpole (WA)

Albany (WA)

Area: 90 km². Population: 30,656. Founded on December 26, 1826. Traditional lands of the Minang people. Albany is Western Australia's oldest permanently settled town. Tourism, agriculture, timber and fishing have taken over from whaling as the main industries. Western Power Wind Farm to the west of town supplies it with up to eighty percent of its electrical demand. A notable person born in Albany is Olympian Rechelle Hawkes, Hockeyroo's captain for eight years and winner of three Olympic Gold medals. Famous for being the last port of call for ANZAC troop ships destined to Europe in World War I. Must-see attraction: The National Anzac Centre.

We check into our motel at Emu Point in Albany and then go to town for groceries. After walking out to Emu Point beach and seeing some of the local sights, we dine at Rustlers Steakhouse. Lately our motel receptionists, including here in Albany, have been somewhat incensed by our taking so little time to stay and enjoy the local surroundings, "after all Albany is the 3rd largest city in WA". It is not, but I hold my tongue.

No doubt our hosts are well intentioned. Nonetheless, I feel it is important to cite some observations. It is a common sentiment amongst most Australians who we have discussed our journey with, that it will be impossible for us to complete our journey, in the two months allocated. We have been told everything from six months to three years, to just impossible to get around, "as the roads don't connect, don't you know?" Some reasons contributing to these time discrepancies may include the following:

First, us Americans, specifically Canadians, tend to be in a hurry especially when crossing our own great land. We eventually need to get to our destination on time. Some of us do not appreciate nuances and prefer rather to just see the highlights of any place. Point us in the direction of the world's largest lobster. Some of us get quite miffed when someone replies, "well everything in this town is a top attraction".

YOU SHOULD KNOW:

If you are a Canadian get used to being called an American in Australia. Our sovereignty from the US is akin to New Zealand's from Australia.

Second, Australians have a knack for taking time to tell a tale and for being told a tale. Despite their rugged exteriors and standoffishness, they are very social beings. So, the concept of travelling around Australia may involve getting into long conversations with everyone along the way and take more than a few months.

Third, may be the challenge of getting anywhere as many Australians are so focused on getting that free camping spot, a highly prized and talked about item by free campers. We witnessed these discussions and the caravan campers who in their ambition to get that perfect free spot, barely got away from one choice location at the side of the road, before setting up at another. And of course, there is all the socialization that goes along with breaking and making camp. So naturally you are not getting too far, unless you begin to run out of supplies and some sense of urgency kicks in.

Here we are in Albany at the end of May and I am looking at the distance travelled in our American haste, almost across the entire southern part of the continent. Now, we must travel all the way up along the West Coast, all the way across the top of the continent in the other direction, and then all the way south along the east coast to Sydney, in a little more than the time it took us to get here from Sydney. The remaining journey is through the most rugged and desolate regions of Australia, where for all practical purposes the road conditions are unknown to us. You know, I am beginning to believe the doubters. I am beginning to lose faith in the plan. What else can we do, but persevere on? It is not as though we are doing the trip on foot, or on the back of a camel, and after all this is a family vacation. What could possibly go wrong?

Friday, May 29. Sunny 11-18°C

We leave early for Bunbury, 358 kilometers away. We interrupt our drive for a visit to the Valley of the Giants, one of the highlights I have been looking forward to seeing, since reading *In a Sunburned Country*. Today is our first and only encounter with the giant Red Tingle Trees, seventy-meter giants with girth's up to twenty meters at the Walpole Wilderness Discovery Centre. The tree top walk gives us a unique perspective of these ancient giants. These trees, many that are over 400 years old have origins in Gondwana, when all the continents were linked together in the supercontinent Pangaea. These trees provide proof of linkage with trees in Madagascar and Africa since the split of the continents.

Gondwanaland or Gondwana was the southern half of the supercontinent known as Pangaea. Gondwana formed through the drift and collision of minor and major plates about 570-510 million years ago. Gondwana then joined with the massive northern landmass Laurasia to form the supercontinent of Pangaea about 300 million years ago and split off again about 250 million years ago. Gondwana included most of the land masses in the Southern Hemisphere. It began splitting up because of volcanic and seismic activity between 180 to 170 million years ago. India was the first to split away, followed by Africa, and New Zealand. South America and Australia were the last continental plates to split from Antarctica some 45 million years ago and were dragged northwards along with their Gondwanan flora and fauna. Australia continues to move northwards at the rapid pace of three centimeters per year. (60)

Gondwanan organisms have origins in Gondwana and are restricted to two discontinuous regions that have become separated over time. The Proteaceae family of plants (Macadamia as an example) have origins in Gondwana, are predominant in the southern hemisphere and are found in southern South America, South Africa and Australia. There are forty species of Myrtle living across landmasses in the Southern Hemisphere. There is also a fossil record from the temperate rain forests with similar species of trees, plants and animals across the Southern Hemisphere continents. Gondwanan Rainforest covered the entire continent at one time. As Australia drifted, and climatic conditions changed, much of the rainforest disappeared.

The Gondwanan heritage of Australia is preserved in the UNESCO World Heritage Sites, Gondwana Rainforests. Comprised of fifty rainforest reserves from Newcastle to Brisbane around the Queensland-NSW border these are fine examples of major stages in Earth's evolutionary history, active geological and biological processes and exceptional biodiversity. Many of the plant and animal species have their origins in Gondwana. Gondwanan rainforests are not only found in NSW and Queensland, the largest Gondwanan rainforest in Australia is the Tarkine wilderness in Tasmania. Gondwana represents an important part in Australia's natural heritage and a fascinating link between Australian plant and animal species with those from other regions of the world such as South Africa and the Indian subcontinent. (61) (62)

The walk through the trees is absolutely exhilarating, taking us forty metres high, giving us a tree's eye view from atop the forest. The walkway is in excellent condition and is wheel chair accessible. As these trees require 1200 mm/year of rainfall for healthy growth there is serious concern about their sustainability, as drought impacts caused by climate change increase in frequency. Drought is also of concern to another Gondwanan that inhabits the site and only emerges in the rain. At the extreme opposite in size, is the hermaphroditic Bothriembryon land snail who lives in the forest litter and whose shell length is no more than thirty millimeters

Red Tingle (Eucalyptus jacksonii) trees in the Valley of the Giants, Walpole (WA)

We spend the best part of the morning here and then depart for our next destination, Bunbury. Driving through at least seventy kilometers of burned out forest, only the tall Eucalypts have survived and everything else in the understory has been consumed by fire. The ground, lower stems and litter are black with char. The old and dead wood has been burned and converted into soil improving charcoal. Forest pests have been destroyed, and mineral soil exposed to seeds refreshing the forest for years to come, as part of the natural fire ecology. Green shoots are already bursting through the black and red soil providing a colourful contrast.

Renewal following fire on route to Bunbury, (WA)

Indian Ocean Sunset, Bunbury (WA)

Bunbury (WA)

Area: 139 km². Population: 68,248. Founded in 1836. Traditional lands of the Kaniyang people. Bunbury is the second largest city in Western Australia. The port services agriculture, timber and mining. A notable person born in Bunbury is Baron John Forrest of Bunbury explorer, surveyor and the first Premier of Western Australia. Famous for being Australia's fastest growing city. Must-See attraction: Dolphin Discovery Centre.

After arriving in Bunbury or Bumberry, as Susan mistakenly calls it, we check into our hotel before going to the beach and then the Dolphin Discovery Centre. It is unfortunately closed by the time we get there. Having some time on our hands, we give the car a well-deserved wash. The shiny white Toyota Camry is coated with red oxide grime. It seems to smile with delight as its beauty is once again revealed. The car wash has been long overdue, as our clothing have suffered the price of accidental brushes with the grimy car. Our choice is to dine at the hotel as we are too tired to make any effort to go out tonight and have big plans for tomorrow.

Saturday, May 30 Sunny 11-21°C

Our original plan was to spend the better part of the day in Bunbury at the Dolphin Centre before driving to Perth. Our plan has changed, as through correspondence with Susan's friend Nancy, we have an invitation to attend a special event in Perth this morning. Our departure is early, but not before taking some time to dip our toes in the Indian Ocean. The water feels a little cooler than the Southern Ocean, yet is still a comfortable 21°C. Although our road trip has already rounded the southwest corner of Australia and has been heading north, today's two hour, 178-kilometer journey from Bunbury to Perth is the first northward leg of our trip up the West Coast of Australia.

Perth (WA)

Area: 6,418 km². Population: 2,021,200. Founded in 1829. Traditional lands of the Wajuk Noongar people. Perth is the largest city and capital of Western Australia, and the fourth largest city on the continent. Government, business administration and services are key drivers for the local economy although tourism, sports and entertainment are also significant. A famous person born, raised and buried in Perth is actor Heath Ledger. Perth is famous for being the most isolated Capital City in the world and the sunniest Capital City in Australia. Must-see attraction: King's Park and its Western Australia Botanic Garden.

Arriving at our hotel in downtown Perth at 9:30 am, the staff are nice enough to check us in early. At 10:00 am we meet in the lobby with Nancy Jones, a local independent film maker. Nancy happens to be a good friend of Susan going back to her university days, when she lived in Vancouver. Nancy is an awesome host. She truly loves Perth, is engaged and knowledgeable about many issues in Australia. Nancy is proud to show us the highlights, and gutsy enough to show us some of the other facets of the Australian story that most Australians are either unaware of or prefer not to discuss.

Nancy has invited us to join her at a very special event that will not only entertain us with culturally significant song, music, and dance but also enlighten us about the struggle that Indigenous peoples endure in Australia. We have a quick coffee and walk over to the Concert for Matagarup-Refugees on our Homelands Event, presented by the Nyoongar people on Matagarup (Heirisson Island) in the middle of the Swan River, near our hotel. The meandering Swan River is aptly named for the black swans that grace its banks and are prominent in the City of Perth emblem. Perth is known as Boorloo by the Nyoongar people who have inhabited the area for over 40,000 years. The wetlands on the Coastal Plain of the Swan are mythically and spiritually significant as well as being traditional plant gathering and hunting grounds. On September 19, 2006, the Federal Court of Australia brought down a judgement recognising Nyoongar native title over the Perth metropolitan area. The judgement was overturned on appeal in 2008.

Matagarup is a registered site with the Government of Western Australia Department of Indigenous Affairs and is a mythological site with open access and no restrictions, officially recorded as a Meeting Place, Plant Resource and Hunting Place. It is also a sacred birthing site and home to the Nyoongar Tent Embassy, sometimes called the Western Embassy that was established in February 2012, on the 40th anniversary of the Canberra Tent Embassy's inception. (63) These Embassies (East and West) exist to remind all Australians, that Australia always was and will always be Aboriginal land. These are important meeting places in the struggle for dignity, respect and recognition of the UN Declaration on the Rights of Indigenous Peoples. The concert is part of the Grandmothers Against Forced Removals and covers the Forced Removal of Children, the Forced Removal of Communities and Deaths in Custody. It includes story telling, poetry, puppetry and music by artists including Manaaki, The Weapon is Sound, Baby Kool, Pitch Black, The Strangerz, Spacehound and the Catalpa Memorial Flute Band to name some.

It is a beautiful day for our fifteen-minute walk over to the camp at Matagarup, arriving at around 10:30am. While crossing the bridge over the Swan River we view a large welcoming banner for the concert. Police are in force and gathered in the parking lot and are not welcome to the camp or festivities. Entering from the parking lot there is a sign that says Refugee Camp and has an Aboriginal flag flying from it. There is a wood carving of an Indigenous person kneeling on the ground weighed down by ball and chain. The main stage has an Aboriginal flag flying from it. The flag has a yellow sun in the middle with a background that is half black representing the people, and the other half red representing the earth. Flying proudly next to it is a Ché Guevara flag and on the other side of it the Maori flag. A sun banner hangs from another tent declaring in red and black print: Always was, always will be Aboriginal Land.

Family groups from different parts of Australia and New Zealand are camped in different spots throughout the park encircling the main stage area. There is a lot to take in. There are many persons both Indigenous and non-indigenous milling about. Some of the younger men carrying spears, are in shorts with bodies and faces painted in white pigment. Tyler interviews a striking aboriginal man with blond hair and blue eyes as he is applying yellow and red ochre pigment to his face. We then speak with an elder and are welcomed as visitors from America.

Welcome Banner at Matagarup, Boorloo (Perth) (WA)

All attending, are smoked in by native elders and then welcomed to country, followed by Corroboree an interaction with Dreamtime through costume, music and dance. The dancers are young males Michael, Lewis and Clinton and the youngest a child, Peter and are accompanied by Bryce on the didgeridoo. We are treated to traditional spirit, emu, and kangaroo dances. The animal dances tending to mimic their behaviour in nature. Three elders speak about the reasons for the meeting today. It is clear to me that whatever may have occurred in the past, these persons gathered here today are proud and defiant. I feel as though I am trespassing, and yet I am honoured to be part of today's event.

"We are treated as refugees in our own land"

"This is our land, not their land, what gives the white man the right to tell us where we can live and what we can do in our country?"

Outspokenness is generally uncharacteristic of the Indigenous people we have met and will continue to see along the way, who if not outright shy, are generally reserved and keep to themselves. A very proud Maori leader speaks and then a Maori Performing Arts Group performs Manawa mai tawhiti – Kapa Haka. Their music, singing and facial expressions are intense, serious, intimidating and yet at times comedic. Witnessing the Haka is in and of itself a once in a lifetime experience. What a Day!

From Tyler's notes, "The next Indigenous Australian protest event we went to was a protest concert at a park in Perth. This protest was much more militant in nature and demanded immediate action on the part of the government. The protest had to do with the homeless, predominantly Aboriginal, being forcibly removed from public parks in Perth by the police. The protestors described themselves as "refugees in our own bloody country". Another protestor said, "they look at us like flora and fauna". Aboriginals until 1967 were officially considered part of the flora and fauna of Australia, not as people. Despite making up only three percent of Australia's population, fifty percent of juveniles in custody are Aboriginal youth. As one protestor said, "I look at them as terrorists". Only one fifth of the money Aboriginal Australians supposedly get from the government makes it to the people. Even though the government says it is informing Aboriginal Australians about the closures of remote communities, there are still many Aboriginals living off the land and who are remote enough not to know about the government's actions. Many Aboriginal Australians see the sex abuse claims made by government, as an excuse to justify illegitimate interventions."

The day of song and celebration raises funds to prevent the displacement of Aboriginal peoples from their ancestral lands in Western Australia. Shirts, food and bracelets are for sale. More stories are told, and numerous songs performed by a variety of artists including folksingers, rappers and rock artists. The appearance of the Irish Catalpa Memorial Flute Band surprises us. We are treated to a great marching band with the Fenian fighting spirit against injustice, and another important piece of Australian history, that is new to us. The band engages communities and is symbolic for struggle against injustice, memorializing the Catalpa.

The Catalpa was a ship involved in a daring prison break-out of six Fenian brothers imprisoned at the infamous Western Australian Fremantle Prison. From 1865-1867 members of the Irish independence organization the Irish Republican Brotherhood, popularly known as the Fenians, were rounded up and arrested by British authorities. 62 were transported to Western Australia, then a penal colony. Although many Fenians had been pardoned, a small militant group remained imprisoned in Western Australia. John Devoy an exiled and key Fenian leader in America received a letter from James Wilson, one of the imprisoned Fenians. He asked for aid in their escape from prison. Devoy discussed the matter with fellow Fenians including John Boyle O'Reilly, who had successfully escaped a prison road crew in WA aboard a whaling ship to Boston.

Devoy raised funds for the raid and acquired the service of a three-mast whaling vessel named the Catalpa. He chose an American captain George Anthony, and the vessel flew the American flag. Two Fenian agents, John Breslin and Tom Desmond, arrived in WA ahead of time, for reconnaissance of Fremantle Prison. Local Irishmen were recruited to cut the telegraph lines connecting Australia on the day of the escape. On April 17, 1876, the Catalpa dropped anchor off the coast of Rockingham and dispatched a whaleboat to shore. Six Fenians Robert Cranston, Thomas Darragh, Michael Harrington, Thomas Hassett, Martin Hogan and James Wilson were freed from their work groups outside the prison walls by Breslin and Desmond. Escaping by whaleboat from Rockingham and after enduring a rocky night at sea during a squall, the men boarded the Catalpa the next morning.

As the story goes, on April 19, 1876 the Western Australian steamer SS Georgette fired a cannon warning shot threatening to blow up the Catalpa's masts. Captain Anthony responded, "That's the American flag; I am on high seas; my flag protects me; if you fire on this ship you fire on the American flag." After narrowly avoiding a battle, the Catalpa safely managed to reach New York Harbour on August 19, 1876. A memorial of six wild geese in Rockingham, WA was erected commemorating the escape of the six men, and Irish Republican organizations to this day visit Australia and celebrate the daring escape. (64) (65) Irish Republican organizations stand in solidarity with the Indigenous peoples of Australia, and with any community that suffers injustice. I always thought they were called the fighting Irish for a different reason.

We buy some mementos of the Matagarup event including a concert shirt to support the cause and come away from the historic event with a better understanding of the plight of Indigenous peoples, not only in Australia, but also in our own country. Sometimes you must step out of your own comfort zone and try to gain perspective of the issues from the other side of the fence. How would I feel and what would I want if I endured what these people had endured for so long? I know that I would be outraged, and I do not know if I could be as patient, waiting generations for governments to do the right thing. Not knowing in advance what the trip would teach us, it has already enriched my life more than I could have ever expected. End the Racism. End the Shame.

Welcome to Country by Elders at Matagarup
First Nation Refugee Camp, Boorloo (WA)

Nancy leaves and meets Susan at the hotel to take her downtown. Tyler and I meander back along the Swan River into Perth taking in the beauty of the day, the birds along the river and the overall idyllic setting for this beautiful modern city to see how the other side of the fence is doing. Along the way we pass the FMG Fortescue building with Greg Almighty planted out front. The twelve tonne iron ore boulder with a pure iron content of 64%, more than epitomizes the enduring spirit and determination of the people who make up Fortescue. It epitomizes the vast natural wealth in the Pilbara region that is scooped out of the ground daily (468,000 tonnes at Fortescue) and shipped off to Asia with a minimum amount of processing. The largest shareholder owning thirty percent is the Minderoo Group, an Indigenous word, suggesting that Indigenous persons may have an interest in it. Not so. The company belongs to Twiggy and Nicola Forrest. Twiggy is the great grand nephew of Baron John Forrest of Bunbury the first premier of Western Australia. Not to be confused with the owner of the largest number of iron ore leases in the Pilbara. Perth based, Hancock Prospecting founded by Lang Hancock discoverer of the largest iron ore deposit in the world, and one of the oldest land-owning families in Western Australia.

"Minerals are not like crops of wheat or wool that grow every year. You have to find more each year and more each decade if Australia's standards of living are to continue." Lang Hancock

"The continuing health and growth of Asia's economies are critical to Australia. As Asia's economies grow, so should Australia's, we are virtually linked" Georgina Hope Rinehart, Chairman Hancock Prospecting Group Pty Ltd. (66)

Nothing is more obvious than the linkage between the Asian and Australian economies during our journey through the Outback. The company is also involved in large coal and manganese projects in other parts of Australia. It is now being brought into the news by the current leader of the company Lang's daughter, Gina Rinehart one of the wealthiest women in Australia, if not the world. Gina has been highly visible in the news, in dispute with her children over the family trust. Miners, Rio Tinto and BHP operate some of these rich resource properties, that we will see during our journey farther north into the Pilbara and then west into Queensland.

Tyler and I have a kebab lunch near our hotel and then walk into the city centre through an impressive multi-level pedestrian mall, a couple of blocks wide and long. We pick up some tourist information for our trip north and a book for Tyler. Along the way, we stop in at the Perth Mint. It houses Australia's largest collection of natural gold nuggets and sells a wide range of jewellery, coins and other objects of interest. A Canadian mining icon, resides next to the mint in Goldcorp house. Goldcorp is the largest gold miner in the world and is headquartered in our home town of Vancouver.

It is striking how the city has blended modern with old buildings. Although it is admirable that the city has preserved the older buildings, these are clearly confined and over-towered by their modern neighbours. While walking back to our hotel, we stop to take pictures of the Swan Bells, a set of eighteen bells hung in a stylized modern 82 metre copper and glass free standing structure. Twelve of the bells are historic, from St. Martin in the Fields Anglican Church in London and date back to between 1725 and 1770. The bells were donated to Western Australia as part of Australia's bicentenary. The bells are known to have rung as James Cook set sail on the voyage that founded Australia. These were tuned and restored at Whitechapel Bell Foundry and are the only set of Royal Bells to have left England.

Entering Stirling Gardens, we walk past a statue of another famous Forrest. Alexander Forrest brother to Baron John Forrest of Bunbury, was also a surveyor and explorer. The statue sculpted in 1916, by Pietro Porcelli, lists him as the first explorer of the Kimberley and as a representative of that district in parliament till he died. He also served as the mayor of Perth for six years. On St Georges Terrace, we view a mob of life size kangaroos sculpted in bronze by Joan Walsh Smith and Charles Smith in 1997. At dusk, the statues appear lifelike in behaviour, hopping or casually sipping from the fountain. A little farther on is the Harmony of Minerals Obelisk a sculpted 45-foot oil drill pipe with chunks of different ore attached to it from all over Western Australia. The ores and the regions these come from are mapped out on the base of the obelisk and are from top to bottom: Dodecahedron (Diamond) from Kimberley Region, Magnesite (Magnesium) from Ravensthorpe, Manganese Ore (Manganese) from Woodie Woodie, Quartz Dolerite (Silver) from Kalgoorlie, Cassiterite (Tin) from Shaw River, Hematite (Iron) from Mt. Whaleback, Galena (Lead) from Northampton, Supergene (Nickel) from Kambalda, Nickel Sulphides (Nickel) from Kambalda, Quartz Dolerite (Gold) from Kalgoorlie, Spodumene (Lithium) from Ravensthorpe, Bauxite (Aluminium) from Jarrahdale, Chalcocite (Copper) from Ravensthorpe, Jaspilite (Iron) from Koolyanobbing, Azurite & Malachite (Copper) from Thaduna and finally Hematite (Iron) from Koolyanobbing. Financed by the mining industry it was erected in 1971 by Paul Ritter and Ralph Hibble to celebrate the millionth citizen of Western Australia. If nothing else, it demonstrates the amazing wealth that is mined from beneath the soil of Western Australia. What is not described in any of the public art throughout Perth,

~ 133 ~

is the forced removals, displacement and resettlement of Aboriginal peoples from their traditional homelands. Unlike in Canada, no Australian government has signed a federal treaty with Indigenous Australians guaranteeing full citizenship rights, land rights and sovereignty obligating the Federation of Australia to binding commitments with the original owners of the continent. Perhaps this is the underlying reason why many Australians fear migration to their nation. What will prevent new migrants from continuing with the tradition of stealing from the old migrants, something that they do not own?

Meeting up with Susan and Nancy at the hotel, we go for a vegetarian dinner at the Annalakshmi at Swan. The Annalakshmi in Perth is one of seven locations in the world. Three are in Malaysia, two in India and one in Singapore established by devotees to "The Singing Sage" Guru Swamiji. Food is prepared by volunteers with selfless love and positive energy, based on the concept of Athiti Devo Bhava – Guest is God. (67) Frankly, Nancy has the edge on Susan, Tyler and I as she has some idea of what is going on. Susan not being a fan of Indian food, is out of her comfort zone. The place is still closed on our arrival, so we sit outside with a few other families and take in the beautiful river view. When the Annalakshmi opens a steady stream of persons line up inside and out. The hall is filled with rows of tables and chairs. We collect our plate and cutlery and are served by volunteers who have prepared different vegan foods. The restaurant is unlicensed and filled with statues of Ganesh burning incense. Drawing in hundreds per meal from all races and walks of life, especially lots of young persons. The food is delicious. As one spot at a table empties it is filled just as quick by a new hungry person. Eat as much as you can, and when you leave you pay what your heart says. Dinner at the Annalakshmi was the perfect way to end a day filled with so many enlightening experiences. Thank you, Nancy!

Sunday, May 31. Partly Sunny 11-21°C

This morning our drive takes us to the only aquarium we will visit in Australia, the Aquarium of Western Australia in Hillarys. It is the largest aquarium in Australia and tenth largest in the world. It has a neat shark and ray tank with an underwater viewing tunnel and some beautiful jelly fish and coral reef tanks. The vast variety of fish and coral in their brilliant colours is wonderful to behold, as close to a reef experience as you can get while staying dry, or so I think. It creates more anticipation for our upcoming Great Barrier Reef visit. The morning is spent looking at the various exhibits. After lunch we drive to Subiaco Domain Stadium to watch the West Coast Eagles trounce the Geelong Cats 120 to 64. Departing early for the game was a good idea, as parking is at a premium and we have a substantial walk to the stadium. The outside of the stadium has a tailgate atmosphere with Barbies on the go, and vendors selling a variety of game souvenirs. Ty purchases a West Coast Eagles shirt and Susan picks out a black baseball cap with a stylized W of two boomerangs representing the Wirrpanda foundation.

The foundation is named for its founding director, David Wirrpanda who is a retired AFL football player with the West Coast Eagles and was selected for the all-Australian team, in 2005. He is an influential Indigenous Australian in sport, community service and leadership in crime prevention. The foundation promotes strong role models and healthy life choices for Indigenous youth. It has programs focused on keeping Indigenous children in school, sports and mentorship programs for Indigenous youth at risk or in the criminal justice system, as well as driver and vocational training programs. Today's game is dedicated to raising funds to involve Indigenous kids in sport. The playing field and stadium are oval, holding 43,000 fans. The game starts at three and goes till 5:30pm. Spending the better part of the game annoying our neighbours about the rules of the sport, we eventually figure it out, and it is truly entertaining. I take some pictures and video to capture the flavour of the day.

Aussie Rules Football could be considered the country's national sport if Rugby weren't such a close competitor. The most popular sport in every Australian state, except for Queensland and New South Wales where rugby dominates. To many outsiders, it seems a bizarre combination of soccer, rugby, and American football. The exact origin of the sport is not known, with some speculating that it is rooted in Gaelic football, and others that it has roots in the Aboriginal Australian sport known as Marn Grook, that may have up to fifty persons playing at once. The codified rules for the game were written in May 1859, in Melbourne. The clubs are structured the same as football clubs in the UK, with the fans being the stakeholders.

This contact sport is notable in that it requires no equipment except for a football (larger and rounder than an American football) to play. Played on a circular field with eighteen opponents per side, points are scored by kicking or running the ball between four tall goal posts in the end zones with six points awarded for the inner posts and one point for the outer posts. The ball is moved by kicking, hand balling, or running with the ball, with specific rules on how the ball may be handled. Hands and whole body may be used to tackle making it one of the roughest sports in the world. With the highest overall spectator attendance of any sport in Australia, it is easily one of the best ways to experience the Australian love of sport.

The Australian Football League (AFL) is the national football league of Australia and is home to the most competitive league in the sport. Although insanely popular in Australia, the sport has struggled to take off abroad. Other countries in the Pacific regions near Australia however, do provide a fan base with Nauru, Papua New Guinea, and New Zealand starting to bring in crowds for the sport. When in Australia it is highly recommended that you see a game, as it is an exciting experience with an enjoyable atmosphere that is action packed. I had received a tip in Canada that it was a must do activity while in Australia, and I agree completely. The day made us West Coast Eagles fans, and we are happy that the team completed 2015 as AFL finalists.

Australian Rules Football Game, Subiaco Stadium, Perth (WA)

Monday, June 1 (Western Australia Day). Cloudy 10-20°C

Susan begins celebrating her birthday by doing some laundry early in the morning. Nancy picks us up at ten am for a tour around Perth and surroundings, by car. Our first stop is downtown, to celebrate Western Australia Day with the many families who are participating in arts and activities inside and out. Today is a great opportunity to see the vibrant plaza downtown between the Museum of WA, the State Library, the State Theatre Company and the Contemporary Arts Gallery. The Perth Cultural Centre has converted their water fountain into an Urban Wetland effectively educating children and adults about the importance of wetlands in improving water quality. Planters in the square contain lemon, orange and olive trees and all are producing fruit. There is a wide variety of stands, balloons, face painting for the kids and music. Some persons are active creating a large mural with plants and beautiful large flowers I have never seen before. We visit the Museum of WA and then the Contemporary Arts Gallery that is featuring some select artworks by the graduating students from art schools across Australia.

Nancy drives us out to Kings Park, the jewel of Perth, showing off a myriad of trees, plants and bird life in a 400-hectare setting on Mount Eliza. We behold a stunning panorama of Perth, the Swan River and the Darling Range. The park displays over 3,000 species of native flora and is a main tourist attraction in Western Australia. Kings Park introduces us to the fascinating boab tree, a native to the Kimberley region in northern WA. It has an unusually wide and swollen pear-shaped trunk and is another fascinating Gondwandan species. At Kaarta Garup we view the meeting of the Swan and Canning Rivers. I am surprised by the large number of plants that are flowering, in what is approaching winter. I wonder about the seasons, and do not have to ponder it for too long as is these are explained through an information board on our walk.

The Nyoongar seasons here in the Swan Coastal Plains are different from our four seasons in Canada. Makuru (June & July) is the season of the First Rains and is known as the Fertility Season when hibernating frogs break through the soft soil and hop to their watering holes. Most tall trees go into bloom and the fish begin to spawn in the rivers. Djilba (August & September) is the season of the Second Rains and is known as the Conception Season when lakes and waterholes fill, and waterfowl are nesting. Kambarang (October & November) is the Wildflower Season where the landscape is carpeted with wildflowers and game is abundant. It is known as the Season of Birth when animals are rearing their young, and Nyoongar do not hunt now, favouring honey and fish instead. Birok (December & January) is the First Summer when there is mass flowering of small shrubs, reptiles begin to appear again, hatchlings and young animals become active and Nyoongar teach their children to hunt young kangaroos, emu and swans. Bunuru (February & March) is the Second Summer known as the Season of Adolescence when large shrubs and bushy trees come into bloom and the Nyoongar teach their children tool making. Djaran (April & May) is the Autumn Season also known as the Season of Adulthood when hunting parties are formed and young people return to their communities often for ceremonies of courtship and marriage.

The lorikeets are abundant, busy chattering and swooping through the giant Coastal Tuart (*Eucalyptus gomphcephala*) trees in their social groups in a display as colourful as the brightest rainbow. The park is blessed with magnificent bird and plant life that sweetens the air with song, colour and subtle perfumes. It is interesting to see the variety of plants and trees that provided Indigenous people with nectars, resins and medicines. Taking a leisurely walk through the gardens we return to the car for our trip to Freemantle.

Freemantle is a busy place today on our arrival and it is challenging to find parking. Walk through the Esplanade down to the fisherman's dock, we are all quite hungry now, and stop for a good feed of fish and chips. I take pictures of the local artwork, including a bronze sculpture of a fisherman on the dock, and of some boats. The local fishing boats are dwarfed by the 61-metre trimaran multihull superyacht *White Rabbit Echo*. Cruising at nineteen knots, the air-conditioned vessel accommodates up to sixteen crew and eighteen passengers in style reserved for the rich and famous.

Freemantle is a southern suburb of Perth. Located at the mouth of the Swan River it was the first area settled by the Swan River Colonists, in 1829. It is named after English naval officer Captain Charles Freemantle who pronounced the possession of Western Australia and established a camp at the site. As a gateway to the west, Freemantle became a significant harbour and port. Its notoriety began in 1850, when the first convict ship arrived. In all, thirty-seven ships delivered almost ten thousand convicts including political and military prisoners that were held in Freemantle Gaol, built by convicts, for convicts. Penal transport ended in 1868, and the Gaol was handed over to the Colonial Government in 1886.

The prison saw lots of activity during the gold rushes in the 1890s, and over time it also served as a prison for women, and as a military prison during World War II. Freemantle Gaol also served as place of execution, meting out capital punishment for murder, with over forty prisoners hanged at the gallows. In 2010, Australian federal legislation prohibited capital punishment in all states and territories. During the 20th century the prison saw an over-representation of young Indigenous prisoners. The prison operated from 1855 to 1991 when it was closed. Freemantle Prison is a UNESCO World Heritage Site and celebrates the convict heritage of Australia complete with tours, an art gallery and gift shop. Freemantle Prison also maintains a registry of every convict and guard, so that Australians can track their lineage back to Freemantle, and if they so desire, apply for a Descendants Certificate. (68)

Australia's modern identity owes much of its foundation to convicts. Crime was a major issue in England in the 18th and 19th centuries because of widespread poverty, social injustice, child labor, squalid living conditions, and overworking of labourers. Gaols in England were overcrowded and after the American Revolution penal transportation to the Americas was no longer an option. Australia became the alternate dumping grounds of the Crown's problems. Stealing sheep, wool or cloth could land you with a seven-year sentence in an Australian penal colony. Most convicts were transported for petty crimes and occasionally so were political prisoners. Few were violent offenders, as serious crimes such as rape and murder were capital and not transportable offences. Most of the transported convicts were English and Welsh (70%), Irish (24%) and Scots (5%), mainly men in their early 20s, with women accounting for only 15% of the convicts sent.

In 1787, the First Fleet of eleven convict ships set sail for Botany Bay arriving on January 20, 1788, founding the first European settlement on the continent in Sydney. Food shortages and sickness ravaged the colony in its initial years. Many of the convicts were illiterate and lacked the farming skills necessary for survival. From 1810 on, Governor Philip founded a system employing the skills that convicts had been apprenticed in. Educated convicts did administrative work, and women were freed if they married. Meanwhile brick makers, carpenters and labourers toiled in building roads, bridges and public buildings. Convicts put in long days, working fourteen to eighteen hours per day, and could earn tickets of leave or even full pardons for good behavior. Many would not serve out their full sentence.

There were other penal colonies including those in infamous Van Diemen's Land that between 1803 and 1853 took in 75,000 convicts. Van Diemen's Land was known for being a harsh and brutal penal colony, and owing to its notoriety was officially renamed Tasmania, in 1856 after becoming an independent state. Along with a cold climate, the impossibility of escape, and brutal punishments the name change to Tasmania did little to wipe away its fearsome reputation. Penal colonies also existed in what are now Victoria and Queensland although at that time these states were part of NSW. South Australia was founded as a free settlement from its birth. Western Australia was the last place where convict transportation ended, with the last convict ship arriving on January 10, 1868.

In all, an estimated 165,000 men, women and children as young as nine years old, were transported to Australia on 806 ships. When transportation ended, convicts made up forty percent of Australia's English-speaking population. An estimated twenty-two percent of Australians are descended from transported convicts. Many convicts rose to prominent positions in Australian society after serving their sentences and found their lives much more fulfilling than might have been in Britain. Many Australians celebrate their convict heritage, even though it was once considered a stain. As an important part of Australia's heritage, eleven former convict sites are UNESCO World Heritage Sites. The convict legacy is a defining characteristic of modern Australia's identity. (69) (70)

We visit the prison, although do not participate in the tour. The prison is a place where none of us feel comfortable. The gift shop sells pyjamas for children that are stamped as the transported convict fatigues were back in the day, in the broad arrows identifying Property of Mother England. Visiting a gallery of art produced at the prison we take time viewing the paintings. Some of the artwork is very good, and includes both traditional line and dot works, as well as, western style paintings of birds and landscape. The prison, for all its warm welcome, is creepy and I am happy to leave. Motoring back to Perth as night falls, we celebrate Susan's birthday with Nancy at Sorrento's, an Italian restaurant with good atmosphere and good food. Susan has really enjoyed the visit with her friend, as brief as it is, a perfect Birthday gift. After an enjoyable time, we say our farewells to Nancy.

Nancy Jones, our amazing host in Perth (WA)

Tuesday, June 2. Partly Sunny 17-22°C

We depart Perth going 190 kilometers north along Indian Ocean Drive heading for the Pinnacles at Nambung National Park. Along the way I stop several times to take pictures of the pure white sand dunes pushing in from the ocean and some of the local plant life and flowers. Arriving at Nambung National Park before noon, we walk and drive through the Pinnacles desert, taking photos of the unusual limestone formations, dating back millions of years. These were uncovered by the shifting sand dunes about 6000 years ago. Thousands of limestone pillars rise through the yellow sands, some as high as 3.5 metres creating a unique geological landscape.

The terrain and climate are changing. The landscape is transitioning from treed to mangrove scrubland terrain interrupted by large, white sand dunes. The temperature is rising on our approach to the warmer climes of the Indian Ocean. The nighttime temperature has increased to 18°C, and the daytime temperature to a comfortable and moderate 22°C. The range in temperature will change again on the next leg of our journey north into tropical climes. We eat lunch by the sea in Jurien Bay, 200 km north of Perth. Our journey then continues north to Geraldton, completing a total distance of 415 kilometers for the day, and checking into our hotel at four pm.

innacles Desert, Nambung National Park (WA)

Geraldton (WA)

Area: 254 km². Population: 35,749. Founded in 1850. Traditional lands of the Amangu people. The third largest city in WA. A major Westcoast seaport for fishing and seven bulk handling berths for wheat, sheep, sand, iron ore, copper, nickel and zinc concentrates. A notable person from Geraldton is Edith Cowan social campaigner and politician who was the first woman elected to an Australian parliament in 1921 and whose face is on the $50 banknote. Fondly known as the Lobster Capital of the World although Shediac, New Brunswick in Canada also claims that title. Must-See attraction: HMAS Sydney II memorial.

After checking in to our hotel, we drive out to the HMAS Sydney II Memorial commemorating the loss of 645 Australian sailors off the coast of Geraldton. The HMAS Sydney (D48) is a reminder of the ultimate price paid by many Australian sailors, soldiers, and airmen. A Royal Australian Navy Leander-class light cruiser, it was purchased from the British just prior to its launch in 1934. Its first deployment was in 1935 to enforce sanctions imposed on Italy by the League of Nations during the Abyssinian Crisis. When WWII began on September 1st, 1939 with the invasion of Poland, the Sydney was assigned to patrol duties and convoy escort in Australian waters. In May 1940, the Sydney was assigned to the British Mediterranean Fleet. This was its first combat deployment. During its eight-month deployment the Sydney sank two Italian warships, participated in multiple shore bombardments, and provided support to the Malta convoys. All these actions occurred with the ship receiving minimal damage and no casualties.

Returning to Australia in February 1941, the Sydney resumed its regular convoy escort and patrol duties. Unfortunately, the Sydney's luck ran out on November 19, 1941. The Sydney engaged the German auxiliary cruiser Kormoran in battle. The battle was fierce. The German merchant raider was damaged and scuttled by its crew. 317 German crew were rescued and held in prisoner of war camps till the end of the war. Unfortunately, the Sydney was sunk in the process killing all 645 crew members aboard. The wrecks of both ships were lost until 2008, with Sydney being discovered on March 16 at a depth of 2480 meters, 207 kilometers west of Steep Point, WA.

For twelve days after the sinking, the government maintained the strictest secrecy about the loss of the Sydney. There were numerous conspiracy theories surrounding the fact that no Australian survivors were found. One involved a Japanese submarine killing Sydney's crew by firing on them with machine guns and taking prisoners back to Japan. Another allegation suggested that the Sydney was carrying gold bullion from Singapore instead of ammunition, and that the Australian and British governments were covering up the truth of the entire matter. Little information was released until 1957, and then that answered few questions about a possible government cover up. In 1997, the Minister of Defense asked a government committee to make further inquiries regarding the circumstances surrounding the loss of the vessel. It received over 400 submissions and tabled a report to Parliament in June 2000 that again left many questions unanswered. It was not until both wrecks were found in 2008, that a proper investigation could be conducted. The final report to the loss of the HMAS Sydney II, that includes conclusions, empirical evidence and investigation of frauds, conspiracies and speculation was made public on July 9, 2009.

The Sydney's defeat was largely owing to its unpreparedness for battle, and the proximity of the two ships, less than 1500 meters apart, essentially point-blank range for naval guns. The Kormoran used the element of surprise with disguised flags and guns, to gain proximity. The Sydney took heavy and accurate damage twenty meters from the bow by a ship launched torpedo, eighty-seven 15 cm shell hits and multiple hits from 3.7cm shells and 20mm machine guns. This resulted in severe fires, seventy percent casualties during the one-hour battle, the destruction of most of the life boats, and the eventual violent sinking of the Sydney. The Kormoran did take fire from Sydney's six-inch guns that caused damage to radio communications, fire suppression, and started an engine room fire that could not be put out as the fire-fighting system was destroyed. Life boats were deployed, 318 men escaped unharmed and the Kormoran was scuttled before the survivors were taken prisoner. (71) In the end, nineteen frauds, speculations and conspiracy allegations were investigated and found untrue. A very drastic loss of tale telling material.

The unique dome of 645 seagulls at the HMAS Sydney II Memorial Geraldton, WA

The main memorial for the loss of HMAS Sydney II is found on top of Mt. Scott in Geraldton, WA. Designed by Joanna Walsh-Smith and Charles Smith it is a significant and fitting tribute to an enormous loss of life in the struggle to defend Australia during WWII. This single incident took one third of Australian sailors during WWII. The memorial has a spectacular view overlooking the city and the Indian Ocean. It is circular in design, symbolizing infinity and eternity. It is surrounded by beautiful gardens filled with red roses, and bougainvillea full of fluorescent red, white, pink and orange blooms. The south-west side of the memorial has a black granite wall engraved with the names, rank and state of origin of each of the 645 sailors lost. The eye catching circular sanctuary consists of seven pillars signifying the national significance of the memorial and the joining of heaven and earth that are crowned by an open-air dome of 645 stainless steel seagulls representing the spirits flying free between water and sky. Although there are other significant aspects of the memorial, none speak more to me, than that of the Waiting Woman Sculpture. At the outer edge of the memorial a waiting woman is frozen in time, leaning into the wind and gazing into the distant horizon in desperate, patient hope. Lest We Forget.

Somber moments and reflection ground us and make us appreciate our freedom. Each of our journeys through life are different. Some are very unpleasant. Others are blessed and filled with joy. The grand design, if any, determining our fortune and fate, remains a mystery. I ponder about life while dining at the Dome restaurant next to the Indian Ocean watching a spectacular sunset, laced with incoming storm clouds. It is our introduction to the spectacular sunsets of Northern Australia. These only get better, the farther north and then west through the Pilbara and Kimberley regions that our journey takes us.

The Waiting Woman, HMAS Sydney II Memorial, Geraldton (WA)

Wednesday, June 3. Sunny 19 - 22°C

Departing from Geraldton at eight am and working our way north on the Northwest Coast Hwy 1, we cross the 26th parallel at around eleven in the morning. Entering a more desolate, treeless land with parched grasses, dried out lakes and dark red earth, we are skirting around the periphery of the Little Sandy Desert. The challenge of today's long drive is remaining unbitten by the countless black flies during our rest stops. I must press on the gas pedal hard when passing super long and wide loads of prefab homes that are headed for the oil, gas and mining fields in the north. We make good time with little to see along the way and sadly skip a visit to Shark Bay as a deviation to this point of interest takes too long to fit into our plans. We arrive at our next destination Carnarvon 475 kilometers later, at around 1:30 in the afternoon.

Carnarvon (WA)

Population: 4,559. Founded in 1883. Traditional lands of the Yinggarda people. Prawn fishing, salt mining, tourism and agriculture (cattle, goats, sheep, wool, bananas, mangoes, papaya, tomatoes, grapefruit and grapes) are the local economic drivers. A notable person from Carnarvon is Troy Cook, Australian Rules Indigenous footballer who played with the Sydney Swans and Freemantle Dockers in the AFL and Perth in the WAFL with a staggering total of 303 games played. Known for its landmark, the OTC big satellite dish. Must-See attraction: Carnarvon Space and Technology Centre.

After stopping by the Aboriginal Centre that is unfortunately closed, we visit the Carnarvon Space and Technology Museum. Properly referred to as OTC Satellite Earth Station Carnarvon, the center was a provider of high quality and reliable communications for NASA's Apollo Moon program. Although Australia is not typically associated with space exploration, it has made some important contributions. Contracted by NASA, Overseas Telecommunications Commission (OTC) provided a link between NASA's Carnarvon Tracking Station, 10 kilometers south of Carnarvon, and mission control in the United States. During the Apollo 11 moon landing, the Earth Station was the first live telecaster in Western Australia, relaying Neil Armstrong's first steps on the Moon. Its role was minimized with the end of the Apollo program, in 1972. During its last years in operation, OTC tracked the European Space Agency (ESA)'s Giotto mission sampling the tail of Halley's Comet, provided launch support for ESA missions, and the launch and tracking of German, Indian and Japanese satellites.

The station was decommissioned in April 1987, remaining actively involved in solar science research hosting a node of the Birmingham Solar Oscillations Network. The satellite earth station is a Western Australian Heritage Site, and home to the Carnarvon Space and Technology Museum that opened in 2012. The museum is a testament to Australia's underappreciated scientific and technological prowess. Australia with its small population and relatively small research budgets has innovated many important products. From its earliest days, these include: the woomra (spear-thrower) and didgeridoo to early modern implements such as the stump jump plough, the refrigerator, the torpedo, the electric drill, the notepad, the tank, and electronic pacemaker to modern devices such as the atomic absorption spectrophotometer, solar hot water, the black box flight recorder, ultrasound, Wi-Fi and the scramjet to name some. The museum is home to multiple space exhibits, a launch simulator and hand casts by astronauts who have visited the site including Buzz Aldrin and Wally Schirra. The large satellite dishes and other communications installations that pop out of the landscape 900 kilometres north of Perth are really the last things that you expect to find here.

Carnarvon Space and Technology Museum, Carnarvon (WA)

We almost check into the wrong hotel today. The hotel we are staying at, has apparently taken the name from a hotel that has been in town for over 100 years. The owner gives us the whole story and the grief he is having with the government about business name infringement, before graciously steering us in the correct direction. Spending the night in a pub hotel is not in our plans for the evening. After checking in to the correct hotel, we drive down along the beach and watch someone kite surfing. Returning to the motel, we relax by the pool. As the breeze rustles through the palm fronds there is not a cloud in the sky and the temperature is a comfortable 18°C, just perfect. The weather is quite temperate. I believe arid-tropical is the correct description, not too hot or wet, yet warm enough to grow a wide variety of tropical and non-tropical fruits, vegetables and flowers including hibiscus and bougainvillea that are in full bloom.

The soil is fertile along the banks of the Gascoyne river. It floods during monsoon season with a record flood of fifteen metres in 2010 that washed away 2000 head of cattle, half of the banana plantation and several houses. Entering town, large Cyclone warning signs remind us that the area is subject to drastic swings in weather that may result in a rainfall increase of up to 6000 percent. The Gascoyne starts 650 kilometres inland draining eight million hectares of catchment area and is known as the upside-down river. It only flows above the river bed for 120 days out of the year and beneath the dry river bed for the remainder of the year. We are now as far west as our trip in Australia will take us. Having reached our furthest point away from Canada, 14,456 kilometres from Vancouver, the distance is somewhat less than the distance of our trip around Australia. We do have that sense as many Australians do, of being far removed from the rest of this busy world. Our son is sick and homesick. I hope that he will catch his second wind soon, as we still have a very long journey ahead, through some tough country.

Thursday, June 4. Sunny 20-24°C

We depart early for Karratha 650 kilometers away in the Pilbarra, going north along Hwy 1, after having a buffet breakfast in the motel restaurant. An Outback tour-group who are checking out of the hotel the same time as us, are travelling in a modified air-conditioned bus that is raised well off the ground, equipped with large stubby tires, all wheel drive, and no doubt lots of equipment in case of emergency. Our drive today is extremely long with no sight seeing along the way other than from the car. Spotting 57 wedge-tailed eagles today, and lots of gold finches who love darting right in front of the car, we cross the Tropic of Capricorn at 10:30 am, and not long after, pass by the Parry Mountains. Taking a random roadside pit stop, I come across a roadside memorial to Ashley David Johnson who did not make it quite to fifty. It is constructed of a concrete slab with an engraved stainless-steel truck hubcap on edge at the base, supporting a cross adorned on either side by stainless steel exhaust pipes, solar nightlights, speakers, beers, and a coffee. R.I.P. Ash. Being very much in the middle of nowhere, the memorial serves as a good reminder, that one slight mistake may lead to a tragic end on this stretch of lonely highway.

YOU SHOULD KNOW:

Our Victoria state license plate slogan reads Stay Alert /Stay Alive. You will frequently receive this reminder from road signs to take a break from driving so that you can be alert. We take one at least every two hours.

Three hours south of Karratha the soil turns to a deep rich red colour and is highlighted by a preponderance of two-metre high, dark red termite mounds that randomly poke through the landscape. It is the unmistakable soil of the Pilbarra, rich in iron oxide. The surrounding mesas, natural pyramids, cliffs and caves, although not as prominent, remind us of the Four Corners country and Monument Valley in the USA. We pass the most westerly Rio Tinto iron ore mine Mesa A/ Warramboo where annually 25 million tonnes of ore is hauled out in giant 190 tonne mining trucks, crushed, and then transferred by rail to freighters at Cape Lambert. There is no mistaking the richness and value of this blood-red soil that smells of money. The operation is on the traditional lands of the Kuruma Marthudunera who signed a land use agreement with Rio Tinto, in 2011. A company sign informs us that the agreement determines how business is carried out on the lands and acknowledges mutual recognition and respect.

The iron ore rich soil of the Pilbarra, (WA) | Susan Bryant

After all the driving today, I think that our journey is going to be a real achievement. This is until we meet a young motorcyclist from Bern, Switzerland who is travelling around the world on a BMW motorcycle. He has crossed Asia from Europe, crossed from Vladivostock to Melbourne by ship, is travelling around Australia and then sailing to South America to travel north and then complete his circumnavigation of the planet. Wow!

Karratha (WA)

Population: 16,475.   Founded in 1968. Traditional lands of the Jaburrara people. Iron ore, sea salt, ammonia, and liquefied natural gas (LNG) drive the local economy. The most notable persons from Karratha are long gone, the creators of the petroglyphs at Murujuga. Karratha means good country and is most known for its industrial development.   Must-See attraction: Murujuga (Burrup Peninsula – the largest Indigenous rock engraving site in the world).

Coming into Karratha we enter a coastal plain busy with gas activity, two gas plants and gas flares well off in the distance on the coast. Karratha is a classic company town and with lots of industrial activity it is growing quickly. The town was originally established to support the processing and transport of iron ore from fourteen mine sites owned by Rio Tinto and its partners. In 1980, the town site expanded again to support the export of LNG extracted from the North-West Shelf, Australia's largest resource development project. It is run by North-West Shelf Ventures and is made up of six partners: Woodside Petroleum, BHP Billiton, BP Plc, Royal Dutch Shell, Chevron and Japan Australia LNG Pty Ltd.

An excellent experience here, is the guided tour of some of the over one million petroglyphs and 2500 archeological sites distributed over an 88-square kilometer area on Murujuga (Burrup Peninsula). The standing stones date back to the last ice age depicting thousands of Aboriginal ceremonies, and animals including whales, kangaroos, emus and even the extinct Thylacine (Tasmanian tiger). Twenty percent of the petroglyphs were damaged because of construction and industrial development. The site was declared endangered by the National Trust of Australia. It has received assistance from the World Monuments Fund through an American Express grant to fund the research necessary to place the site on Australia's National Heritage List. Access requires a four-wheel drive vehicle and should be guided to get the most from the experience. We regrettably forgo this experience due to time and cost considerations. Checking into our hotel that has a kitchenette, we then shop for groceries and Susan makes us a delicious home cooked meal of steak and pasta. Its been a long travel day and we melt into our beds with heavy eyelids.

Friday, June 5. Sunny 22-29°C

Today our return journey to Canada begins in a roundabout way. Having reached the half way point in our road trip, although our journey is taking us deeper into the Australian continent, we are slowly on our way back home. Travelling 240 kilometers north-east along the Northwest Coast Highway 1 to Port Hedland, we stop for coffee at Whim Creek. The well-equipped roadhouse provides us with lattes and entertainment from talking cockatoo's, "Hello Harriet". Our next rest stop is at a mozzie (mosquito) filled creek where I take pictures of budgerigars and ghost gums. The bright green and yellow of the budgies, highlights well against the ghost white bark of *Corymbia aparrerinja* commonly known as ghost gum. A local traveller warns us that these distinct trees have a reputation for their limbs breaking off unpredictably, damaging persons and property. After hearing the warning, we are more cautious about enjoying the generous shade that these twenty metre trees offer.

Loading Iron Ore for export at Port Hedland (WA)

Port Hedland (WA)

Population: 15,044. Founded in the 1880s. Traditional lands of the Kariyarra people. Port Hedland is the second largest town in the Pilbarra. With its natural deep anchorage harbour, it is the largest bulk export port in Australia and the world. It ships 446 million tonnes per annum primarily of iron ore, as well as salt, manganese, and copper concentrate. The town also supports the liquefied natural gas (LNG) industry. A notable person from Port Hedland is wildlife artist and illustrator Frank Knight. Port Hedland is most known for being the largest bulk export port in the world. Must-See attraction: Staircase to the Moon may be viewed here during the full moon, between March and October.

Arriving in Port Hedland, after travelling though the Outback is surreal. Within fifty kilometers of the town we come across many service vehicles from BHP and other companies, zipping across the landscape along various service roads. These snorkeled four-wheel drive vehicles that were originally white in colour are pasted with the bright red mud of the surrounding countryside. The plain is flat, stretching out to the coast whose horizon is dotted with massive bucket-wheel conveyors, processing plants and cranes. A mountain of bright white salt greets us at the rail overpass going into Port Hedland. We are awestruck by the size of the major industrial complex that spreads over many kilometers and supports the world's largest bulk commodity port. BHP Billiton has two separate port facilities here and 1,000 kilometers of rail leading to seven inland mines in the Pilbarra providing high paying employment to people from all around the world. The 440 million tonnes of iron ore exported annually from Port Hedland is staggering when compared to total annual iron ore exports from North America (Canada - 35 million tonnes, US - 13 million tonnes). The combination of rich gas and iron ore resources, good transportation networks, and excellent port access with proximity to the Asia Pacific market has played a significant role in making Western Australia the nation's economic powerhouse with $138 billion dollars in annual exports.

We check into our beachfront motel and then visit the port to have a look around, shop for mozzie lotion and go to the post office to mail off some postcards. After getting back to the hotel, Ty and I take a long walk down Saltie Lane accompanied by song birds and the odd wedge-tailed eagle. The beaches here are better known as a nursery for flatback sea turtle eggs than they are for Salties. We tally eleven bulk carriers waiting offshore to be loaded, while keeping a keen eye out for dolphins. The air temperature is Mediterranean-like and the beachside houses have lush and colourful gardens, with bougainvillea in full display. After walking for five or six kilometers, dinner is at the Dome restaurant near the downtown waterfront before tucking in early, as tomorrow is another long journey. Our hotel is situated close to the town water tower. At night, it is lit with alternating red and blue lighting shooting up the tower stem converging on the conical holding tank in violet radiance. The bright image is striking against the pitch blackness of an Outback night. Tonight, is perfect for viewing the Staircase to the Moon. Unfortunately, being unaware of it, and that it is occurring during our meal, we miss it.

Saturday, June 6 (Queensland Day). Sunny 24-32°C

Beginning our journey at 7:30am, travelling along the Great Northern Highway #1, our trip today takes us 612 kilometres to Broome. Today is another pure driving day. While checking out, I am told that the trip will be very scenic, and to make sure to stop in and visit the crocodile sanctuary. It is easy to spot on the way into Broome. Of course, as a gullible Canadian I accept these statements as truth, instead of Aussie humor, that may be as facetious as the tales are long. The route is not scenic. The low-lying shrub land is punctuated by dead feral cattle and frequently fly-covered, live beige cattle camouflaged in the scrub, grazing at the edge of the road. I am presented with a dilemma. If I drive too fast, it is difficult to spot the cattle and anticipate whether at a moment's notice, the cattle will wander on to the highway, as they often do. Not compromising on safety, we nonetheless, make good time. Our pit stops along the way are brief and uneventful. Arriving at the outskirts of Broome at around two in the afternoon. The crocodile sanctuary is not signed well at all, and we drive right past it. Thank goodness for GPS navigators.

Broome (WA)

Population 12,766. Founded in the 1880s. Traditional lands of the Yawuru people. Pearls and tourism are the economic heart of the community. Broome is named for a notable Canadian, Sir Frederick Napier Broome, who became Western Australia's governor in 1882 and facilitated self-government for Western Australia. Known for Cable Beach and its pearls. Must-See attraction: Camel riding on Cable Beach.

Smiles from the ultimate cold-blooded killers, saltwater crocodiles
Broome (WA)

We continue to our hotel and check in before returning for the crocodile spectacle. The Malcolm Douglas Wildlife Park is open to visitors between two and five pm during crocodile feeding. It has been recommended to us, as the best place in Australia to see crocodiles. A lot of these living dinosaurs are here for viewing, along with other Australian birds and wildlife. One may pet baby crocs and see the big crocs scrap with one another while vying for a prime spot to catch some rays or a chicken. Our lasting impression after our experience here today, is that seeing a "Saltie" in the wild, is best be from a distance. These are versatile animals with killer instincts, having survived on earth for over 100 million years and human beings may be part of their diet.

This fearsome reptile is one of Australia's most dangerous animals, and one you absolutely do not want to encounter in the wild. The saltwater part of their name is misleading, as the creatures can swim in both salt and freshwater. Estuarine crocodile (*Crocodylus porosus)* is its species name, although most Aussies commonly call them "Salties". This crocodile is the largest species of any living reptile and is the largest terrestrial and riparian predator on Earth. Males may reach six meters in length, weigh up to one thousand kilograms and live up to seventy years. Females are usually smaller, reaching three meters normally. Saltwater crocs can swim across large stretches of ocean and inhabit various areas near water including mangrove swamps, estuaries, deltas, lagoons, and lower stretches of rivers but may be found inland along rivers over 300 kilometers from the coast. Their distribution is the largest of any species of crocodile, ranging from the Eastern coast of India across to Southeast Asia, down to and across Northern Australia.

The Saltie is a hyper-carnivorous apex predator that relies on ambushing its prey. It can take down any animal that enters its territory including other predators and humans. Because of their sheer size and distribution, the saltwater crocodile is the most dangerous crocodile in the world. A large male has the most powerful bite of any animal on Earth. Exerting two thousand kilograms per square centimeter of pressure, it can crush a full-grown cattle skull with a single bite. A saltwater crocodile is an eating machine that will essentially eat any animal tissue. Humans entering their territory are treated as prey. The power and size of this crocodile gives them an advantage over humans, and so does their speed. Salties can swim as fast as 29 kilometers per hour and move on land as fast as eleven kilometers per hour in short bursts. These speeds are usually only reached in surprising explosive bursts with deadly agility, of an otherwise lethargic animal. Saltwater crocodiles are extremely territorial. Adult males will share territory with females. Conflict usually arises with other adult males and territorial struggles may lead to cannibalism. Saltwater crocs mate in the wet season, with females laying and protecting their eggs in muddy nests. It is estimated that of the fifty to seventy eggs laid, only twenty-five per cent of the eggs laid will hatch, with one per cent of hatchlings surviving to adulthood.

One or two fatal attacks on humans occur every year in Australia. Wildlife officials are incredibly diligent in marking billabongs, rivers, lakes, and beaches where Salties are present, and it is a matter of life and death to heed these signs. (72) (73) The saltwater crocodile is a fearsome animal, and it is not to be toyed with. It is recommended to stay away from these highly dangerous, cunning and agile animals. Getting close to one in the wild, may be the last thing you will ever do. Susan is very content to hold and pet a baby croc whose mouth is tightly strapped shut. I prefer not to handle it even though I have had my share of pet turtles, snakes and iguanas. I feel more than a little uncomfortable, treating something that has no hesitation eating me, as a pet. I'm happy to respect this amazingly adaptable creature from a distance, no matter what its size.

Following our croc visit, we drive into Broome. Broome today is a quaint coastal tourist town and reveals little of its seedy past as a coastal pearling town, filled with opium dens and prostitutes. Its legacy includes: deaths of enslaved Aboriginals including pregnant women who were considered the best divers, as well as hundreds of Malaysian and Japanese pearl divers; the bombing by the Japanese during WWII; and the significant devastation to the town caused by 22 Cyclones since 1910. We dine peacefully with no knowledge of these past events at the Land of the Pharos. Great food at a reasonable price and the Baklava is to die for. After dinner, we go down to Cable Beach to catch the very last glimmer of orange light as the sun has already set. Again, we miss the natural phenomena and optical illusion that looks the same as its name, Staircase to the Moon. It is best viewed from Roebuck Bay as the full moon rises over the mudflats at low tide.

Sunday, June 7. Sunny 19-32°C

Having a leisurely day today of no travel, we take our time getting out of bed and have a late coffee overlooking scenic Cable Beach. Cable Beach attracts 45,000 tourists a month from all around the world during tourist season. I must add here, that the quality of coffee, lattes and chai tea in Australia is excellent. Whether in large cities or small towns, it is easy to find a good cup of java in Australia. Cable Beach gained its name honestly, when in 1889 an undersea telegraph cable was laid from

Broome to Java, eventually connecting Australia with Singapore and England.

There are many Europeans here on vacation, as is easily distinguished by the Scandinavian, German and French accents. Our waitress is from France. As many of the young persons working here in the hospitality industry, whether from France, Ireland, Germany or Canada, she is here to work and travel, seeking adventure and possibly a new home. The Australia Working Holiday Visa program provides a once in a lifetime opportunity for those between the ages of eighteen and thirty, from thirty countries that have reciprocal programs, to travel and undertake casual employment to supplement their travel. We meet several young persons from different countries during our journey, who are taking advantage of the program to see Australia.

World famous Cable Beach on the Indian Ocean, Broome (WA)

The day is glorious, as I survey the 22 kilometers of sun-kissed white sand beach from the red ochre cliff crest. There is a stiff yet comfortable ocean breeze bending the palm fronds and suspending dozens of wedge-tailed eagles in midair seemingly not moving at all, just hovering. I received an email earlier today from a friend, and sadly a competitor from an industry I used to work in, has passed away. Although I never met him, I knew of him by reputation as someone who significantly contributed to building a substantial company. I hope that he got to smell the roses, as I am presently. I decide to dedicate the memory of this gorgeous day to him. Today's sad news just reinforces in me, the importance of making the most out of one's life while one can.

Broome early in its history gained notoriety as a pearling town. Indigenous peoples had been collecting and trading shells and pearls amongst each other for millennia. They began trading with Makassan trepangers who came for sea cucumber for the Chinese medicinal and food markets, and then later with the Europeans. The first European pearling industry started in Shark Bay in the 1850's. By 1910, 3,500 persons were pearling in the waters off Broome making it the world's largest pearling centre, supplying up to seventy percent of global demand. The industry's early history is tarnished with enslavement of Indigenous peoples; mistreatment and nonpayment to Malay labourers; and considerable loss of life caused by shark attack, the bends, and cyclones. The shell at the time was highly prized for buttons. As plastic buttons came into use, demand for shell dropped off dramatically. (74)

Today the industry is focused around the cultivation of beautiful South Sea pearls, in the only significant wild stock pearl fishery in the world that exports about $70 million of pearls, annually. Divers hand-pick wild *Pinctada maxima* oysters from ocean beds near Broome between January and July. Workers then seed the oysters by inserting a bead of mussel shell into the oyster's gonad. The oysters are returned to the sea bed in net panels and are turned over on a regular basis for the next three months to ensure a round pearl. The net panels are then transferred to farms in sheltered bays and suspended from floats and maintained stress free for another two years before pearls of desirable size and quality may be harvested. (75)

We stop in to the showroom for Cygnet Bay Pearl Farms, the oldest operating pearl farm in Australia, located 200 kilometers from Broome, on the Dampier peninsula. The showroom in Broome, contains many exquisite pearl strands, pendants and earrings, most that are well out of our price range. For those that truly appreciate fine pearl jewellery, this showroom is not to be missed. We are quite fortunate to see the world's largest pearl on display here. There is no mistaking that there is something special about this pearl. Measuring 22.24mm in diameter and weighing 156 grams the pink & white round pearl is part of the Brown family's private collection. It is the only pearl of its size and quality in the world and is estimated to be priceless. (76)

We go to the local market to see what the artisans have for sale. Susan cannot resist pearl earrings and a pendant depicting the Ribbon Staircase to the Moon. Susan has also arranged for all of us to go for a camel ride in the afternoon at Cable Beach. I must say that I am reluctant about participating as it is not part of my original plan. Tyler and Susan are supposed to ride, and I am supposed to do the photography. Susan has decided that I should not get off easy, and despite my considerable weight, she is able to secure a huge camel by the name of Tiny, that can handle both Tyler and myself. At the end of the day, we get our pictures as well.

As I have been horseback trail riding quite often in my life, I consider the camel ride as a gimmicky tourist experience and I am not expecting too much from it. I am pleasantly surprised. I have heard that camels may be quite moody and mean, yet these animals are pleasant and calm. The camel ride although brief, is exhilarating and quite different from horseback riding, as you are much higher off the ground. Tyler really loves it and would love to do it again some time. We have a wonderful stroll down the beach. Our long chain of camels turns around after entering the nudist section of the beach, and strolls back to where we started, as the sun begins to set.

Having beverages and calamari as the sun sets over Cable Beach, we then dine in our room on a delicious BBQ chicken dinner, picked up from the local grocery store. I am somewhat concerned about the next leg of our journey. Some of our hosts in Broome have questioned our visit to Derby. There it is again, "there's nothing there, Mate". Where have I heard this before? There has been some negative news on the Tele lately about Derby regarding Indigenous drug abuse and crime. Entering country where thirty percent of the population is Indigenous, care must be taken not to trespass on Aboriginal lands, as we are not carrying any Aboriginal land travel permits. We will use respect rather than fear as our guide for this leg of our journey. It has worked well for us so far.

Riding Tiny at Cable Beach, Broome (WA) | Red Sun Camels

Monday, June 8 (Queen's Birthday). Sunny 19-32°C

Being in no rush this morning, we begin by taking in coffee and the beautiful scenery at Cable Beach before heading 220 kilometers northeast to Derby. Our departure is delayed as Susan keeps inputting Darby (our neighbour's dog) instead of Derby into the navigator. Just as Bumberry, Susan cannot get Darby out of her head. The trip is quite uneventful as we skirt around the Great Sandy Desert. Although the temperature reaches 32°C in the afternoon, it is mild compared to the blistering 45°C temperatures that are reached here in November. At our lunch stop we meet and chat with former ranchers from New South Wales who as many other Grey Nomads are caravanning throughout Australia as part of their retirement. Boab trees are now becoming a familiar site in the landscape. The boab tree (*Andansonia gregorii)* is the only Australian baobab tree, another Gondwanan relic, with six other species of baobab trees growing in Madagascar and Africa. Boab trees are unmistakable, generally reaching twelve meters in height and have broad swollen trunks that may extend to over five meters in diameter. These trees are good at storing water and have been used by Indigenous peoples for food, water, shelter, clothing, art and medicine.

Boab Prison Tree, Derby (WA)

Derby (WA)

Population: 4,865. Founded in the 1880s. Traditional lands of the Nyikina people. Mining (oil, diamond, lead, zinc), agriculture, administration and tourism are economic drivers for the community. A notable tree from Derby is the Boab Prison Tree. Derby is known for the highest tides anywhere in Australia. Must-See attractions: Norval Gallery and Mowanjum Art and Cultural Centre.

On the outskirts of Derby, we stop at the notorious Boab Prison Tree. Its history as described in the signs is tied to the early history of the pearling industry and the kidnapping and enslavement of Indigenous peoples known as black-birding. Prior to the founding of Derby and the Derby gaol, the tree was used as a rest area for the chained captives on their forced marches from throughout the Kimberley. Captives included pregnant women who were desired for pearl diving, as it was believed that they could hold their breath longer. (74)

While reading the information signs one cannot help but feel shame that something of such spiritual significance to Indigenous people was used for such a horrendous purpose against them. The tree is one of many Larrkardiy around Derby that are considered by Indigenous people to be imbued with special mystical forces, falling into a category called malaji. It has been recorded as a site of significance under the Aboriginal Heritage Act 1972. According to Ngarrangkani (Traditional Law) anyone who trespasses without authority or injures a malaji exposes themselves to retribution by these mystical forces. If that is not enough to deter vandal carvers and trespassers, then one is reminded that the hollows of these trees are inhabited by snakes. The information signs also reveal that termite mounds (Jilkarr) in the Kimberley are to be treated with reverence and respect. In former mortuary rituals, deceased persons were interred in active mounds that the termites resealed to accommodate the remains. Aside from religious belief and practice, both Larrkardiy and Jilkarr assisted in the health and well being of Indigenous persons by providing them with nutrients and medicines

After our visit to the Boab Prison Tree, we travel to the Mowanjum Art and Cultural Centre and receive a warm welcome. We are shown into a theatre, and learn about the displacement of these people from their traditional lands to Derby, having retained their culture by practicing their art. The Mowanjum Culture is made up of persons from three traditional territories of the Worora and Wunambul people who lived along the coast and inland north of Derby, and the Ngarinyin people who lived in the central Kimberley. These different peoples were brought together at a Presbyterian mission and at government settlements in the early 1900s, and have since been displaced and resettled several times, to their current location on the outskirts of Derby. These three groups of persons are known as the Wandjina tribes. Wandjinas are the creators of the land. These cloud and rain spirits that appear to be ghost or alien-like are quite haunting. The Wandjinas are painted against rich red and gold ochre backgrounds often incorporating serpents and lightning using distinctive dot painting. Part of the gallery contains a cave with paintings, as found on their traditional territory. The gallery contains beautiful and captivating art. It is an active space for young and old participating in the creative process.

After our visit at the cultural centre we go to the Norval gallery, run by Mark Norval and his partner Mary. The gallery has an eclectic look and feel to it. With a wonderful mini-boab and cacti garden out front displaying a few iron sculpted creatures, it is a busy place with artists scurrying around preparing canvasses and working on different art pieces. Mark and Mary are both teachers who work with Indigenous artists and help to display their work, as well as Mark's own elaborate and stunning works of art. They are both gracious hosts as we browse through their gallery. Mark gives Tyler a gift of a fossilized Mako shark tooth taken out of the Derby pier and allows us to view his extensive vinyl album collection out back. After purchasing a few small paintings out of the large assortment on display we meet one of the artists. Tanisha is proudly wearing her West Coast Eagles jersey and is busy on another project yet graciously takes time for a picture. Enjoying our brief visit here, we highly recommend a stop in to the gallery if you ever find yourself in Derby. Thank you, Mark and Mary!

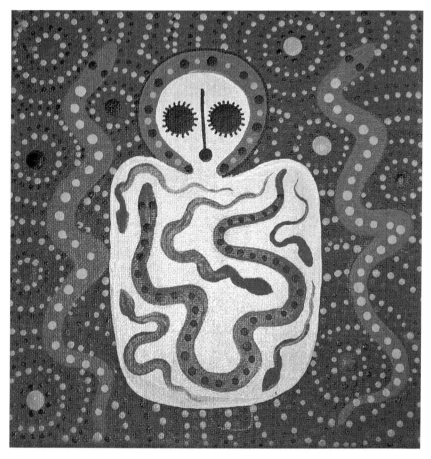

Wandjina painting by Tanisha Allies, 2015
Derby, Kimberley region (WA)

We check into our hotel and then go down to the wharf for dinner. Derby is the Bay of Fundy of Australia, known for having the highest tidal change of over ten metres. The sunset over the pier is breathtaking, a typical Kimberley sunset. It is easy to see what inspires the stunning art in this magical land. Our journey on the morrow will be lengthy, so we hit the hay early.

Sunset, Derby (WA)

Tuesday, June 9. Cloudy 19-30°C

Leaving Derby at eight am our travel today takes us 548 kilometres to the only sizeable town along the way, Halls Creek. This leg of the road trip is very isolated with only one roadhouse at Fitzroy Crossing, half way to our destination. The roadhouse is a general meeting point for many Indigenous people as it provides access to services. It is well patrolled by several of their dogs that loiter around the gas pumps in a possessive manner. The local Indigenous people only speak to us when we say hello, and even then, remain quite still as if there is an invisible barrier between us. I have no sense of friendly or warm greeting, and respect that there is probably a good reason for that. We quickly move on, as there is still a long journey ahead of us. Our companions along the route are feral cattle at the roadside, both live and dead; wedge-tailed eagles soaring above us or picking at roadkill; and a landscape dotted with termite mounds. The termite mounds change colour from gray to iron oxide red as soil conditions vary between limestone and iron rich mineral soil.

A common sight in the dried-out riverbeds on our journey
Jarlalu Bridge (WA)

The only excitement of the day is during a river crossing along a narrow dike through a river at one of the 24-hour campgrounds in search of a toilet. The signs clearly advise us that crocodiles inhabit the area and that attacks cause injury or death. That only makes our crossing that much more disconcerting, as it is bumpy and narrow. One wrong move of the steering wheel and we may easily hang up or drop in. Only the many cattle near the riverbank give me any comfort that these crocs are probably already well fed and will not be interested in these three greenhorns trespassing into the kill zone. The risks one takes when your spouse wants to pee in the relative comfort of a filthy Outback outhouse.

TIP:

Public rest areas throughout Australia need improvement. Most lack running water, are filthy and have overflowing waste bins. Bringing along your own toilet paper and hand sanitizer is well advised, as many roadside public washroom facilities lack either.

Halls Creek (WA)

Population 1,211. Founded in 1887. Traditional lands of the Jaru people. Trading center for cattle stations and aboriginal communities. A notable person to Halls Creek is the prospector Charlie Hall who the town is named after. Charlie found a 28-ounce gold nugget on site December 25, 1885. Halls Creek is known for the ensuing gold rush that lasted less than 3 months, bringing more than 15,000 persons to Halls Creek. Must-See attraction: Wolfe Creek Crater.

We arrive in Halls Creek at three pm and go to the Tourist Centre before checking into our hotel. As our vehicle is not four-wheel drive, we skip going out to the Wolfe Creek Crater and visit the pub early. One of our bar tenders is a young gentleman from Winnipeg who is on a work travel permit. He has clearly found himself a place that is well away from the hustle and bustle of Winnipeg and warmer. Dining on burgers, we get an early night's sleep so that we may set off early on Wednesday.

Wednesday, June 10. Cloudy 17 - 30ºC

Our drive of 300 kilometres north to Kununurra via the Great Northern Highway merges with the eastbound Victoria Highway #1 for the last 43 kilometers. As we enter the East Kimberley the landscape changes visibly to red striated cliffs topped with boulders, as if arranged by a mischievous giant. We have been travelling in the Kimberley, since our arrival in Broome. The Kymberley region is three times the size of England and is one of nine regions in Western Australia. In the northeast corner of WA, its striking geology and outstanding sunsets attracts visitors from around the world.

Kununurra (WA)

Population: 4,573. Founded in 1961. Traditional lands of the Miriwoong people. Agriculture (melons, mangoes and Indian sandalwood); tourism and mining are economic drivers for the community. Notable from the Kununurra area is the Argyle Pink Diamond. Kununurra is known for the Ord River Dam and Lake Argyle, one of Australia's largest freshwater reservoirs. Must-See attractions: The mini Bungle Bungles.

Kununurra was established as part of the Ord River Irrigation Scheme. The Ord River is fed by 46,000 square kilometers of watershed on the Kimberley Plain and is held back by the dam at Kununurra. The diversion dam created Lake Kununurra stretching 55 kilometers upstream to the larger Lake Argyle Dam. Lake Argyle is the second largest artificial freshwater lake in Australia and was originally built to provide irrigation for rice farms intended to support markets in China. Magpie geese ate the rice faster than it could be planted, so the crops were turned over to sugar cane for the Asia market and more recently to Indian Sandalwood and a variety of produce and fruit crops. The reservoir irrigates 150 square kilometers of cropland now yet may support up to 450 square kilometers. Although the dam has caused major changes to the environment, the reservoir has also created an environment that now supports 26 species of fish, 270 species of birds and some 35,000 freshwater crocodiles (77).

At the south-west end of Lake Argyle, 185 kilometers from Kununurra is the Rio Tinto Argyle diamond mine. Known for being one of the first diamond mines to exploit a volcanic pipe that has produced more than 800 million carats of rough diamonds, since 1983. It is one of the worlds largest producing diamond mines, and the largest for natural coloured stones including champagne, blue, pink and red diamonds. Most of the stones are cut in India and marketed in the US, Japan and China. (78)

Reaching Kununurra, we cross the diversion dam and then drop into the tourist info centre to scope out the local attractions. The young lady at tourist information is super helpful outlining some of the highlights we should try to get in during our short stay. We go for lunch and then out to the Hidden Valley in Mirima National Park where we view the mini Bungle Bungles and do a scenic cliff top walk. The sandstone interspersed with darker bands of higher iron ore content, were laid down in distinctive layers and folded by tectonics over the millennia, then carved by the weather, leaving these stunning geological sculptures.

Geology typical of the Kimberley, Kununurra (WA)

The park has a great interpretive trail describing the Miriwoong people's connection to the land and their use of the different trees growing in the area. The **Theriwoong**, the sandpaper fig (*Ficus scobina*), provides fruit that ripens in March and April, wood used to make fire by drilling one stick into another, and leaves abrasive enough to sharpen wooden tools. Virtually every tree here has a special use, from the **Merndang** paperbark (*Melaleuca dealbata*) for shelter and hats, to the **Daloong** wild mango (*Buchanania obovate*) for sustenance. The **Woolewoorrng** woolybutt (*Eucalyptus miniata*) when hollowed out by termites makes a good Gooloomboong, commonly known as didgeridoo, used for making music, spear throwing or as a fighting stick.

Following our trip to the park we visit the local Indigenous art gallery Artlandish and view some great Indigenous art pieces from Western Australia, Northern Territory and Queensland. Purchasing the 2nd Edition of Didgeridoo by John Bowden, we hold off on buying an actual didgeridoo as the gallery has not identified the musical pitch of their displayed instruments. Prices are good, ranging from $250 for the plain, to $350 for local and $450 for some of the more ornate musical instruments. I hold off on purchasing a didge as we will learn more about what features to look for in a didge, from the book and during our journey.

Susan purchases some small items and then we shop for some essentials before heading up to Lookout Point to watch our final Kimberley Sunset. While watching the sun set, we get into a discussion with locals about health care and gun ownership policies in our two countries. Canada and Australia both have universal health care programs and there is common satisfaction amongst us with our health care. All agree that the US is gun crazed, seemingly valuing gun ownership over their own lives. We cannot understand how any country can tolerate tens of thousands of injuries and deaths by guns every year, as if in a war with itself. Australia put tighter gun controls in place over twenty years ago, when one man with a semi-automatic rifle killed 35 Australians and injured eighteen. Australians were outraged, and the changes were dramatic including a national gun buyback program. The firearms policy put in place has reduced mass shootings and mortality caused by firearms significantly. The evidence is irrefutable and proves that policies based on common sense save lives. The sunset this evening is a stunner. We stay till there is just enough light left to still find our way back to the car.

Dining at the Pumphouse restaurant, a renovated pump house on the Ord River, we are welcomed by a sky full of screeching flying foxes bursting out of the trees as the last day light fades out. We have a wonderful dinner. Leaving the restaurant for the evening and while driving back to our hotel Tyler says, "We've been here too long". I'm not sure if Tyler is commenting on the length of our visit in Western Australia for eighteen days, or that he has just had enough of the whole trip. For some reason, he cannot wait to move on to Northern Territory. The likely reason is that it gets us closer to home, although he seems to have a fascination for the sheer remoteness and rugged beauty of that region. He will not have to wait much longer.

Sweet Memories of the Kimberley
Kununurra (WA)

~ 173 ~

Northern Territory (NT)
Area: 1,420,970 km². Population: 243,700. Founded in 1825.

To get any sense of Australia's ancient history and raw natural beauty a visit to the Northern Territory is a requirement. Although sparsely populated and only designated as a territory by the Australian government, NT is home to some of Australia's most important cultural heritage sites. NT is comprised of two regions, North Australia is the northern area around Darwin, and Central Australia is the area around Alice Springs. North Australia is a tropical wetland, that is close in climate to Southeast Asia and in the wet seasons may have great monsoons. Central Australia is a more arid landscape, home to the great deserts that are stereotyped as making up much of the whole country.

The Northern Territory was first settled by Indigenous Australians over 50,000 years ago according to archaeological records. Before Europeans arrived, Makassan traders from Indonesia contacted Indigenous Australians and regularly traded with them for sea cucumber or trepang as it was a delicacy sold in China. Europeans first sighted NT's coast by ship in the 17th Century. The British attempted to settle NT three times in the 19th Century and failed owing to starvation and despair. Finally succeeding on their fourth attempt in 1869, with the establishment of the Port Darwin settlement. Northern Territory was briefly under the control of NSW before being transferred to the control of South Australia.

In 1911, the Commonwealth was given control of the Territory and the NT was briefly divided into North and Central Australia from 1927-1931. During WWII Darwin became a military town because of its proximity to the South Pacific zone of operations. The Japanese bombed Darwin destroying much of the old town, and what remained of the old town was further destroyed by Cyclone Tracy in 1974. The Territory was finally granted responsible government with a legislative assembly by the Commonwealth in 1978.

NT's main sources of income are mining and tourism. Bauxite, manganese, and uranium mines are found throughout the Territory. Tourism however, is the major economic driver. Specifically, two popular parks: Kakadu and Uluru-Kata Tjuta. Kakadu in the Top End of the Territory is best known as being the filming site for *Crocodile*

Dundee and is home to some brilliant Indigenous rock art. Uluru-Kata Tjuta (Ayers Rock) in the center, is home to a large red monolithic rock that is of great spiritual importance to Australia's Indigenous peoples. Besides these two parks; there is the tropical capital of Darwin, home to informative war museums and beautiful oceanside views; the town of Alice Springs, a hub for purchasing Indigenous art; and Arnhem Land, a secluded area of Indigenous land never settled by white colonists. If you are looking to understand the Indigenous peoples of Australia better and see some of the greatest natural wonders of Australia, the Northern Territory is an absolute must-see. (79)

Thursday, June 11. Sunny 19 – 32°C

After waking up early we make a 426 kilometers beeline for Katherine in Northern Territory. Crossing the border into NT at 8:30am, we have entered a new time zone losing 1.5 hours. The fruit inspection station that we expected at the border is non-existent. The only significant change is in highway speed that has increased from 110 kilometers per hour to a generous 130 kilometers per hour maximum. The faster speed limit is quite unnerving on a bumpy, curvy two-lane highway and there is no temptation to speed, though I do slow down at times. Stunning "Big Sky Country" scenes of the Pinkerton and then Stokes Mountain Ranges unfold as we proceed through Timber Creek and then across the Victoria River. The drive is one of our more scenic trips through Savannah land interspersed with Palm trees hugging shady cliffsides. The boab trees are disappearing as we proceed farther east.

I capture some photographs of three Brolga, large grey Cranes with bare red heads and grey crowns as well some brave wedge tailed eagles that allow us to get closer than usual. We also stop for a photo shoot at the Victoria River, one of the largest rivers we have seen lately that surprisingly has water in it. Along the way, the lifting and folding of iron rich sandstone escarpments stands in testament to the continent having been lifted out of the sea by great geological forces including the collision of continents. As Victoria Hwy 1 starts curving north towards Katherine the landscape becomes more vegetated with tree and plant species that we have never seen before. Arriving in Katherine at 3:30pm and checking into our hotel, we prepare our plans for the coming days and book a river trip up the Katherine Gorge after returning from

Darwin. Deciding to sup at the hotel, the restaurant offers home cooking including delicious meals of kangaroo and crocodile. Tyler and I go native with no regrets, while Susan sticks to something more traditional. The meals are awesome. We tuck in and get a good night's rest.

Shaded cliffside palm grove (NT)

Friday, June 12. Sunny 20-28°C

Our drive today takes us 315 kilometres north along the Stuart Highway #A1 towards Darwin. This highway is the major north/south artery through the middle of Australia to the heart Alice Springs, and then farther south to Adelaide. On our departure some military transport trucks pass by carrying the impressive Abrams M1A1 tanks of the 1st Armoured Division based in Darwin, boasting the red Roo insignia. Otherwise, the trip is uneventful for us, moving at a good pace with a lot more traffic than we are used to. The air is warming and heavier with humidity, and the vegetation is becoming more tropical the farther north our journey takes us.

No worries about making good time here
Stuart Highway north of Katherine (NT)

Darwin (NT)

Area: 112 km². Population: 136,245. Founded in 1869. Traditional lands of the Larrakia people. Tourism and mining (gold, zinc, manganese, bauxite, and offshore oil and gas) are economic drivers for the Northern Territory's most populous city and its capital. Named by the captain of the HMS Beagle after British naturalist Charles Darwin who had sailed with them earlier on their second voyage. Darwin is known for being a small, relaxed, yet cosmopolitan city. A gateway to Asia and some of the most spectacular natural parks in the world. Must-See attractions: Dinner on the wharf and a sunset cruise.

After reaching Darwin on the Timor Sea at 1:00 in the afternoon, we check in with our car rental agency first to see if our vehicle requires any service. Explaining that we have already put 11,000 kilometres on the vehicle, the fleet manager advises us, "Don't worry about it, it's a new vehicle". Ok, enough said, as it has not given us any trouble thus far and is running just fine. We drive to our hotel on the Darwin waterfront, near the convention centre. Enjoying beverages and sandwiches on the verandah while we wait for our room, we relax knowing that the next two days ahead of us involve sleeping in, no long-distance driving and holiday enjoyment. After lunch and checking in, we walk the long and difficult route up and around the hill to Darwin city. We find the easy way, a public elevator and ramp, later in the day on our return down to the waterfront.

We take a picture of the Beagle Bell and a statue of Charles Darwin, who it turns out never set foot here. Ironically, just as the many Asian tourists anxious to see a mammal in the wild at the Twelve Apostles, Darwin was disappointed to only actually ever see a marsupial mouse while on his brief visit to Australia. It is in Australia where I hear for the first time in my life about the impact of Darwinism on Indigenous communities. It is not something I was taught in school either by the creationists or the scientists. When studying excerpts of *On the Origin of the Species* in biology class, in Canada during the 1970s, I learned about species adaptation and survival of the fittest in context to birds in the Galapagos, although not in its complete racist and colonial context.

Charles Darwin's book, *On the Origin of the Species by Means of Natural Selection or the Preservation of Favoured Races in the Struggle for Life* (complete title) introduced the scientific theory that populations evolve and was to some measure influenced by observations of the colonization of Australia and the treatment of Indigenous peoples. Darwin considered several reasons for the decline of Indigenous peoples in Australia including alcoholism, foreign diseases and the demise of traditional food sources. He was blind to the displacement of Indigenous peoples from their lands, observing "wherever the European has trod, death seems to pursue the aboriginal" coming to a broader conclusion "the varieties of man seem to act on each other in the same way as different species of animals – the stronger always extirpating the weaker" paving the way for some vicious social policies in the 19th, and 20th centuries. (80) (81)

I always held Darwin on a pedestal, for his observations and perspectives on evolution. I was never informed about or comprehended, that we are living in the hangover of Darwinism, intended by Charles Darwin, or not. The stronger extirpating the weaker articulated through colonization and imperialism has wiped out thousands of indigenous civilizations globally. It has justified theft and the concentration of wealth in the hands of a very few, as more citizens of our planet are marginalized, ecosystems destroyed and as species extinction accelerates. One can only hope that the machines that are learning quickly to become independent from us, will not apply Darwinism and scientific reduction on our species, in the same way.

We go to the tourist centre for some helpful advice and then walk into the pedestrian mall, looking at Indigenous art and books. For dinner we wander down to Stokes Hill Wharf with what seems is the rest of Darwin, to enjoy some Thai food and watch the fish being fed from the docks. It is a relaxed, cool and pleasant way to spend the evening.

Saturday, June 13. Partly Sunny 24-32°C

After doing laundry we walk in to town and enjoy Croque Monsieur and Croque Madame at the Pearl restaurant in downtown Darwin. I never ate a Croque before, so it is a pleasure trying something new for breakfast. After breakfast we window shop although I must say that the books and Indigenous art are the only items of real interest to the guys. Afterwards we drive out to the Defense of Darwin Museum.

The Defense pf Darwin Museum tells the story of those men and women who lived and worked in Darwin during World War II. It includes an immersive experience of the first bombing of Darwin, by the Japanese on February 19, 1942. The largest single attack by a foreign power on Australia, 188 Japanese aircraft attacked both airports and the wharf, sinking eight ships and damaging another ten of 46 in the harbour, destroying the oil storage tanks and many of the buildings in Darwin. Australia's Pearl Harbour began with a first attack that lasted forty minutes, with the Japanese losing four planes. It was followed by a second attack an hour later that included 54 land-based, long-range high-altitude bombers that pounded the RAAF base for 25 minutes and destroyed twenty military aircraft. Both attacks effectively cut off cargo shipping to support Java and the Philippines and signalled the beginning of 97 air raids against Northern Australia between 1942 and 1943. The initial air raid caused significant chaos in Darwin. Fear of imminent invasion resulted in many of its inhabitants fleeing inland. Many RAAF servicemen deserted their posts owing to incompetent leadership and destroyed airfields, with 278 still missing three days after the attack. The military police called in to restore order, got drunk and looted private property adding to the chaos. More than 250 persons died, ten vessels were sunk, and all key infrastructure was destroyed. The Northern Territory came under military control for the duration of the war. Administration moved to Alice Springs, as Australia rebuilt its infrastructure for defensive and then offensive air operations. Darwin was bombed a total of 64 times. Civilians were authorized to return to Darwin, in February 1946, although many chose not to. (82) (83)

Taking photos of artillery field pieces, jeeps and bunkers, none has as more important message about war, than the picture of one of the many poems written by Australian Vietnam Vets:

THAT PLACE

Vietnam was a wonderful place
It took the smirk right off your face

You arrived bright and bushy tailed
only to be aged quickly into an adult male

The aging process lingered on
Until the sanity strings were not so strong
As time went by your resistance faltered
Even though those of your time could not understand
Why you had altered

The alterations some could be seen
The screams, the tears, the violence and the scenes
And the casualties, the kids, the wives,
and the family friends
All became part of the never end

The real danger was the silence within
That boiled and simmered again and again
Never ending and reviled
by graphic images on the tube each night
Awakened abruptly from sleep with indelible sights

Instilled survival responses still come to the fore
But do we really need them anymore
I think we do and it won't be long
Till some stupid politician bastard starts beating his
drum

- Tango Two Charlie

The irony is not lost on us that yesterday's enemy is today's major economic partner as we view the outer perimeter of Darwin harbour. It is home to two large LNG plants. One is operating, and the other is under construction. These plants compress natural gas to a liquid form that is transported by large ocean-going vessels (89,000 to 145,000 cubic metres). The ConocoPhillips plant at Wickham Point known as Darwin LNG was completed in 2005 at a cost of ($1.5 billion,2005). It is a co-venture with Inpex, Eni, Santos, Tokyo Electric and Tokyo Gas. It is connected by 500 kilometers of subsea pipeline to the Bayu-Undan gas reserve (est. 3.4trillion cu ft.) producing 3.7 million tonnes per annum (84).

Under construction is the massive project Ichthys, a co-venture between Inpex, Total, and other partner petroleum companies and utilities from

Taiwan and Japan. It is being constructed for $34 billion and is expected to complete by 2017. The project will draw gas by undersea pipeline 890 kilometers from the Ichthys field (reserves twelve trillion cubic feet and 500 million barrels of light oil) and is expected to produce 8.4 million tonnes LNG and 36 million barrels of light oil per annum. (85)   These two projects are just two of several projects in Australia. Australia is now the third largest exporter of LNG globally after Qatar and Malaysia however, its position could change depending on the markets and the completion of $135 billion worth of projects that are now underway in Australia. Other nations such as Canada who are just embarking on LNG projects for export have a monumental challenge ahead of them to compete with Australia.

This evening we are taking the fish and chips sunset cruise of Darwin Harbour and get a good view of all the cranes and activity at the new LNG plant before heading towards Cullen Beach to take in an another absolutely stunning sunset. Our tour guide Jessica came to Darwin looking for a guy. In her words, "The odds are good, but the goods are odd". According to the locals, Darwin is a classic boomtown for fortune seekers and persons trying to hide from their family. It brings in all kinds and tilts the gender scales to a large proportion of males. Fifteen years ago, there were no high rises, and today there are quite a few, indicating recent rapid growth. Disappointment is expressed that some of the promised growth that was supposed to occur locally, has been exported. New apartment buildings stood empty for a long time, while approximately 8,000 temporary foreign workers were flown in and out of on-site work camps. The food and other supplies including materials for the plants were outsourced offshore. This should be a lesson for us Canadians, and others, who expect employment and contracts associated with an LNG boom.

Adding to the local male population, is a seasonally-rotated unit of 1,100 US marines and their air support. Housed at the RAAF base in Darwin, these troops participate in joint exercises with Australian forces on an annual basis. These troops and talk of the US navy maintaining a year-round fleet in Darwin has created tension between Australia, the US and China. In addition, the M1A1 Abrams tanks of the Australian 1st Armoured Regiment are stationed at Robertson Barracks, just twenty kilometers south of Darwin. As part of Australia's 1st Brigade, the armoured regiment has seen action in East Timor, Iraq, and Afghanistan in the last decade. The Australian naval base Coonawarra, is home to eleven Armidale class patrol boats with crews of 21 each. These boats conduct border patrol and enforce against illegal immigration and illegal fishing, by vessels primarily from Indonesia, and other countries including Vietnam and Taiwan.

Globally, pirate (illegal, unreported and unregulated) fishing is highly organised, mobile and elusive employing an estimated 22,000 slave labourers including children. It nets between 11-25 million metric tonnes of fish valued at between $10 to $23 billion annually, representing at minimum twenty per cent of the total catch. It is estimated that eighty per cent of the shark fin, and fifty per cent of the salmon marketed, has been illegally caught. (86) Australia's Exclusive Economic Zone stretches between three and 200 nautical miles from the coastline. Only Australian registered boats that have GPS installed, can fish commercially in the zone. The Australian Fisheries Management Authority has the responsibility of managing nine million square kilometers of fishery. With the assistance of satellites and the Australian navy it enforces the rules and regulations of the fisheries. (87)

Thirty per cent of the global illegal fishery occurs in Indonesia yet a significant portion slips into north Australian waters in the Timor Sea, the Sea of Arafura, as well as into the Indian and Southern Ocean. Speedboats that can outrun most naval vessels have been employed in large numbers for shark finning. This illegal activity involves the removal and retention of shark fins and discarding the remainder of the shark overboard, often when it is still alive. Shark fin is sold for as much $400 per kilogram although whole fins of whale or basking sharks sell for as much as $20,000 and are still in high demand, despite international campaigns to curb demand in Asia. The locals tell us that some of the pirate fisherman set up artificial islands. These are known in the trade as FADs (fish attracting devices). FADs are often made of polypropylene and are known to be effective for attracting skipjack, yellow fin tuna, albacore, dolphin, marlin as well as a variety of sharks. Many of these floating devices have their own encrypted GPS and remain moored and submerged both outside and inside territorial waters.

Sunset off Cullen Beach, Darwin, NT

Despite all the industrial, military and tourist activity, and Darwin's big city look, it still has small town appeal. It is easy to turn your boat into the sunset and feel all alone. Jessica slips out of the boat, into the water and wades ashore to pick up our fish and chips from an onshore restaurant. The water temperature is cold for Darwin 24.7°C. In the summer, it apparently gets up to 29°C. Jessica is fearless about the whole exercise and returns quickly with a warm fresh fish and chips dinner. She must have a lot of confidence in the 26 live traps set for saltwater crocs along the beaches and harbour of Darwin. One of the blokes on the boat says, "they used to catch eighty Salties a year before the hunting ban and now they are catching 240 per year from the Darwin area." Crocwise boaters don't clean fish from their boat and don't fall asleep on their boat. I did not see any signs about eating fish in a boat. I enjoy my meal, take in the sunset as the warm breeze blows gently and the water laps against the edge of the boat. I let my worries about the world slip away and immerse myself in Paradise.

After sunset, we head back to the wharf and watch from water level as persons throw scraps of their meals to the fish. No sharks or crocodiles, just lots of giant Southern Ocean sunfish. These enormous fish that reach three metres in length, come up to the surface on their silvery side, appearing as a large sun disc. Using a parrot-like beak these fish quickly devour any food that hits the water with the same intensity as when devouring jellyfish and molluscs. After docking, we stroll back to our hotel under a starlit canopy for a good night's sleep.

Sunday, June 14. Partly Sunny 24-32°C

We have breakfast near the hotel and then drive out to Humpty Doo in hopes of shopping at the Didgeridoo Hut. Unfortunately, it is closed because of renovation. We drive back towards Darwin and visit the George Brown Darwin Botanical Gardens. We stroll through a good portion of the 42 hectares of beautifully laid out gardens, with many of the tropical plants and trees of Northern Australia and Southeast Asia in bloom. A bronzed frilled lizard and a Desert Rose with its spectacular large pink blooms welcome us into the gardens. The path eventually leads us to the vast Palm gardens and walkways leading into the dense, dark tropical woodlands. Our senses are over stimulated by the intensity of bright Hibiscus colours, the bizarre patterns of Lichens populating stems, the fantastic aerial roots from delicate Orchids to amazing Banyans, the fragrant smells of Wattle and a variety of bird calls, unlike any we have ever heard before. We are walking through a wonderland of diversity. The humidity eventually wears us down and after touring through a local craft market, we make our way back to the car, and head back to our hotel. Susan goes into town to shop, without her anti-shopping anchors. Tyler and I go for a beer and lunch on the hotel verandah to swap a few footy, fishing and travel yarns with Marty and Robo from Melbourne.

After Susan gets back from shopping we take a brief air-conditioned rest in our room. Then we are off to the night market out at Mindal Beach, to dine by sampling from the various food booths and to look for a didgeridoo. Mindal Beach is packed with what appears to be most of the population of Darwin. There are all kinds of buskers, musicians and food wagons selling everything from basic burgers and fruit smoothies to more exotic Asian foods. A terrific didge player is playing a series of four different didges, each tuned in their own key and micro-phoned, accompanied by a drummer. Walking through the market we eventually find the didge dealer who is selling authentic, tuned didgeridoos made and decorated by artists from Arnhem Land.

View of city from Mindal Beach, Darwin (NT)

Arnhem Land, the home of the didgeridoo is one of five regions in NT. It is 97,000 square kilometres in the northeastern portion of NT some 500 kilometres east of Darwin on the northern tip of the West Coast of the Gulf of Carpentaria. Arnhem Land has a population of 16,000 persons of whom 12,000 are Yolngu traditional owners who have occupied the land for at least 50,000 years. The land is bordered by the spectacular Kakadu National Park on its western flank, The Sea of Arafura to the north and the Gulf of Carpentaria to the east. The land was named after the city Arnhem in the Netherlands by Captain William van Colster when he sailed into the Bay of Carpentaria on behalf of the Dutch East India Company, in 1623, on his ship the Arnhem. Arnhem Land has tremendous scenic beauty and diversity, ranging from towering escarpments and savannah woodlands to lush tropical forests, legendary rivers and rugged coastlines teeming with fish, migratory birds, Dugongs, turtles and Salties. The isolated area is Indigenous land and requires special permits for access, and properly equipped vehicles for overland travel via unsealed roads, if not flying. After leaving Darwin, our trip will take us well south away from the coast detouring around the

Gulf of Carpentaria, on roads that are paved and more suited to our vehicle.

The didgeridoo is actually the Euro-Australian name given to the instrument by Herbert Basedow in the 1920's, basing the name on the earthy, mystical sounds made as players practiced with the instrument. The instrument is known to the Yolngu as Yidaki and has just as many Indigenous names as there are identifiable language groups. The origin of the instrument is likely no more than 2,000 years old, and its use spread to other parts of Australia and more recently around the world. There are forty Indigenous nations between the Gulf of Carpentaria in the north-east to Derby in the north-west whose traditions, art, music and culture include the didgeridoo. "Didgeridoos got some spirit in there; look after it and it will look after you – abuse it and it will abuse you back". (88) After practicing playing the didge, Tyler and I can both testify that the statement is fitting and true.

The didge is made from the trunks or limbs of trees that have been hollowed out by the termite (*Coptotermes acinaciformes*). The termites live in and eat out the central heartwood portions of living and dead trees of certain tree species in monsoonal regions of northern Australia. Swamp Bloodwood (*Corymbia ptychocarpa*), Darwin Stringybark (*Eucalyptus tetrodonta*) and Darwin Woolybutt (*Eucalyptus miniata*) are some of the species used, although didges have been made from hollowed out Bamboo and even PVC pipe. Often the limbs are softened by soaking, and then the termite tunnel material is pried out using a thin hard stick. Sometimes slivers inside are removed by pouring hot coals down the tube. Knotholes and cracks are sealed with beeswax. The beeswax is also used to form a mouthpiece and then the pipe is sounded and cut to length, to give the desired pitch. (89) Typically, didges are about four feet long, although these do come in all shapes and sizes and I have seen one shaped as a saxophone.

Didge Power, Port Coquitlam (BC)

The didgeridoo player may produce a continuous sound by employing a technique known as circular breathing. Difficult at first, it requires some practice and over time becomes natural. Playing the instrument requires a relaxed state of mind. The harder you try to play it, the worse the results. Relax for best sounds. Many sounds are achievable including droning, overtone, punctuation, purring, vocalizing, and the replication of animal sounds of the snake, dingo, kangaroo and kookaburra and of course the sound "didgeridoo". Allow your imagination to wander and let the instrument come to life. Its power will surprise you.

As Tyler and I are both interested in a didge with good pitch and artistic decoration we view quite a few and test them for sound before picking a Bloodwood instrument from Katherine. It has a deep pitch in D-sharp and is painted with a crocodile at its base, water lilies and mullets by the artist Dukduk. It measures four feet and weighs about five kilos. I ask to have it packed in bubble wrap and buy a didge Bag to protect it for its long journey back to Canada. As we begin deciding on booths to select a meal from, someone close by throws up a couple of times. That causes us to reconsider eating at the market, and instead we decide on a pleasant sit-down meal at a Greek restaurant on the water, not far from our hotel.

Monday, June 15. Partly Sunny 24-32°C

Checking out of our hotel early today, refreshed and with a full load of clean laundry, we are ready to tackle our trek south and then eventually east out to the coast and the Great Barrier Reef World Heritage Area. Before that, there are still have many kilometers to travel and much to see. Leaving the humid tropical climes of Darwin. we drive south 100 kilometers to Litchfield National Park, home to many of the tree species used to make a didgeridoo. The 1,500 square kilometers park encompasses traditional lands of the Koongurrukun, Mak Mak Marranunggu, Werat and Warray Indigenous peoples. We spend the morning driving across the north end of the park via its paved road to view its stunning natural wonders. Our first viewpoint is of the amazing Magnetic termite mounds that look the same as worn gray tombstones and are aligned in a north-south direction to minimize exposure to the sun and regulate temperature in the mound. Not far from these are the giant Cathedral termite mounds of the Spinifex termites (*Nasutitermes triodiae*) towering a good five metres over us mere mortals.

Magnetic Termite Mounds, Litchfield National Park (NT)

Termites are not ants and are more closely related to cockroaches. Termites are socially similar as ants in developing colonies that range from several hundred to several million individuals. Also, similar as ants, termites have castes of blind, sterile female and male workers and soldiers. Termite colonies will maintain several fertile kings and queens. Queen termites may live up to fifty years. Termites are widespread on most continents playing a significant role in the carbon cycle, breaking down plant and wood detritus. (90)

Cathedral Termite Mound, Litchfield National Park (NT)

We travel to the Bulley Rock holes, then Florence Falls and Wangi Falls that have all cut through the sandstone plateau over thousands of years creating deep narrow tropical rainforest gorges. These provide swimming holes in spectacular natural settings that may be visited by crocodiles in the wet season, although are usually clear in dry season. Our final visit in the park is to Tolmer Falls, whose caves are home to the rare ghost and orange horseshoe bats. We view these waterfalls from high above in a stunning setting, where their waters empty out into a lush tropical forest below, that spans out as far on the horizon as one can see. The park is home to wallabies, dingoes, possums, flying foxes and the impressive yet harmless Nephila spider. The black and yellow female Nephila spider may grow to the size of a human hand, yet the male is barely visible, something Susan thinks should be true for males of all species. Just after noon, our journey begins out of the park and heads south on the Stuart Highway. It has been hot and humid. Noticing a distinct and welcome drop in humidity, as we stop to take a picnic lunch later in the afternoon at the Adelaide River, some of us Canadians are just not built for tropical weather. We travel on to Katherine, 315 kilometres south of Darwin, and overnight before our next day's adventure.

A happier moment between mother and son, Florence Falls
Litchfield National Park (NT)

Katherine (NT)

Population: 6,094. Founded in 1926. Traditional lands of the Jawoyn people. Agriculture (mango), mining (gold), defense and tourism are economic drivers for the community. A notable person born in Katherine is Indigenous advocate Mick Dodson who was named Australian of the Year in 2009. Katherine is known for Nitmiluk National Park and the Katherine Gorge. Must-See attraction: the Katherine Gorge.

Tuesday, June 16. Sunny 20-32°C

Today we take a thirty kilometre drive out to Nitmiluk National Park for a river cruise up the Katherine Gorge to enjoy the scenery and learn about the cultural significance of the gorge to the Jawoyn people. This spectacular gorge carved through the porous sandstone over the last 23 million years has been shaped by earthquake fault lines and the river itself. The headwaters of the Katherine river that originate in Nitmiluk National Park flow through Katherine becoming a major tributary of the Daly river flowing into the Timor Sea.

Flying Foxes hanging out in Nitmiluk National Park (NT)

The Jawoyn Burr or Dreaming concerns the past, present and future of the land, its gorges, its plants and animals, its rocks and rivers and all living creatures. Bula the Creator came from the northern salt water country and with his two wives eventually went underground north of Katherine in the "sickness country". Bula left his image as paintings in rock shelters however, the area is very dangerous and not to be disturbed for fear that earthquakes and fire will destroy the world. Another important spiritual being from the north Nagorkko came from the saltwater country and divided the people into two main moieties – Yirritja and Dhuwa and through this social grouping taught the people proper behaviour and correct marriage relationships. Nagorkko also gave the law mowurrwurr or clan groups and showed different clan groups what was edible and not edible.

Bolung the Rainbow Serpent is believed to inhabit the deep green pools of Nitmiluk and is an important giver of life, although may also act as destroyer, taking the form of lightning and bringer of floods. Fishing, drinking water, and swimming by new initiates and pregnant women is restricted in these pools. Bolung must not be spoken to or disturbed. Nitmiluk is the name given to the gorge by the Dreamtime figure Nibilil for the cicada's song- nit, nit, nit, nit that was heard at the entrance to the Gorge. (91) More than 4,000 rock art sites have been found on Jawoyn land including the remote and very significant archeological and rock art site Nawarla Gabarnmung. It has 36 pillars carved out of the rock holding up the ceiling, with a stone axe dating back 35,500 years and charcoal in the pits dating back 45,000 years. The Jawoyn people who own the land co-manage the park with the Northern Territory government.

The signs displaying "No Swimming" because of the presence of saltwater crocodiles are perfectly clear. Despite these signs, some of the German tourists still insist on bringing swimwear along. After paying admission, and taking the path down to the river, we pass by trees filled with chattering flying foxes who are just settling in for a sleep. After boarding, our river vessel journey takes us up through the first and second of thirteen gorges on the Katherine river. Saltwater crocodile live traps are in place right across from the swimming hole as we depart. Viewing a rock painting on the canyon wall halfway between the first and second gorge, we sight three freshwater crocs basking on sandbar nesting areas on our return. It is a crystal clear blue day and the cool temperature on the water is refreshing. The sandstone retains huge reserves of freshwater that it releases slowly through the cliff walls in certain parts of the gorge. Approaching the gorge walls, we see sections of moss covered rock raining water into the river. It is easy to spot where powerful tectonic forces have cleaved fault lines through the sandstone and changed the course of the river through the gorge, as pointed out by our guide.

Katherine Gorge, Nitmiluk National Park (NT)

On completing our boat tour our captain tells us, "the Jawoyn people do not use the word goodbye unless it is for a funeral. They say, "See you later." Now I am going to use the Aussie for goodbye, "get off my boat!"" The Aussies have a great sense of humour. You just must be Australian to get it. From Nitmiluk our navigator is set for Daly Waters and our drive takes us 273 kilometres south on the Stuart Highway. We will be visiting and lodging at one of Australia's most famous pubs, much to the chagrin of Susan and Tyler, who at this point in our vacation, prefer staying at resorts.

Australian Pubs are public houses licensed to sell alcoholic beverages and have played a key role in the British colonization of Australia.

Proliferating in the 1850s, during the gold rush, these large colonial era pub hotels with their shaded verandahs played an important role in providing the golden elixir of ice cold beer, lodging, meals and often served as a post office and general store. Generally, centrally located near a beach or in a prominent part of town, many still stand in modern cities and towns, operating as these have since foundation. Although Australian pubs have garnered a reputation for being lively, loud and male dominated, during our trip we have seen them welcome families, serve good meals and provide important lodging, especially in more remote locations. More-over every pub has its own characters and although many of the pubs appear similar on the outside, most offer something different inside.

Last Gas and Beer for 576 kilometres, Daly Waters Pub
Daly Waters (NT)

Daly Waters (NT)

Population: Estimated at between 30 to 50. Founded in 1872 when the Overland telegraph reached the site. Traditional lands of the Jingili people. The Daly Waters Pub is the economic driver for the community. Named by a notable surveyor-explorer, John McDouall Stuart who led the first successful colonial expedition across Australia from Port Augusta in the south to Darwin in the north, preparing the route for the Stuart Highway and the Overland Telegraph. Daly Waters is known for the Daly Waters Pub. Must-See attraction: The Daly Waters Pub.

The Daly Waters Pub is unlike any pub I have ever seen and is what makes it so special. Timing of our arrival is perfect, as the bougainvillea vines covering the front and roof of the pub are in full splendid Fuchsia coloured bloom. The bright blooms distract us from noticing the camouflage painted helicopter planted on the roof of the service station and gas bar on the opposite side of the street. After fueling up, we check into our cabin. Not really knowing what to expect, we are pleasantly surprised by how modern, clean and spacious our accommodation is. Given the season, we remain calm about all the holes in the ground accompanied by snake warning signs surrounding the cabin. Much more effective than a guard dog.

The pub built in the 1930's by Bill and Henrietta Pierce has witnessed murders, shootouts in the main street, cattle stampeding through town and more than the odd drunken brawl. (92) I mention none of this to the family, instead relaying that the pub had been visited by the famous travel writer Bill Bryson, failing to mention that Bill never did make it to his room. It is the original Outback Pub. Its that place where you expect the stuff of legends and tall tales. Entering the Daly Waters Pub, we enter a world of traveler's nostalgia, whether in the pub itself, or out in the beer garden. It is impossible to miss the hats, bras, sport shirts, licence plates, driver's licences, company id cards, business cards, thongs and shirts commemorating trips around Australia or around the world. Patrons come in by the bus load and happy hour has them lined up out the door as the girls with their Irish lilt and cute smiles do an amazing job of keeping the taps flowing with golden thirst quenching elixir of frosty cold beer.

This Pub has something for everyone, Daly Waters (NT)

Settling into a corner table and enjoying happy hour while playing billiards we then have the most massive burgers ever. I go Australian all the way, expecting a coronary event at any moment, as I chew through the plate size bacon and egg, cheeseburger. The entertainment out in the beer garden is country music whose target audience of grey nomads show up faithfully to listen, dance and of course imbibe beer well into the wee hours under a starlit canopy. Before heading back to the room, we leave a few of our own mementos including a maple leaf branded church key hanging over the door to the beer garden.

Wednesday, June 17. Sunny 16-28°C

We are up at dawn and have breakfast in the beer garden while staff are washing down the patio. A truck has just finished dropping off a delivery of over a dozen pallets, mainly holding of kegs of beer. Based on the previous evenings consumption, that is likely a Daly delivery. Pulling out of town, we pass kangaroos hopping near the roadside as our journey heads south on the Stuart Highway. We are forced to pull off the highway at one point, as a piece of mining equipment taking up the whole width of the highway, is transported north. We have been diligent about taking advantage of gas whenever it is available as the opportunities are few and far between. Today there is an exception to that rule. We do not pull into the first gas station on the way, as a large water buffalo has strolled off the highway and is headed straight towards the petrol pumps. That is just more trouble than it is worth, so we keep going. Otherwise, our 567-kilometer journey to Barkly Homestead at a steady pace of 120 kilometers per hour is uneventful. The treed savannah gives way to a shrubby savannah just before our turnoff from the Stuart Highway to the Barkly Highway. The detour is significant as we will not be travelling farther south towards Alice Springs and Uluru, the most famous rock in Australia. Taking the Barkly Highway, is taking the road less travelled. It will take us east to Queensland and the coast, allowing us to eventually complete our circumnavigation of Australia.

Encounter with a wide load, Stuart Highway (NT)

Barkly Homestead (NT)

Population: Estimated between 20 to 40. Traditional lands of the Wakaya people. Situated on the Barkly Tablelands it is the only roadhouse between the Stuart Highway and the Queensland border. Named after a notable person, former governor of Victoria, Sir Henry Barkly. The Barkly Tablelands has less than 6,000 persons living in an area of more than 283,000 square kilometers. Barkly Homestead is open every day and is a welcome stop for road weary travelers. Can't miss attraction: The Barkly Homestead Camel.

Barkly Homestead (NT) is a welcome rest stop
576 kilometers from Daly Waters (NT)

We check in at 2:30pm and are told not to miss happy hour and the big rugby match, State of Origin, Queensland vs New South Wales. The hotel is busy, and the event is not to be missed. So be it! We show up late after happy hour, no thanks to my son and dear spouse wanting to watch a popular show called the Eggheads. We settle into the bar amongst rugby fans and the local cowboys, dressed complete with chaps, the first we have seen in Oz. The cowboys sure fit the stereotype of square jaws, handsome and lean, except for the old veterans that are handsome and crippled. Good blokes, all dressed fancy enough to catch the eye of their favourite girl and develop a serious broken heart and hangover to go with it. There are some cute police officers travelling through, so who knows what may happen. After dining and getting tired of waiting for the game to start, we retire back to our cabin and watch New South Wales beat Queensland, to tie the two out of three series.

Thursday, June 18. Sunny 16-28°C

I have a restless night of sleep because of a loud and malfunctioning heat pump that the hotel management is unable to turn off for some reason. This makes for a long drive today. We are greeted outside our cabin by the pleasant sight of a flock of cooing crested morning doves digging through the dirt, occasionally harassed by some cockatoos. We have breakfast in the bar as it is being hosed down, after an active evening. We then drive towards the border with Queensland, 250 kilometers east. Crossing the border, we set our watches ahead five years and half an hour as per the sign at the gas station, and travel east another 200 kilometers to Mount Isa. Having not travelled on worse roads than these anywhere in Australia, if these are the best roads that Queensland, "The Smart State" as proclaimed on their licence plates, offers then we are in trouble. The roads in NT were far superior to these bumpy, windy, and narrow roads. Crossing the Outlander Way, the terrain changes to pastureland and the road stretches out to the horizon as far as we can see, giving us the sensation that we are in the prairie lands of Canada.

An unwarranted slight to Northern Territory based on our experience
Camooweal (QLD)

Queensland (QLD)
Area: 1,852,642 km². Population: 4,750,500. Founded on June 6th, 1859.

The second largest state in Australia, Queensland is a paradise and a prime tourist destination. Beautiful tropical rainforests in the north and gorgeous beaches line the East Coast. Despite having a murky past as a poorly run backwater, Queensland has developed into one of Australia's most tourist friendly states. The original inhabitants of Queensland were Aboriginal Australians of the Murri and Bama peoples, and Torres Strait Islanders. Pre-European contact, Queensland was home to Australia's largest Indigenous populations. Willem Janszoon, the first European to land in Australia, landed in Queensland in 1606. He and his party explored the west coast of the Cape York Peninsula near what is now Weipa. When James Cook proclaimed all of the East Coast of Australia as British territory in 1770, he made it so that NSW, Victoria, Tasmania and Queensland made up one large colony. When the colony of New South Wales was founded in 1788, Queensland was considered a part of NSW.

Exploration of Queensland continued in the following decades until a penal colony was established in 1824 by John Oxley at Brisbane. Penal transportation ceased in 1839 and the colony became a free settlement in 1842. In 1859, Queensland became a separate state named in honor of Queen Victoria. Despite being the home of the world's first Labour government in 1899, Queensland is considered one of Australia's most conservative states, and a prominent Liberal and National Party stronghold. Regressive and corrupt governance under the National Party in the 1970s and early 1980s stagnated development in Queensland. (93) (7)

Inland, Queensland consists of a combination of quite humid pastureland and desert with low rainfall. The north is tropical and wet, the south-east is more temperate, and the coastal strip is home to gorgeous beaches. Tropical cyclones present regular threats to Queensland and precautions have to be taken at certain times of the year. Queensland is home to many great Australian tourist destinations. The capital of Brisbane is a beautiful, modern and cosmopolitan city that is always worth a visit. Port

Douglas is home to beautiful resort beaches and provides great access to the Daintree Rainforest and the Great Barrier Reef, and Townsville is a nice spot to relax and look out at the surrounding mountains and ocean. Opportunities to see Australian natural wonders abound in Queensland with the Daintree Rainforest, Great Barrier Reef, Lone Pine Koala Sanctuary, and the Gold Coast. Queensland is a beautiful summer paradise that even in Australia's normally temperate Fall, remains quite gorgeous. It is absolutely one-hundred percent worth a visit if you want to see wildlife and rainforests that will blow your mind.

An aerial garden of vegetative diversity amongst the tree tops
Daintree Rainforest (QLD)

Mt. Isa (QLD)

Population: 22,785. Founded in 1923. Traditional lands of the Kalkadoon people. Mount Isa is the administrative, commercial and industrial center for northwest Queensland. Its mine, is one of the single most productive in world history, based on its combined production of lead, silver, copper and zinc. A notable person from Mount Isa is professional golfer and entrepreneur Greg Norman (The Shark) who was ranked #1 golfer in the world for 331 weeks. Mount Isa is most known for its mine although the Mount Isa Rodeo & Mardi Gras are well known and very popular. Must-See attraction: Dinosaur Discovery Centre.

We pull into Mount Isa in the early afternoon. The remote community is dominated by one of Australia's largest mining operations. Mount Isa Mines Ltd. produces lead, silver, copper and zinc. Its great smoke stack reminds me of the Inco Super-stack in Sudbury, Canada. Mount Isa is a town of over 22,000 persons. Over twenty per cent are employed directly by the mine operations with many other locals providing supplies or support to the mine in one form or another. The mine was developed in 1924 after the discovery of lead, silver and zinc ore bodies a year earlier. It has struggled at times, especially in the early years. It also developed into Australia's largest company at one time, and innovated several refining, milling, smelting and flotation processes.

The company runs as two streams of business now. The copper business unit produces six million tonnes of ore per year. It incorporates two underground mines at Mount Isa, the largest network of underground mines in the world; a copper concentrator; and a copper smelter. The zinc business unit is one of the largest zinc mines in the world with an estimated 650 million tonnes of reserves in four mines producing nine million tonnes of ore each year. It also incorporates a zinc lead concentrator, filter plant, lead smelter, and supporting services. It produces lead bullion in four tonne blocks as well as silver bullion. The company contributes about a billion dollars annually to the Queensland economy. It has invested $290 million in environmental initiatives, complying with regulatory standards since December 2013, although it does have a legacy of high sulphur dioxide and heavy metal emissions in years prior to that. Since 2013, Mount Isa mine has been owned by Anglo-Swiss Glencore PLC, the largest company in Switzerland and one of the largest commodities trading companies in the world. Glencore was founded by Marc Rich, the world-famous commodities trader. On the FBI's most wanted list for tax evasion and dealing oil with Iran during the Iran hostage crisis, Marc was later pardoned by Bill Clinton. (94) Glencore is a world leading integrated commodity producer and marketer, trading over ninety commodities. It leads in supplying copper and zinc and has strong market share in the supply of many other metals and minerals, coal, oil, and agricultural products, generating over US$173 billion in revenue, in 2015. It employs over 160,000 persons, in over fifty countries. Glencore has recently agreed to sell forty per cent of its agribusiness to the Canada Pension Fund for US$2.5 billion (95).

Mount Isa is prosperous, and Rodeo Drive has a Walk of Fame paved with the names of the legendary rodeo riders and champion stock including Spinifex. Spinifex was a horse so famous that Australian National Treasure - Slim Dusty (winner of 37 golden guitars) wrote a song about him. Australia's largest rodeo has been held here for three days each August, since 1959. The rodeo launches with a Mardi Gras parade of floats attracting about 30,000 persons each year. The rodeo puts up over $200,000 in prize money, attracting competitors from all over the world who compete in bull and bronc riding, steer wrestling and roping events.

View of Mount Isa Mines Ltd., Mount Isa (QLD)

We try to visit the Kalkadoon Cultural Centre to learn more about these people firsthand. Unfortunately, it is closed. The proud and independent

Kalkadoon were one of the last indigenous people in Australia to resist settlement of their lands. Over a period of one hundred years, the Kalkadoon fought organised troops in open combat using stone age weapons against rifles. In September 1884, over 900 Kalkadoon had gathered rocks, boomerangs and spears at a place now known as Battle Mountain about 100 km northeast of Mount Isa. After successfully staving off a first charge by sub inspector Frederick Charles Urquhart and 200 para-military cavalry, armed with carbines, the Kalkadoon warriors were eventually outflanked and cut down in successive waves of charges and rifle fire. (96) (97) The massacre marked the end of aboriginal resistance in the region however, not the spirit to fight for what is theirs.

A memorial obelisk reads: "This obelisk is in memorial to the Kalkatunga tribe, who during September 1884 fought one of Australia's historical battles of resistance against a Para-military force of European settlers and the Queensland Native Mounted Police at a place known to-day as Battle Mountain – 20 kilometers southwest of Kajabbi. The spirit of the Kalkatunga tribe never died at battle but remains intact and alive today within the Kalkadoon Tribal Council "Kalkatunga heritage is not the name behind the person, but the person behind the name."" (98)

Nearly two decades after filing claim, on December 12, 2011, Honourable Justice Dowsett of the Federal Court formally recognised the Kalkadoon people as the native title holders of nearly 40,000 square kilometers of land. The determination followed long negotiations with the Queensland government and 30 landholders in northwest Queensland who have entered into Indigenous land use agreements with the Kalkadoon. The Kalkadoon now hold exclusive rights to 4,000 square kilometers and non-exclusive rights to the remaining land.

In the judgement of the Honourable Justice Dowsett:

21 Mount Isa and its mines are important Queensland icons. The grazing industry here is also very much part of the Queensland story. As the evidence demonstrates, the Kalkadoon have played a significant role in the development of both industries and, as a result, of this city. Indeed, the Kalkadoon people are, themselves, an important part of the same Queensland story. The evidence demonstrates that they were willing to fight to defend their country and culture, just as other peoples have done for thousands of years all over the world. Their efforts to achieve recognition of their traditional ownership have not been unopposed. Very many problems have been overcome in order to permit me to make the orders which I am about to make. The Kalkadoon have borne the adverse consequences of the clash of cultures which inevitably accompanies mass migration, of which the European settlement of Australia is a typical example. The recognition of Kalkadoon traditional ownership of this land goes only a small way towards the recognition of their suffering since 1861.

22 I do not come here today to give anything to the Kalkadoon people. I come on behalf of the Australian people to recognize their traditional ownership of this land in a way which will bind all people and for all time. My order binds the Commonwealth of Australia, the State of Queensland, the Mt Isa City Council and the Boulia, Bourke, Carpentaria, Cloncurry and McKinley Shire Councils, together with all other people and companies.

23 I now make orders in terms of the draft which I initial and place with the papers.

24 On behalf of all Australians I congratulate the Kalkadoon people upon this recognition of their traditional rights. Particularly I congratulate you on behalf of the Judges of this Court and our staff. We all wish you well for the future and express our determination that your contribution to our history, and the price which you have paid for our prosperity, will not be forgotten. We look forward to sharing the future with you. (99)

As it stands native title rights may include the right to live on an area, access the area for traditional purposes, visit and protect important sites, hunt, fish and gather important resources such as water wood and ochre and to teach law and custom on country. It may confer the right to possess and occupy an area to the exclusion of all others, although only on land now held by or for indigenous people or on land that is unallocated or vacant crown land. As of June 30, 2014, 291 native title determinations were registered with the Federal Court of Australia's National Native Title Tribunal covering an area of almost two million square kilometers of Australia over 25% of its land mass. (100)

Travelling along Highway A2, the Flinders Highway, better known as the Dinosaur Trail, we feel it is appropriate to visit the Dinosaur

Discovery Centre. Most of the major dinosaur finds in Australia were discovered within one hour of Mount Isa at Riversleigh, including specimens of carnivorous kangaroos and the Tasmanian tiger. After viewing the various displays at the Discovery Centre, we drive up to lookout hill for a great panoramic view of Mount Isa. Ordering pizza on the way back to our motel we dine outside in the BBQ area and share tales with the son of the innkeeper, young Daniel, about our strange homeland. It is 12,269 kilometers away from Mount Isa with snowy mountains and rain forests that have no parrots. He has his world geography book in hand and sees that mountain lions and grizzly bears live in these forests. He asks a question, and we respond, yes, these creatures do eat children. And so, myths of fear and adventure are perpetuated. Daniel responds as bold little boys everywhere do, "I'm not afraid of anything", and I do believe him.

Friday, June 19. Sunny 12-24°C

Today our drive takes us to Hughenden, 521 kilometres along the Dinosaur Trail. Home to many Australian dinosaurs including the largest carnivorous marine reptile, *Kronosaurus queenslandicus* measuring between nine to ten metres in length and weighing eleven tonnes. Winding through the iron rich mountains near Mount Isa we eventually reach two significant markers 76 kilometers east of Mount Isa and just west of Dingo Creek. One monument is for the ill-fated Burke and Wills expedition, and the other is for twelve Indigenous persons who had helped the bungled expedition and were killed, by a subsequent failed rescue mission.

In 1860 to 1861, Robert O'Hara Burke and William John Wills led an expedition of 19 men, 23 horses, six wagons and 26 camels carrying twenty tonnes of provisions from Melbourne, Victoria north 3,250 kilometres to the Gulf of Carpentaria. The expedition was in a race with the experienced surveyor-explorer, John McDouall Stuart. In July 1859, the South Australian Government had posted a significant reward of 2,000 pounds for the first successful north-south crossing of the Australian continent, west of the 143rd line longitude. Although Burke and Wills are memorialized in statues, art, film and postage stamps, their legacy as uncovered by a Royal Commission, is one of an incompetently led expedition that fell apart and was poorly documented. "Without a doubt, a complete disaster." (101) Seven expedition members including the leaders perished. Only one member of the expedition, a soldier, John King managed to come within fifteen kilometres of their intended destination and return. King could tell the story, only by the grace of Indigenous people who kept him alive, and a rescue mission that brought him back to Melbourne. Less well documented in historical records, except by the perpetrator in his journals, is the slaughter of twelve Indigenous Yarrinookoo on October 30, 1861 by Native Police led by Frederick Walker. Walker was leading a rescue mission for Burke and Wills, not knowing that the men had already perished. (101) (102) (103) Such is the tragedy of more than one great Australian tale and its failed heroes.

At Cloncurry the Burke Development road heads north past the Burke and Wills Roadhouse to Karumba on the Gulf of Carpentaria, the same way that Burke and Wills traveled through this tough country. Steering clear of the opportunity to go north, our journey continues east, as the road conditions as posted on the information signs, indicate that the highway is not flooded and is open through Julia Creek, Richmond, Hughenden and Charter Towers. The information is encouraging as it signifies that we can drive to the East Coast of Australia without having to detour farther south.

The landscape transitions into pastureland, that is completely parched by a long enduring drought. Along much of the roadway there is nothing other than parched dirt, punctuated with dead Roos and livestock. Driving past a tall modern sign from Suncorp Bank promoting "Agribusiness Supporting Rural Communities" with "Farewell from McKinlay Shire" printed along the bottom, the embedded irony is difficult to ignore, given the impact of the severe drought and continuous grazing on the land. We stop and wave to a train engineer hauling what appear to be empty concentrate cars back to Mount Isa along the rail line, running parallel to the highway. The road itself is narrow, bumpy and just downright dangerous in some spots, for the posted speed limits. It is a shamefully inadequate highway compared to the highways in NT. So far, we have seen no evidence, that we are five years ahead of NT, here in the Smart State.

Hughenden (QLD)

Population: 1,154. Founded in 1874. Traditional lands of the Yirandali people. Agriculture and tourism are the lifeblood of the small town. A notable person from Hughenden is Andrew Crombie who unwittingly discovered Kronosaurus queenslandicus. Hughenden is most known for the Porcupine Gorge. Must-See attractions: Porcupine Gorge and the Holden Café.

orcupine Creek carves its way through Porcupine Gorge (QLD)

In Hughenden, after checking into our hotel we go to the Flinders Discovery Centre to get directions out to the Porcupine Gorge and a local lookout. Our drive out to Porcupine Gorge is 61 kilometres north of Hughenden along the paved Kennedy Development road. The Porcupine Gorge is promoted as the little Grand Canyon of Australia. To compare the gorge to the Grand Canyon is a real stretch even for Australia, nonetheless, an enjoyable visit if in the area. Capped by sheets of basalt lava flow, the strata of sedimentary sandstone layers have been carved 120 metres deep by Porcupine Creek, during the last 170 million years.

Challenged by a bull on the roadway up to the gorge, we take extra care driving below the speed limit on the way back. Judging by the the lack of traffic, a speedy rescue from this roadway is unlikely. We decide to spend the sunset up at Mount Walker, overlooking Hughenden. At a sixteen percent incline the paved road up to Mount Walker lookout far exceeds the maximum grade standard of seven percent for North American roads. Throwing the Camry into low gear on our roller coaster ascent, the 360° panorama at 478 metres up top, is well worth being pinned back in the seat on the trip up. We head back to Hughenden as the sun sets and come across some Australian bustards, *(Ardeotis australis)* strolling through the tall grass. These beige, one metre ground birds have been an important source of food for Indigenous peoples. The birds blend well into the surroundings, have well developed legs for running, and will only take flight if necessary.

Serving up memorabilia and good food, the FJ Holden Café
Hughenden (QLD)

We dine at the FJ Holden Café. It is a must see filled with Holden and Elvis memorabilia. It serves up great meals fast and at fair prices, a rare treat in Oz. Across the road next to the iconic Grand Hotel, a four metre *Muttaburrasaurus* has one of his yellow eyes fixed on us, as we stroll out to our vehicle. The car is sheltered from the sun, in a covered carpark running up the middle of the boulevard, end capped at the far end, with two sawed-off twenty-foot wind turbines with a curved roof between them forming a unique rotunda. A lot of work has gone into making something out of the main street. On the return to our hotel we are accosted by a large band of roving pure white crested cockatoos who sure know how to wake up any neighbourhood in a hurry.

Saturday, June 20. Sunny 11-26°C

Our trip today takes us 383 kilometres east to Townsville. We view a 35-foot Comet Windmill up close, at a rest stop in Prairie. It is a time-tested, beautiful machine working with nature to deliver life sustaining fresh water. Comet windmills have been successfully pumping water in the Australian Outback for over 130 years. These efficient low maintenance windmills can draw water from 1000 feet, supplying as much as 250,000 gallons of water per day. Gaining elevation as we pass Torrens Creek we stop at the summit of the Great Dividing Range at 550 meters in elevation in the south end of White Mountains National Park. A remote 108,000-hectare range of sparsely treed, pure white sandstone mountains and gorges stands out dramatically against the surrounding spinifex grasslands. The home to bearded dragons and pink-crested galah cockatoos plays an important role as a water intake area for the Great Artesian Basin. It is too cool for the dragons to make an appearance. We spot a pair of flirting galahs in an Acacia, while taking some pictures of the scenery looking down from the summit.

Flirting galahs,White Mountains National Park (QLD)

Missing my early morning coffee, I am hoping to pick one up along the way. 33 kilometers west of Charters Towers I pull into Balfe's Creek at the local pub, motel, and caravan park. We walk in through the tavern entrance and get a big "Welcome to Paradise", by the proprietor himself. I ask, "Can you make me a latte to go"? He replies, "Ain't got no lattes mate, but I can make you a coffee". He goes back into his office and puts on the kettle and brews up two instant coffees in mugs, mine being twice the size of his. I guess I forgot to mention that I was looking for coffee to go. What fun is that?

"My name is John, people in these parts, they call me Honest John, friend of the working man." We introduce ourselves and explain how we managed to find ourselves in Balfe's Creek. Tyler and Susan are getting a little anxious, as I work on a mug of coffee that should be good for three pee breaks. John sucks back five cigarettes in the meantime, while we discuss energy self-sufficiency, the Queensland drought and other big topics such as the Great Australian Aquifer. John tells us a fantastic tale about how the Aquifer is fed from thousands of miles away in Papua, New Guinea and pushes up tiny, translucent creatures through the water bore holes.

The beauty of Australia is its people. They pride themselves in the tale, not so much in the facts, as those usually only improve in the retelling (there is always some kernel of truth). The magic is in the telling of the tale. The delivery is always well done, takes time, and sucks you in. We always feel we are interrupting when saying, "Sorry, we must move on, otherwise we'll never make it home". John – if we had started our journey with you, who knows, we might still be in Balfe's Creek today. Thank you for sharing and your hospitality. We did consider heading north to Cooktown, as you recommended however, that road beyond Cape Tribulation is just a nasty piece of work.

The Great Australian Aquifer is formally known the Great Artesian Basin. It is one of the world's largest groundwater resources covering some 1.7 million square kilometers, 23% of Australia, primarily in Queensland, northern sections of New South Wales and South Australia, and limited parts of western Northern Territory. The Basin ranges in depth from less than 100 meters to 3000 meters and is estimated to hold almost 65 million mega litres of water. It is held in several complex multilayered aquifers within continental sandstone that was formed during the Jurassic and Cretaceous periods, when much of inland Australia was below sea level. Most of the water entering the Basin, filters down from riverbeds on the western side of the Great Dividing Range. Much of the water moves through the basin very slowly and it is thought that some of the water in the Basin is up to 2 million years old. At maximum pressure of 1300 kilopascals, the average water temperature is 35°C, although it may be as high as 130°C subsurface, heated by past volcanic activity and radioactive decay of uranium, thorium and potassium. (104)   Although some of the geological basins extend to Papua New Guinea (PNG), I could find no recorded evidence of recharge water coming from PNG.

The Great Artesian Basin is the only reliable source of relatively good quality water for many drier parts of Australia and has sustained Indigenous peoples and groundwater dependent ecosystems for millennia. In some areas, it is a provider of geothermal energy. Some aquifers and caves are home to stygofauna, small animals that have lost their eyes and pigments. (105)   The Great Artesian Basin sustains the lives of 180,000 persons and 7,600 enterprises in over 120 towns. It supports pastoral activities, the mining of copper, uranium, bauxite and opals, oil, gas and coal seam gas. Many of the natural springs are sacred and cultural sites of importance to Indigenous people, integral in their ceremonies and stories. The Great Artesian Basin Coordinating Committee is cross jurisdictional for basin management activities, including research, monitoring, planning and actions including the sealing of old bore holes to preserve water and Basin pressure. There are numerous sustainability challenges. Not least of these are the many competing uses, the significant waste of water (90%) from open stock bores, and the reluctance of water users to fund upgrades to the infrastructure (104).

Australia is the driest inhabited continent on earth and has one of the highest per capita water consumption rates after Canada and the US. There is no question that water security is very important to Australia. In some regions, you may easily pay much more for a litre of water than a liter of petrol. During 2013-2014, an estimated 92,000 giga litres (GL) of water were extracted from the environment twelve percent higher than in 2012-13. Of the total, fourteen percent was extracted by water providers and the remaining 86% was used mainly by the Electric and Gas Supply industry. Most of the water used for energy, was non-consumptive (hydro-electric) with 78,000 giga litres returned to the environment in regulated discharges. Surface water represented 96% of the water supply with groundwater supplying three percent and desalination one percent. Agriculture accounted for 12,393GL or 62% of Australia's water consumption. Of that almost one quarter was used to grow cotton. Australian households accounted for 1,906 GL or ten percent of total water consumption. Although households used only thirteen percent of net distributed water, expenditure by households for distributed water represented 67% of all expenditures on distributed water. It is graphically obvious that there is a large disparity between who is using water and who is paying for it. The highest price paid was by South Australian households with an average price of $4.29 per thousand liters. The cost of water may explain the increasing use of rain storage tanks across the country for eight percent of total household consumption in 2014. (106)

The Constitution of the Commonwealth of Australia states that natural resources policy including water is a responsibility of the states. Some states operate integrated statewide utilities although others have transferred the responsibility of water provision to the local municipal level, many who in turn contract commercial services. Water reservoirs play a major role in water supply especially for the large cities that may have multiple rivers, watersheds and reservoirs in their supply chain. Water demand especially from rivers may fluctuate wildly depending on rainfall conditions. The Federal Government has had to step in, especially for funding, and where water demand was becoming controversial between states, users and long-term sustainability. Intervention has fluctuated between governments and party politics. Most major cities have established desalination plants that supply anywhere from fifteen to fifty percent of their water supply when needed. We see evidence throughout the country of conservation, of both energy and water. It is evident in the solar water heaters on the roofs of our hotels, the signage in our room requesting us to respectfully limit showers to three minutes, recommended reuse of towels, turning off power when leaving a room, the road trains carrying massive rainwater storage tanks to various communities, the roadside washrooms fed by rainwater or greywater and the extensive use of drip irrigation. It is encouraging to see the level of conservation at the consumer level in Australia.

Leaving the Outback, the landscape transitions from scrubland to well treed forest as we pass through Charters Towers. Heading into Townsville the scenery is dramatic, with lush tropical forested coastal mountains giving way to the East Coast of Australia and the South

Pacific Ocean. Our arrival on the coast is a significant milestone for us, as we feel assured that we can complete our journey as planned. The balance of our trip will be at a more relaxed pace, with more breaks.

Drawing water for over 130 years, Comet Windmills
Prairie (QLD)

Townsville (QLD)

Area: 140 km². Population: 189,238. Founded in 1865. Traditional lands of the Bindal and Wulgurukaba people. Townsville is the largest urban center on the north-east coast of Queensland. Contributing to the local economy are over 10,000 businesses including refining of copper, zinc and nickel, administrative offices, tourism, James Cook University, the Australian Institute of Marine Science, the Great Barrier Reef Marine Park Authority, a large army base and an RAAF base. A notable person from Townsville is the editor-in-chief of WikiLeaks, Julian Assange. Townsville is most known for "The Strand", it's seaside foreshore including jetty, park, café's and pools. Must-See attraction: The view from Castle Hill is spectacular.

View of city, The Strand, Cleveland Bay and Magnetic Island
Townsville (QLD)

The temperature is moderate with persons swimming in the ocean from palm shaded beaches under cloudy skies. We check into our hotel and hit the beach for seaside fish and chips and walk along the beautiful Strand in downtown Townsville. The town is filled with weekend traffic, as everyone is trying to make the most of the Strand. Parking is at a premium, as there is also a flea market and a military event taking place at Jezzine Barracks, that is closed to the public for the day. Following lunch and our walk along the beach we drive the car up to the top of Castle Hill. It is a narrow, steep, circuitous climb for the car and there are many athletic men and women challenging the hill on foot. We must be cautious in avoiding them and oncoming traffic, while not accidentally slipping over the cliff's edge. The trip to the top, even on foot is well worth it, for outstanding views of Townsville, the surrounding Pacific Ocean and islands. Having arrived in another special region of Australia we are ready to fully embrace it. In the evening we go to Ciabatta's for fine Italian dining and enjoy a lovely meal.

Sunday, June 21 (Father's Day). Partly Sunny 12-28°C

This morning we make a beeline for Port Douglas, 418 kilometers north along the Bruce, Coral Coast and Captain Cook Highways that all make up Highway A1. Heading north towards Cairns, the landscape quickly changes from forested hillsides to sugar cane and banana plantations nestled between coastal rainforest. These lush tropical crops extend for miles on either side of the highway interrupted occasionally by the sighting of a narrow-gage cane train. The lush green beauty of the plantations, mask some darker facets of plantation history in Australia. The most enduring legacy of the period, is the cane toad. 3000 of these toxic toads were introduced in Queensland to control the cane beetle, in 1935. The cane toad has since become one the most invasive and problematic species, growing in population to over 200 million across Northern Australia.

As North Americans, when the topic of slavery comes up, we tend to think of the Trans-Atlantic slave trade or sometimes the Arab slave trade. Australia has a long history of slavery, as well. Slavery in Australia comes as a surprise to many outsiders however, not to those familiar with Australian relations with Indigenous Australians and Melanesians. Black-birding is the coercion of persons to serve as labourers, through tricks and kidnapping. The practice was used to get slave labourers to work on Australian sugar plantations and in the pearling industry. Queensland plantation owners had a great need for labourers. Between 1863 and 1904, an estimated 55,000 to 62,500 South Sea Islanders were forcefully displaced and recruited as labourers, through black-birding. These labourers were Melanesians who came from eighty South Pacific

Islands including Vanuatu, Papua New Guinea, the Solomon Islands, and the Loyalty Islands, as well as Polynesians from Niue. The Queensland government attempted to regulate the trade, by requiring every ship recruiting labourers, to carry a person assigned by the government to make sure labourers were willingly recruited. Unfortunately, these supervisors were often corrupt, and easily bribed, or ignorant to the plight of the enslaved Pacific Islanders. (107)

The labourers were often called Kanakas who for all essential purposes were slaves. To avoid prosecution, the labourers were referred to as indentured labourers. Aboriginal Australians from the Cape York Peninsula were also kidnapped and employed on the Queensland plantations. The methods of black-birding differed greatly with some persons willingly boarding to work, others being tricked, and some being kidnapped. In some instances, entire villages were black-birded with the promise of trade or a religious service on-board the ship. Many died during the voyages by ship, owing to unsanitary conditions and even more persons died working in the fields. There are no known statistics of the exact number of persons black-birded. Between 1904 and 1908, most of the remaining 10,000 Pacific Islanders were deported, a result of *The Pacific Island Labourers Act* of 1901, shutting down the practice. Black-birding, was not the only form of slavery in Australia. Indigenous Australians were also made indentured servants on ranches throughout the country. The pearling industry took food, timber, water and slaves from the mainland and throughout the Torres Islands, reducing the island populations by half, by 1900. Indigenous Australians were forced to free dive in deep waters without equipment, with pregnant women preferred, as it was believed that they could hold their breath longer. It resulted in many accidents and deaths. (74)

The soil is rich, the climate humid, and the sky threatens with brief bursts of sweet water. Taking a brief java stop at Godfathers Café, we then continue to slog through the traffic. We have grown unaccustomed to busy roads and are impatient after our traffic-free experience in the Outback. Three quarters of the way into our road trip, bypassing the city of Cairns, our route eventually enters the curvy scenic coastal highway carved out in the cliffs, heading to Port Douglas. We will have an extended stay at this destination, for some well deserved "Rest and Recreation", and are anxious to get to our hotel and settle in.

Port Douglas (QLD)

Population 3,205. Founded in 1877. Traditional lands of the Kuku Yulanji people. Tourism is the greatest driver for the local economy. The 42nd US President, Bill Clinton vacationed here in 2001 during the September 11 tragedy. Steve Irwin "The Crocodile Hunter" perished offshore from Port Douglas. Port Douglas is most known for its natural beauty and situation close to two World Heritage Sites. Must-See attractions: The Great Barrier Reef and Daintree Rainforest.

Daintree River and Rainforest, Daintree National Park (QLD)

Port Douglas is a popular tourist mecca. The town is populated with an abundance of British tourists as we check into our hotel on Macrossan Street, near 4-mile beach. We are tired and decide to take the rest of the day to shop for a home cooked meal, and grab a late sushi lunch and beer, before walking on the beach. We BBQ surf & turf, eye steak and fresh local prawns tonight. The best meal in Australia. The love of my life whips up as good a meal in our hotel room as any gourmet restaurant in Oz.

Monday, June 22. Partly Sunny 17-23°C

Following breakfast on the balcony, we do some laundry and administrative chores and book our trip out to the Great Barrier Reef for Wednesday. We then drive up into Daintree Rainforest on a self-guided tour. At 1,200 square kilometers, Daintree is the largest continuous rainforest in Australia. It is also the oldest intact lowland tropical forest on the planet, between 110 and 200 million years old, dating back to Gondwana, showing off spectacular biodiversity both new and ancient. Thirteen different rainforest types have been identified ranging from the tall forests of the lowlands, to the heath growing on the mountaintops that receive as much as 9000mm of rain per year. Sixty percent of the annual rain falls between December and March and the area is prone to an average of two cyclones per season.

Of the nineteen primitive flowering plants found on earth, twelve of them reside in Daintree. Its biodiversity is unrivalled in Australia, containing thirty percent of Australia's frog, marsupial and reptile species, 65% of Australia's bat and butterfly species and twenty percent of the bird species. Seventy animals and 700 plants are only found in Daintree. It is home to Australia's largest snake the Amethystine Python that reaches 8.5 metres in length, the Ulysses Blue Swallowtail butterfly that typically has a wingspan of 14 centimetres, and the Cassowary. The Cassowary is a tall land bird that can run through dense forest at fifty kilometres per hour, jump 1.5 meters high, and swim in the ocean or across large rivers. These creatures amongst enormous multi-buttressed tropical trees covered in hanging vines and aerial ecosystems surrounded by ancient ferns and cycads, all in a spectacular setting of mountaintops that reach down to the white sand beaches of the fringing coral reef. (108) We must see it.

The drive to the National Park itself is not far, though there is a bit of a wait to catch the ferry for the crossing over the Daintree River. Our first stop is at the Discovery Centre, for a self guided walking tour along a multi-tiered boardwalk through different layers of the forest canopy. We educate ourselves on the history of the forest, its structure, its diversity of plants and animals, and how Indigenous people lived within it. It is very instructive and covers a great many aspects of the ecosystems within different parts of the forest and how these interact. There are a few different scientific stations, as well as an interpretive centre equipped with the latest interactive technology covering ecology, evolution, flora, fauna, fungi and climate change. One of the research stations, is one of 22 global stations that are part of the Global Malaise Program, contributing to the International Barcode of Life. It collects arthropods (primarily insects and spiders), sending them to the Biodiversity Institute of Ontario, in Canada. Unique specimens are assigned a barcode and index number. We see a variety of epiphytes (mosses, ferns, orchids, bromeliads) growing mid-stem or higher on tree trunks, creating spectacular mid-air ecosystems. The diversity in trees is amazing, including rosewood, Noah's walnut, Alexandra, black palm, and white aspen a tree from the Citrus family. In addition to a range of mahoganies and a nutmeg we also see trees with bizarre local names such as Idiot Fruit, Wait-a-While, and Vicious-Hairy-Mary.

After a light lunch at the Discovery Centre we drive along the Cassowary Highway up to Cape Tribulation in search of the elusive cassowary. This mysterious flightless bird is native to New Guinea, Australia and the islands in the body of water between the two landmasses, known as the Torres Strait. The cassowary is by far one of the strangest bird species inhabiting the planet. The southern cassowary is the only species of cassowary living in Australia and is notable by its characteristics. The 1.5-metre tall bird has a black bristly quill plumage, a blue face and neck, a red nape and wattles, and a horn-like casque (helmet) that may measure fifteen centimeters. Cassowary feet have three toes with a twelve-centimeter sharp dagger claw on the edge. It is very agile in its environment.

The cassowary has a fearsome reputation, as it is known for not backing down from humans and is rumored able of disemboweling a human being with one strike. Despite its reputation there is only one documented human death by cassowary attack, and exceedingly more cassowaries have been hunted and killed by humans. Nonetheless, the public are warned to be cautious about encountering cassowaries in the wild. The southern cassowary forages for food on the forest floor. Its diet consists mainly of fallen fruit, although it may include insects, fungi, and small vertebrates. It is a solitary bird and only pairs during mating season. Cassowaries are shy and unless provoked, will avoid humans. Unlike other birds, the male tends to raise the chicks. The cassowary is unfortunately vulnerable to extinction. In Queensland, it is considered an endangered species with threats including road building, feral animals, and hunting. It is estimated there are 10,000-20,000 southern cassowaries left globally, with 1,500-2,500 of them left in Australia. These birds are a national treasure. Conservation efforts are strictly enforced to preserve these birds that face a high risk of extinction if their natural habitat is not protected. (109)

Southern Cassowary (QLD)

At Cape Tribulation, we park the car and walk down to the beach to enjoy the scenery. This is as close to "The Reef" and as far north on the East Coast of Australia that our travel by car will take us. Despite large multilingual yellow and red signs warning that "Crocodiles Inhabit this Area - Attacks May Cause Injury or Death", a group of visitors are wading through the beachside mangrove swamps, right in the kill zone. My son just shakes his head remarking, "never underestimate the stupidity of people".

After taking pictures, we meander towards the parking lot along a trail and encounter two turkey sized birds rapidly chasing one another. The birds are squabbling over a cricket that is jumping frantically trying to escape, jumping between our legs in its effort to get away. These birds are fast, fearless and ruthless hunters. Our first impression is that these may be young cassowaries. We get a touch nervous about having a chance encounter with the parent cassowary. Based on our preliminary information, that could be dangerous, the same as being between a grizzly bear and its cubs. It makes for some entertaining video footage, especially now that we know that these birds were just common Australian bush turkeys. Who's the turkey?

Unfortunately, we miss Cooktown. It was the 2nd largest tent city in Australia after Brisbane during Gold Rush days. It is named after James Cook who took seven weeks of safe harbour there, after his vessel the Endeavour took serious damage on the Endeavour Reef off Cooktown. Attempting to go north of Cape Tribulation to Cooktown we realize immediately, with the multiplicity of potholes in the road, and a vehicle in the oncoming ditch whose axle and body are completely transfigured, that continuing will be complete folly. We change course, turning around and driving south for tropical fruit ice cream instead. Afterwards, our drive takes us to the spectacular viewpoint at Alexander Point to take some Kodak moments before returning to our hotel to enjoy Greek Salad & BBQ chicken dinner on our balcony accompanied by sea breezes blowing through the Palms.

Tuesday, June 23. Partly Sunny 16-21°C

The tropical rains came down hard last night and the beach is misting as the sun burns off the moisture. I pick up lattes from our favourite little bookstore in town and we have a quick breakfast. Ty and I set out to Four-mile beach and walk the length of it from the cliffs to the furthest visible point from the cliffs, and back again. The winter waters of the Coral Sea are a bone chilling 26°C and vacant of jellyfish as we walk the beach barefoot in the water up to our knees, massaging our feet and exercising our calves. It is a relaxing and refreshing two-hour walk in the wind and the waves as the sun burns off the mist and warm things up. A kite surfer impresses me with his ability to make it out as far as the horizon goes in heavy winds and navigate his way back into shore with ease. All our senses inform us that we are in Paradise.

Tyler climbs some vines in the Rainforest at Mossman Gorge (QLD)

After our walk, we drive out to Mossman Gorge, a world heritage site tropical forest. It has survived for 135 million years and is considered the evolutionary cradle of Australia's flora and fauna. The trail has placards along it that describe many of the trees and how these are used by Indigenous people and animals. It is very pleasant and feels as if we are getting lost in an ancient world, as we walk deeper into the tropical forest along the gorge. This diverse forest is at the southern edge of Daintree National Park. The trees are covered in vines slithering up tree trunks like fat pythons, and epiphytes that create giant mid-air nests for a variety of plants. From a clearing along the edge of the gorge we view Manjal Dimbi, a sacred mountain to the Kuku Yulanji, before re-entering into the darkness of the rainforest where we are accosted by some more bush turkeys. The forest abounds with stem inhabiting fungi such as walnut-like gels, delicate yellow capped mushrooms to fanned turkey tails, as well as beautiful hanging gardens of parasitic mistletoes. The wavy buttresses of some of the towering tropical tree stems are other worldly and impressive. Exiting the trail over a boardwalk bridge, the magic stays behind us as we re-enter the modern world.

Feeling comfortable enough that we will not have any trouble finding petrol on the remaining journey, we give away our spare petrol can to visitors passing through from New South Wales. We then drive back to Port Douglas, so that Susan can escape her frustrating men, and enjoy some retail therapy. Enjoying beer and pizza we then retire early, as tomorrow promises to be a big day out at the Great Barrier Reef.

Wednesday, June 24. Rain/Partly Sunny 16-22°C

The day starts out with another tropical downpour, although by the time I pick up lattes, my umbrella is no longer required. Today we set out to the Great Barrier Reef (GBR), the worlds largest structure made by living organisms. It is approximately 2,300 kilometers long, extending up the eastern seaboard of Australia and consists of a network of 2,900 individual reefs and 900 islands covering almost 345,000 square kilometers. The next largest reef is in the Caribbean Sea and is one tenth of its size. We will be heading out to the Agincourt Reef, a ribbon reef on the very outer edge of the Great Barrier Reef, two kilometers from deep ocean, running parallel to the continental shelf. Some 400 species of coral in various colours and designs (stag horns, brain, mushroom, plates) make up the reef that hosts over 1,500 different species of fish and a wide array of marine mammals and sea turtles.

We lather up with sun screen, optimistic that our good weather totem (Susan), will provide us with a sunny day despite the gloomy prospects of stormy conditions. The aluminum Wavepiercing Catamaran that holds up to 450 passengers and 28 crew, leaves shore at ten am. It propels us at 34 knots out to Agincourt Reef, 72 kilometers away, in just over an hour. The experience includes coffee breaks and a hot lunch served on a massive ocean platform. It provides a base for helicopter trips over the reef, semi-submersible reef trips that allow patrons to view the reef without getting wet, and dive platforms equipped with gear for snorkeling and scuba diving. Susan, Tyler and I take the semi-submersible sub a few times to survey the reef and its noteworthy coral and creatures. Tyler and I then go to the snorkeling platform, pick up our gear including a pool noodle and jump in the water. The pool noodle alleviates a lot of treading and lets us make the most of our experience without tiring out to soon.

At 24°C these Canucks find no need to wear scuba suits
Great Barrier Reef (QLD) | Quicksilver Cruises

The sighting of various corals, giant clams, sea turtles and hundreds of varieties of colourful fish of every description is magical, as anyone who has ever snorkeled or dived on a reef knows. The experience is one that everyone should have the opportunity to do once in a lifetime, at least. Approximately two million persons visit the GBR annually. The reef employs more than 64,000 persons and generates over $6 billion in revenue. Although pollution, overfishing and tourism itself all threaten the reef, the biggest concern to the Great Barrier Reef Marine Park Authority is climate change. Climate change influences ocean warming and acidification contributing to coral bleaching, slowing coral growth and increasing coral susceptibility to disease. Saving the magic of the Great Barrier Reef, and the survival of our own species are great reasons for society to reduce carbon emissions. We are on the reef till three pm and then fly back across the water into Port Douglas under sunny skies, rainbows, incoming storms, and choppy seas. It is an unforgettable day!

Thursday, June 25. Sunny 16-24°C

Our departure from Port Douglas is with regret today. It has been our first stay in Australia with four nights in one location. We are relaxed and have just begun to feel at home in this tropical paradise with its hint of Tofino. After cleaning the BBQ and kitchen, laundering clothes and packing we drive to Townsville 418 kilometers south along the Cassawary Hwy #1. Just north of Cairns, we stop in at Outback Opal Mines to view and purchase some opal jewellery.

Opal the "Eye Stone", is the national gemstone. Australia supplies 95-97% of the worlds precious opals. According to an Indigenous legend, opals were formed when a rainbow fell to earth. Opal is a mineraloid with a water content usually ranging between six to ten percent. It has a unique closely packed lattice of silica spheres that depending on thickness, influences the play of colour or the diffraction of light passing through its microstructure. Opals may display nearly every colour in the visible spectrum in a single piece, although many are collected and cut for their specific colour characteristics with black opals being the rarest. Although NSW is home to black opal and South Australia produces eighty percent of Australian opals, we have waited till Queensland to purchase, as our interest is in the boulder opals which are only found here. Boulder opals are mined from ironstone. They are usually cut with a natural look using the ironstone as a backing to a thin layer of opal resulting in dark body tone and colour vibrancy similar as black opal. (110)

Opal is the birthstone of persons born in October. Legend and mythology have painted the stone both as the evil eye, and earlier, prior to and in the middle ages as a stone of good fortune, healing and love that could also confer the power of invisibility if wrapped in bay leaf and held in the hand. Having two family members with birthdays in October, it is only right that while in the land of opals, we purchase the appropriate gifts for them, and so we do. We are confident that their auras, will only bring out the best in these gems.

Our trip is punctuated by a midday breathalyzer stop just south of the Murdering Point Tropical Fruit Winery. Fortunately, we did not stop in and do the tour, for I might have just sampled the fare. No matter how hard and how long the cop makes me blow in to the device he gets a big fat zero point zero. Unfortunately, for some other tourists, their campers are pulled over, and are being thoroughly strip searched. The roadside police action must cause tourists travelling north to think twice about the invitation of nearby promotional billboards welcoming tourists to the winery. The maximum limit for blood alcohol content in Australia is 0.05%. It was introduced over 25 years ago to curb the high number of road fatalities. Spot checks are random, occurring at any time, in any location. Breath testing for alcohol as well as saliva testing for THC, Methamphetamine and MDMA does not require probable cause.

We arrive in Townsville at four pm, check into our hotel and then drive out to Jezzine Barracks and climb to the top of the Barracks gaining a new perspective of Townsville. The fifteen-hectare heritage precinct of Jezzine Barracks and the Kissing Point headland are significant both to the local Indigenous people who know it as Garabarra and to the military who established a fort here in 1870. It was in continuous military use between 1885 and 2006. The area includes a coastal walkway connecting the Strand to Rowes Bay with observation decks at Kissing Point Fort, the crossed boomerang amphitheater, traditional plantings and a regimental plaza as well as an army museum.

Kissing Point Fort was completed in 1891 as part of Queensland's colonial defence plan to protect the rich pasture lands, nearby goldfields and shipping in Townsville harbour with a small battery of 64-pound rifled guns. Since Federation, the 3rd Regiment (Kennedy) and the 31st battalion trained and mobilized from Kissing Point. These troops saw action in the Boer War, the First and Second World Wars and conflicts up to and including East Timor. Kissing Point was renamed Jezzine Barracks in 1964 in honour of the 2/31st infantry battalion who distinguished themselves during the second world war in June, 1941 by taking and holding the clifftop town of Jezzine in Lebanon, from the Vichy French, under heavy fire. (111) James Heather Gordon of Western Australia was awarded the Victoria Cross after he took it upon himself under heavy machine gun and grenade fire, to creep forward alone and take out a machine gun post and its four machine gunners with his bayonet. (112) The Army Reserves were moved to Lavarack Barracks in 2009, and Jezzine Barracks was handed over to the community of Townsville.

US and Australian flags fly proudly here, in commemoration of when Townsville was home to the 5th US Airforce prior to the battle with the Japanese for New Guinea. The evidence clearly indicates the close bond that exists between these two countries, geographically far apart, yet very close as brothers in arms. We capture some beautiful sunset pictures down by the outdoor seaside pool before stopping in for a casual seaside fish and chips dinner.

Poolside at The Strand, Townsville (QLD)

Friday, June 26. Sunny 18-22°C

Departing from Townsville at nine in the morning there is an air of calm anticipation in our vehicle. We have travelled a very long distance together through some tough country and have experienced a range of emotions, from pure highs to lows and sometimes just plain monotony. Sensing that we are nearing the end of our journey it will be relatively easy going from here on in, and before we know it we will be winging our way home. Relaxed as we cross the tropic of Capricorn going south, we stop in the seaside community of Bowen for coffee and pie at Jochheim's Pies. The award-winning bakery has seating for 65 persons and the place is full. I take the opportunity to enjoy a savoury meat pie, my first and last in Australia. It is delicious.

We go down to the seaside and stop in at the tourist kiosk, looking for regional brochures and maps for the remainder of our journey. The young lady in the kiosk lets us know, "Oh you really should stop and do some snorkelling out here. Our reefs are amazing". That is very inviting. We take a walk out on the jetty to take in the beach and stunning scenery. Right at the entry to Bowen Wharf are numerous signs. The one that catches my immediate attention is "Warning Sharks Frequent These Waters". Australian humour again. If we were thinking about snorkelling, we sure forget about it quickly, been there, done that, lived to tell about it. Observing thousands of tiny blue crabs scurrying across the wet sand., we unfortunately miss the sea turtles that frequent the jetty as we are here at low tide.

Beach at low tide, Bowen (QLD)

The scenery on our way south along Hwy 1 is mainly sugar cane fields interspersed amongst coastal mountains and beaches, punctuated by the odd sugar mill every 100 kilometers or so. Australia's sugar cane industry that began as plantations with indentured labourers, consists of over 4,000 cane farms, many that are family run. 95% of the farms operate in Queensland, in a fifty-kilometer wide strip running 2,100 kilometers between Mossman and the Atherton Tablelands in the north to Grafton in Northern NSW. Widely recognized as a low-cost producer,

Australia is the third largest raw sugar supplier in the world exporting eighty percent of its supply with an annual production value of approximately AU$2billion. It is the seventh largest agricultural export with 4,400 cane growers supplying between 30-35 million tonnes of cane and between 4-4.5 million tonnes of raw sugar, processed in 24 sugar mills annually. (113) Most of the transport from cane fields is done via narrow gage rail. The industry has been thriving. It faces some sustainability issues. Securing water entitlements for perpetuity is high on the list. We arrive in MacKay after 389 kilometers of easy travel along the Cook Highway and check into our hotel near the Marina.

Lush sugar cane crops north of MacKay (QLD)

Mackay (QLD)

Population: 120,000. Founded in 1860. Traditional lands of the Yuwibara people. Mackay contributes significantly to the Australian economy. It is the gateway to the Bowen Basin coal mining reserves where over 100 million tonnes of coal are extracted annually from 34 mines and exported to Japan and China in addition to supplying domestic use. Sugar is the other major industry with tourism, marine and retail playing minor roles. A notable person from Mackay is the jockey and thoroughbred horse trainer George Moore who was made an Officer of the British Empire in 1972 and inducted into the Sport Australia Hall of Fame in 1986. Mackay is known as the sugar capital of Australia as its region produces a third of Australia's sugar. Must-See attractions: Rats of Tobruk and Orchid Display House, Queens Park.

View of Marina, Mackay (QLD)

A visiting soccer team sponsored by Emirates, leaves the hotel for practice or a game as we check in. We go for a walk along the marina promenade and over to the beach to take some pictures before heading back to the hotel for a rest. We enjoy a tasty Thai food dinner down by the Marina. The meal is delicious, as is the excellent Dopff Gewurztraminer, something the Alsace still has over Australia.

Saturday, June 27. Partly Sunny 18-22°C

We are woken at 7:15am by the hotel fire alarm. There is a wedding today and twelve women were drying their hair in one room, raising the temperature enough to set off the alarm. Lucky for their hairdos, the rooms are not equipped with fire sprinklers. We leave MacKay and cross the 21st parallel at nine am heading south towards Gladstone, 444 kilometers away. Our trip passes through cane fields, banana and macadamia nut orchards into pasture lands interspersed by Eucalypt forests and Koala warning signs. We are back in Koala country. Half way through the trip we pull off into Marlborough and have lunch and a pint in the local pub. We add our names along with thousands of travelers before us, to the pub wall. The town including the post office is for sale to anyone interested in buying a town whose local characters match its name. Susan deeply apologizes for causing a scene by smashing the glass and making a mess with her soda pop, as do I, for mistakenly stepping behind the bar looking for a cleanup rag. "You can't be doin that here Mate". Unruly tourists. What do you do with them?

hainsaw in action, Marlborough Pub, Marlborough (QLD)

Gladstone (QLD)

Population: 31,778. Founded in 1863. Traditional lands of the Bailai, Gooreng Gooreng, Gurang and Taribelang Bunda nations. Gladstone's local economy centers on its heavy industries and natural deep-water port. Sixteen wharves ship 98 million tonnes annually of thirty different products, primarily coal (71%) and alumina (24%). A notable person from Gladstone is "Mr. Gladstone" William Robert Golding. alderman, harbor master, mayor and author who worked to achieve recognition of the port, negotiate financing, and plan infrastructure for the growth of Gladstone. Gladstone is known as the Engine Room of Industry. Must-See attraction: Enjoy coffee and the view from Auckland Hill Lookout.

Arriving in Gladstone, we are welcomed by a massive coal fired electric power plant. NRG Gladstone Power Station has a generating capacity of 1680MW burning four million tonnes of coal annually to support a thriving aluminum industry. Home to many industrial complexes including Queensland Alumina (worlds largest alumina refineries), Rio Tinto Alcan Yarwun Alumina Refinery, Boyne Smelters Ltd. (Australia's largest aluminum smelter), Cement Australia Gladstone (Australia's largest cement plant), and Orica Australia that produces 9,000 tonnes of chlor-alkali, 590,000 tonnes of ammonium nitrate, and 80,000 tonnes of sodium cyanide annually. The port is the fourth largest coal exporting port in the country, shipping 42 different types of coal. The port ships 29 other products including alumina, aluminum, ammonium nitrates, grain, cement and general cargo. (114) The scene reminds me of Rhineland Germany, only in a more tropical setting.

We check into a hotel downtown, with a beautiful view of the harbour. It is without a doubt, the best value hotel we have stayed in to date, with two bedrooms, two bathrooms, a kitchen dining area and laundry room. After going out to buy groceries, Susan prepares a fine meal, Greek salad with BBQ chicken. Our family chills out watching TV, and I drift off into the deep sleep of a hibernating bear.

Auckland Hill Lookout, Gladstone (QLD)

Sunday, June 28. Rain/Partly Cloudy 16-22°C

This morning our thoughts are with our good friends, Tom and his bride to be, Karen. It is the date of their wedding day in Toronto. Strangely enough, it is still a day away for them, because of the difference in time zones. Tom was my first road touring partner way back in 1976. In our teens, we borrowed my Dad's little red VW beetle for a short road tour. After installing a CB radio and flared tailpipes that blew off the occasional red flame, we dubbed ourselves with the CB handle "Little Red Spartan". Traveling across Canada to Vancouver we got bored with the rain in Vancouver and headed south to Los Angeles, returning via Las Vegas, Salt Lake City, Yellowstone, and Fargo over a period of 5 weeks. It was a great adventure with many good memories and the first of many road trips. I send off a congratulatory email with some passages from Aboriginal Creation Stories to commemorate their special day. Our hearts dance with delight on this joyous day.

After checking out, we drive up to the Outlook Café on Auckland Hill to buy some lattes and take pictures of the industrial vista that is Gladstone. There are just as many power and sail boats in the water, as there are storage tanks and silos. No doubt the local industry brings a high degree of prosperity to the local community. After navigating our way out of town, we continue 429 kilometers south along the Bruce Hwy 1 to Noosa

Heads on the popular Sunshine Coast. We are tempted to drop into Bundaberg as Tyler and I have been enjoying its golden nectar of Ginger Beer, throughout our travels in Australia. We skip Bundaberg as our schedule is being affected by heavy highway traffic. It is a Sunday and we are in thick weekend traffic returning farther south to Brisbane. Oh, how I long for the empty Outback highway.

Noosa Heads National Park (QLD)

Noosa Heads (QLD)

Population: 3,999. Founded in 1879. Traditional lands of the Gubbi Gubbi people. A suburb of the Shire of Noosa its local economy is driven by tourism based on its beautiful beach tucked between the Noosa River and Noosa National Park on the Sunshine Coast. A notable person whose mother was removed from her traditional lands here, Dr. Eve Muwewa D. Fesl OAM, CM, Ph.D., athlete, poet and Gubbi Gubbi elder, is the first Indigenous person to graduate with a Ph.D. from an Australian University(Monash). She received the Order of Australia Medal in 1988 for her work with ethnic community and maintenance of Aboriginal languages. Noosa Heads is most known for its cosmopolitan village atmosphere set within natural beauty. Must-See attraction: The wild koalas in Noosa National Park.

Driving past Pomona into Noosa Heads we get a close-up view of Mount Cooroora, an imposing monolithic 439-meter volcanic plug. Home to the world-famous King of the Mountain Festival, the rock face reminds me of El Capitan in Yosemite, not in size, but in the way the sheer cliffs dominate over us. We drive on to Noosa Heads and check into the posh Sheraton hotel. It is well situated in town between restaurants and shopping, steps away from the beach. While driving into town it is not apparent at first that this is no ordinary small village. Stepping onto the main drag it becomes clear how this cosmopolitan location attracts over one million visitors a year from all over the world. Our hike takes us along the beach and eventually into Noosa Heads National Park in search of koalas. The light is fantastic. I get some great photos of surf, surfing and sunset interspersed with far off cloud bursts over open ocean. This is surfing country with hundreds of surfers in the water outside of the flagged boundaries of Noosa beach, riding along the rocky coastline of Noosa National Park, known for its permanent rips. To top it off, it is cloudy and as dusk approaches there are still many persons out in the water during prime shark feeding time. It is surprising that there are not more shark attacks in Australia.

Surfing at dusk, Noosa Heads Beach (QLD)

I get some photos of Mount Cooroora way off in the distance along with pictures of three distinctive cloud bursts, waves and surfers crashing the park shoreline. These images will remind my senses, of the magic of this moment and place, for years to come. On our return at dusk we wander along Hastings street as shop windows light up and torches blaze in the outdoor tents of restaurants. Doing a little window shopping for things we cannot afford to buy, and checking different restaurant menus along the way, we finally settle on an Italian restaurant for the evening. It is raining and cold. Being seated comfortably in a tent on the patio, the propane heaters and torches warm up the atmosphere. Dinner is a wonderful suckling pig in honey with Gorgonzola cheese, accompanied by live Spanish acoustic guitar. We are cherishing the last days of our journey.

Monday, June 29. Rain/Overcast 16-22°C

Sleeping in, we take our time checking out as the weather has turned for the worst, and the journey ahead of us today is our shortest trip, 140 kilometers south into Brisbane through heavy traffic. Navigation into Brisbane is more problematic than we expected. We lose our satellite tracking in the tunnels and the tunnels fork more than once. Finally, after making numerous river crossings in the Brisbane delta, probably more than we need to, we locate our spacious fully equipped apartment. This will be our base for the next few days in the capital of Queensland.

City Cat Public Transit on the Brisbane River, Brisbane (QLD)

Brisbane (QLD)

Area: 15,826 km². Population: 2,274,600. Founded on May 13th, 1825 as a penal settlement. Traditional lands of the Yuggera people. Brisbane is the capital and largest urban center in Queensland, and the third largest in Australia. Brisbane has a growing economy in information technology, financial services, higher education and public-sector administration as well as petroleum refining, paper milling, metal working and tourism. It is home to contact offices for major domestic and international companies. A notable person from Brisbane is Sir Charles Kingsford Smith who in 1928 made the first trans-Pacific flight between Oakland, California and Brisbane, 11,566 kilometers in a Fokker F.VII monoplane named Southern Cross in 82 hours with three stops. Brisbane according to Lonely Planet is Australia's hippest city. Must-See attraction: Take a river tour of Brisbane on a City Cat.

View of Central Business District taken from a City Cat, Brisbane (QLD)

Changing into our warmer clothing to face wet winter weather conditions we go out for lunch and then do a big grocery shop to last us for the duration of our stay in Brisbane. Afterwards, we hike into the Central

Business District (CBD) and go to the tourist information centre to get our bearings and determine the best way to get around the city via bus and fast river catamarans. Doing some window shopping along the way we return to our apartment and retire for the evening.

Tuesday, June 30. Partly Cloudy 12-21°C

After an easy-going morning, we drive out to Lone Pine Koala Sanctuary and spend a great day with the animals of Australia. Founded in 1927, Lone Pine is the world's oldest and largest Koala sanctuary, with over 130 Koalas. Located in Fig Tree Pocket, a suburb of Brisbane, it sits on an eighteen-hectare site that houses over 95 animal species of Australia including the notorious Tasmanian devil, the elusive platypus, kangaroos, wallabies, wombats, parrots, emus and various reptiles. We get lots of pictures and opportunities to get close to the kangaroos and emus while feeding them.

There are two camps regarding zoos, aquariums and animal sanctuaries. One questions the ethics of zoos, and abhors the maintenance, handling and feeding of animals from the wild in captivity. The other supports putting the public in touch with animals, to educate, and assist humans in appreciating the wonder of the other species we share the planet with. After travelling the length and breadth of Australia for two months and being in a great variety of natural settings, we know how rare it is to see most of these animals at all, let alone up close. Most persons these days view nature and wildlife from in front of a screen. Perhaps, humans need being in a great variety of natural settings, we know how rare it is to see most of these animals at all, let alone up close. Most persons these days view nature and wildlife from in front of a screen. Perhaps, humans need more live interactions, rather than fewer, if we humans are ever going to learn to fully respect the lives of the other species on the planet. Leaving Lone Pine there is an important sign at the exit that reads, "The earth is not only for humans". We couldn't agree more.

Family photo, Fig Tree Pocket, QLD | Lone Pine Koala Sanctuary

Wednesday, July 1 (Canada Day) (Territory Day). Sunny 11-21°C

I set out early in the morning, as I am attending the Population Geographies Conference at the University of Queensland. The easiest and most scenic route is via the City Cat. High powered catamarans run up and down the Brisbane River between the University of Queensland,

St. Lucia, through city centre to north shore Hamilton. On route, I meet statisticians and planners from Melbourne, Victoria. After introductions, we discuss topics such as the nonsensical Canadian voluntary short-form census (viewed by statisticians and researchers as a collection of meaningless demographic data), the practicality of Melbourne hook turns, and the development of a high cost desalination plant in Melbourne. The river trip goes by quickly and before we know it, we arrive at the large and scenic campus of the University of Queensland, St. Lucia. My new acquaintances are helpful in making the search for the location of the conference much easier than it might have been, had I been alone.

Good data is the foundation for good decision making, and what becomes clear to me after listening to the opening plenary and sessions on population and aging, is that obtaining good data and making good decisions is challenging. Despite the massive amount of data generated by POS systems and social networking, little of it is being used to assess migration and demographic changes. Although conflict and opportunities for education and employment are listed as key drivers for global migration, surprisingly little mention is given to climate change. This is questioned by a professor from the University of the South Pacific during the opening plenary question period, who clearly sees climate change as an underlying driver.

Population and the Environment sessions review research and development on Terra Populus, a tool providing high quality spatio-temporal data describing people and their environment; and a host of topics reviewing international migration induced by environmental degradation. In the afternoon, I enjoy a warm and sunny ride back on the Cat to CBD. I am left with lots to think about regarding our ever-growing population, the demands it is putting on our environment, and how we are losing our ability to maintain our communities in many areas of the world. It is forcing mass exodus of 55 million persons of concern (refugees, asylum seekers and internally displaced persons) in 2014, (115) a trend that is doubling every five years. It is staggering to know that more than twice the population of Australia is homeless. Unlivable ecosystems with diminishing resources contribute to increasing conflict, instability and inevitable flight in countries with weak economic and political structures just as forewarned in 2010, by the executive summary of the U.S. Navy Climate Change Roadmap. (116) Human behaviour on the planet must change dramatically before we will see an improvement in these statistics.

Getting back to the apartment, I pack up the didge, wrapping it with some clothing for additional protection, and begin making some preparations for our return to Canada. Tyler and Susan return from their day trip that included a tour of the Brisbane river and shopping for a DVD set of Danger 5, an Australian television series, Tyler has been hoping to purchase while here in Australia. Susan prepares a delicious gnocchi dinner and we settle in for the evening, watching TV. One show, Bogan Hunters catches our attention providing us with a brief glimpse of the Bogan subculture of Australia. It is in your face, ignoring most conventions of civil behaviour and respects few boundaries, if any. Tyler is laughing, not taking it seriously while his parents are gobsmacked. What can I say? It is not everyone's cup of tea.

Thursday, July 2. Sunny 8-20°C

Cleaning up the apartment and packing for our return home, we give our cooler and tyre inflation kits to a family staying in our hotel and leave Brisbane at 10 am heading 392 kilometers south along the M1 to Coffs Harbour. The highway in spots, is wide and divided, and in other places, narrow and bumpy two-lane highway. We are now travelling through diverse coastal landscape varying between pasture lands, vineyards, cane fields and berry orchards.

Coffs Harbour (NSW)

Population: 45,580. Founded in the 1870s. Traditional lands of the Gumbainggir. Once based mainly on bananas, the local economy now relies on blueberries, fishing and tourism. A notable person from Coffs Harbour is Deborah Knight, journalist and news presenter on Weekend Today and Nine News. Coffs Harbour is most known for its Must-See attraction: The World's Largest Banana.

Arriving in Coffs Harbour at 3pm, we check into our hotel use the afternoon to take care of some things. We vacuum and wash considerable dirt and grime from the car, mail postcards, pick up the next morning's breakfast, and fuel up. Tomorrow is our big push into Sydney. It will take us roughly 7 to 8 hours of driving on crowded highways. We dine at the resort tonight to avoid any unnecessary driving.

Friday, July 3. Sunny 8-17°C

We are up at six in the morning and on the road by 7:30 am for a 550-kilometer drive south along the Pacific Highway to Mascot, home of Sydney's Kingsford Smith International Airport. Initially the trip is along winding two-lane highway as many sections of the highway are being improved and under construction. The highway eventually widens out to four and then six lanes with the speed limit increasing to 110 kilometers per hour making for safer and faster travel.

Arriving in Mascot after our long journey, we check into our hotel and unload most of the contents of the car including all our baggage. It is our last stop before flying home. We use the balance of the day to orient ourselves for activities tomorrow, that include a journey to the Blue Mountains and the return of our trusty vehicle. Being travel weary, all of us would jump at the chance to fall asleep and wake up in our own beds at home. There are still some great things to see and a few miles to put on yet.

The Three Sisters, Blue Mountains (NSW)

Saturday, July 4. (US Independence Day) Sunny 7-14°C

This morning we drive out to the Blue Mountains to view the Three Sisters. The drive in heavy traffic winds its way into the Blue Mountains along a modern highway. It is a beautiful day with clear skies. The view point for the Three Sisters provides a spectacular panoramic view of the Blue Mountains and the valley below. The wind is blowing hard and it is chilly, even for us Canadians, although we do not have the benefit of the winter clothing that most of the visitors are wearing.

After taking in the scenery we decide to warm up and visit the Waradah Aboriginal Centre. The Centre has a Gallery with art and artefacts, as well as a great live performance with music, dance and a narrated description of their cultural significance that is informative and fun. The centre has great exposure to visitors from around the world, as their location is so close to the Three Sisters. It is a fantastic opportunity for those travelers that will not get into the Outback to engage, if just momentarily, with Indigenous people and learn something about their culture. The experience reaffirms much of what we learned while on our journey and is very worthwhile. Thank you!

Waradah Aboriginal Centre, Katoomba (NSW)

Proceeding to Scenic World, the timing of our visit on a weekend is far from perfect. After snaking through Disneyesque lineups for a few cliff-side rides, as scenic as these are, most of the afternoon evaporates. We drive back to Mascot, top up the car with petrol and return our vehicle with 35,380 kilometers on the odometer. We have completed our journey of 17,780 kilometers after 61 days on the road in Australia. The car returns attendant is not certain what to make of our vehicle return. This is not the typical weekend or weekly rental return. She goes out to the lot to view the vehicle, to make sure that it is still intact and undamaged before we leave. We take a cab back to the hotel, happy and relaxed passengers. It has been an epic journey. We are tired and travel weary and have booked our morning pick up from the hotel. We pack up our things, have dinner at the hotel and go to bed early, ready for our flight home in the morning.

Sunday, July 5. Sunny 7-15°C

All of us are up at six in the morning to catch our flight that departs at 10:20 am. Hurry up and wait. There is already a long lineup at the tax office in the airport for those that want to recover their Goods and Services Tax paid on items. Frankly, I had every intention of getting tax refunded for some of our purchases. It does not look as if the wait will be worth it, so I don't. We are determined to make this flight home and check in early. The airline staff are helpful in arranging safe passage for the didge. It travels home, checked in as a stroller. Our flight is delayed till 11 am, so we eat breakfast before going through security. The airport is busy with Qantas international and domestic flights. Security drags out as it usually does. The security bag screener is quite humorous, unlike most screeners, asking travellers to remove laptops, wombats, goannas and liquids from their carry-on luggage for inspection. Our flight home will be approximately fourteen hours (1.5 hours shorter than our flight to Sydney). Although we are travelling east and would normally lose the better part of a day flying from Vancouver to Toronto, we will arrive in Vancouver at 8am on the same day, three hours earlier than our departure from Sydney. As promised, we gain back the day we lost when coming to Australia. Only in Oz.

The direct flight from Australia although long, is relatively comfortable in the Boeing 777. Watching a lot of movies on the way, before we know it our plane lands in Vancouver. We are grateful that we did not route our flight through Bali, as flights to and from Bali are on hold now, because of atmospheric ash from a Volcano in Japan. Clearing customs is a breeze and then we catch a taxi home. Coincidentally the cab driver has a daughter studying medicine in Townsville. Small world. We get into a long discussion regarding cost of living differences between Australia and Vancouver. Arriving home to high heat, heavy smoke from forest fires and drought conditions for the last two months, it seems that we are getting an Outback welcome home. We air out the house, and turn on the water main, before retiring to the comfort of our beds for four hours to try to beat our jet lag. We are spent, feeling and looking the same as exhausted balloons. Sinking into our beds and succumbing to sleep we relish in the great reward experienced by most travellers after a long journey. We are Home Sweet Home!

Retrospect

It has been two years now since our epic journey. This story would have been difficult to write had I not decided to start a simple journal and take over 6,000 pictures and video clips along the way. I have already discussed the motivation behind the story and I must say that it has been a pleasure writing it. I truly have lived every moment of the trip again and have learned much more about the amazing continent we call Australia. I look back at both my professional and personal objectives prior to the trip, that began with the line "see, listen and learn" and I must say that I have accomplished that, and much more. Many of my family, friends and colleagues asked if I was writing a book about Sustainability. I answered in all honesty, "No, it is going to be a Travelogue." It was the initial inspiration, and I truly hope that it is the result. If it offers readers a little more than that, it was intended to, and I hope you gained as much insight about Australia and its place in our world, as I did.

To those adventurers with the desire to undertake such a journey, but lack the means, I offer these thoughts. We made a considerable financial commitment to this journey and could have easily renovated our kitchen instead. For those with less means, I suggest the following. Australia has a fine hostel system and Greyhound operates through most of Australia other than Western Australia, although Greyhound can get you to Broome from Darwin. There are other options such as purchasing a used vehicle, and we met travellers along the way who used other modes of transportation including motorcycle, bicycle and even travelled on foot (bring lots of water). There is a Coles, Woolies or both in nearly every town, and usually there is enough bush tucker along the way. We met young people from other countries including Canada who were travelling and working along the way. Australia is a land of opportunity. It is a vast and diverse country with lots to see and great opportunities for adventure. The more time you have for it, the better.

Regrets

To Tasmania. Originally, we planned on visiting your state as part of our route. Many will say, "Well you really haven't seen all of Oz till you've been to Taz". True. Given the time of year and the challenge ahead of us in the given time, our decision was to miss you. For that we are the worse off and regret it.

We also missed going to the Bungle-Bungles, the Reversing Falls, Uluru, The Margaret River, Broken Hills, Kalgoorlie, Shark Bay, Murujuga, Kakadu, Cooktown, Dave's and Andy's and countless other places of interest in Australia. We regret not chatting with every Australian along the way, as we missed many a good yarn. There are many excellent reasons for us to return to Australia, if you will have us.

I have been diligent in determining the correct spelling of Indigenous languages and family groups. I have been faithful in depicting events during our journey as accurately as possible and have investigated many tales that led us down various rabbit holes. I regret any errors.

I have taken liberties with generalizations especially about nationalities in the story. These are my captured sentiments in the moment of a journal. I realize that all humans are different and that I should not be stereotyping. Easily removed especially after much thought during editing, I have chosen to leave them in being true to my story. I regret if you feel offended. Please forgive me if you are.

Acknowledgements

"We value virtue but do not discuss it. The honest bookkeeper, the faithful wife, the earnest scholar, get little of our attention compared to the embezzler, the tramp, the cheat."

John Steinbeck

To the Indigenous peoples of Australia. When and where we did encounter you, we were smoked in or welcomed by you to your land and you generously shared some of your stories with us. Learning from you, something about your cultures and struggles, we returned to Canada with another gift from you, a new perspective and respect for our own First Nations peoples. We thank you!

To all the people of Australia. Thank you for allowing us to visit. You are blessed. You live in a beautiful land filled with beautiful plants and creatures and a bounty of mineral wealth that may be scooped up in your bare hands. Your culture is ancient, rich and fraught with struggle. You are a great nation, one you may genuinely be proud of, when you reflect and acknowledge your complete history, and embrace your Indigenous peoples with the respect they deserve. You are a nation of treasures.

To my weary travelling companions who went along for the ride, even though you really didn't know what you were getting yourselves into. To my partner Susan; Thank you for your trust, support, and your love. To my son Tyler; Thank you for your patience with your parents and your contributions to the book. You are the writer and artist I will never be.

To my late parents Rottraut and Ivo Knoll. Immigrants to Canada who succeeded in providing better lives for their children and promoted a love for reading and discovery. Most of the daily tasks that went into raising us, as the many gifts of love that completed our lives were underappreciated. I remember you with love.

I also acknowledge the following family and friends for reviewing the manuscript, and for sharing their impressions and suggestions: Karin Jordan, Darrin Noble, Tyler Knoll. Thank You.

Trip Trivia

Oceans and Seas encountered during road trip:

South Pacific Ocean, Tasman Sea, Southern Ocean, Great Australian Bight, Indian Ocean, Timor Sea, Coral Sea

Our Favorite Place names:

Cooloongup, Bumberry(Bunbury), Jingalup, Kalgoorlie, Mundaberra, Nar Nar Goon, Paramatta, Toowoomba, Warrnambool, Koolyanobbing, Wooloomoloo, Humpty Doo

Our Favourite Australian words and expressions:

Barbie: BBQ; Bonzer: a good thing; Mate: a buddy or friend; Ta: Thank you;

Woolies: Woolworths Ltd., Australia's largest retail chain; Dunny: Toilet; Blokes: Guys

G'day, How you goin? How goin? Goin? Greetings; Sticky beak: busy body; Footy: football;

Ripper: awesome

Favourite scenery during road trip:

Chris: 12 Apostles, Port Campbell National Park (VIC)

Susan: The white sands of Lucky Beach, Cape Le Grande National Park (WA)

Tyler: The Rainforest, Daintree National Park (QLD)

Favourite activities during road trip:

Chris: Australian Rules Football, Subiaco Stadium, Perth (WA)

 Susan: Sunset Fish & Chips cruise off Cullen Beach, Darwin (NT)

Tyler: Camel Riding, Broome (NT)

Favourite music albums listened to during road trip:

Tyler: To Pimp a Butterfly by Kendrick Lamar, AM by Arctic Monkeys, Liquid Swords by GZA

Chris: Ultimate Creedence by Creedence Clearwater Revival, Channel Orange by Frank Ocean, Torches by Foster the People

Susan: 21 by Adele, Love in the Future by John Legend, Sogno by Andrea Bocelli

Audiobooks listened to during trip:

Three Hundred Aesop's Fables as translated from Greek by George Fyler Townsend, The Adventures of Sherlock Holmes by Sir Arthur Conan Doyle, Call of the Wild by Jack London, The Hand of Fu Man Chu by Sax Rohmer, The Adventures of Tom Sawyer and Adventures of Huckleberry Finn by Mark Twain, Frenzied Fiction by Stephen Leacock.

Books read during road trip:

Chris: The Rough Guide to Australia by Rough Guides, Aboriginal Stories of Australia by A. W. Reed, Aboriginal Legends – Animal Tales by A. W. Reed, The Last of the Nomads by W. J. Peasley, Didgeridoo- A Complete Guide to This Ancient Instrument by John Bowden, The Australian Aboriginal Didgeridoo: A Comprehensive Introduction.

Tyler: Dispatches by Michael Herr, Inherent Vice by Thomas Pynchon, Fear and Loathing in Las Vegas by Hunter S. Thompson, Hells Angels by Hunter S. Thompson, American Desperado by John Roberts & Evan Wright, Kingdom of Fear by Hunter S. Thompson.

Favourite meals during road trip:

Chris: Eye steak and local prawns – home cooked by Susan, Port Douglas (QLD)

Tyler: Thai rice and prawns cooked in pineapple, George's Thai on the marina, MacKay (QLD)

Susan: Rack of Lamb, Cooper's Ale House, Wallaroo (SA)

Unanimous: Favorite Desert – Baklava, Land of Pharaoh's, Broome (WA)

References

1. **Hema Maps Pty Ltd.** *Australia Touring Atlas, Ninth Edition.* Eight Mile Plains, Australia : Hema Maps Pty Ltd., 2011.

2. **The Encyclopedia of Earth.** Southern Hemisphere. *The Encyclopedia of Earth.* [Online] 8 27, 2012. http://www.eoearth.org/view/article/156180/.

3. **Australian Government.** 1:20M Australia General Reference, Map Edition 2. *Australian Government, Geoscience Australia.* [Online] 2007. http://www.ga.gov.au/metadata-gateway/metadata/record/gcat_65187.

4. —. About Australia. *Department of Foreign Affairs and Trade, Australian Government.* [Online] 2016. http://dfat.gov.au/about-australia/Pages/about-australia.aspx.

5. —. About Australia Indigenous Australia. *Australian Government, Department of Foreign Affairs and Trade.* [Online] 2016. http://dfat.gov.au/about-australia/land-its-people/Pages/indigenous-australia.aspx.

6. **Behrendt, Prof. Larissa.** *Indigenous Australia for Dummies.* Milton : Wiley Publishing Australia Pty Ltd., 2012.

7. **Rough Guides.** *The Rough Guide to Australia 11th edition.* s.l. : Rough Guides, Random House , 2014.

8. **New South Wales Government .** History and Geography. *New South Wales Government .* [Online] 2016. https://www.nsw.gov.au/about-nsw/history-geography.

9. **Transport Canada.** Disinsection On Board Aircraft (Advisory Circular No. LTA-002). *Transport Canada, Government of Canada.* [Online] 03 17, 2009. http://www.tc.gc.ca/media/documents/ca-opssvs/lta-002.pdf.

10. **Australian Dictionary of Biography.** Goossens, Sir Eugene Aynsley (1893-1962). *Australian Dictionary of Biography.* [Online] 1996. http://adb.anu.edu.au/biography/goossens-sir-eugene-aynsley-10329.

11. **Australian Government.** Sydney Opera House. *About Australia, Australian Stories.* [Online] 6 24, 2013. http://www.australia.gov.au/about-australia/australian-story/sydney-opera-house.

12. **Bondi Beach.** The History of Bondi Beach. *Bondi Beach.* [Online] 2016. http://bondibeach.com/history-of-bondi-beach.

13. **Australian Government.** Canberra - Australia's Capital City. *About Australia - Australian Story.* [Online] 1 7, 2016. http://www.australia.gov.au/about-australia/australian-story/canberra-australias-capital-city.

14. **Reconciliation Australia.** Five Fast Facts - The Aboriginal Tent Embassy. *Reconciliation Australia.* [Online] 2016. https://www.reconciliation.org.au/wp-content/uploads/2013/12/Five-Fast-Facts-Tent-embassy.pdf.

15. **Australian War Memorial .** Australian military history overview. *Australian War Memorial .* [Online] 2016. https://www.awm.gov.au/atwar/.

16. **Australian Government.** ANZAC Day. *Australian Government, About Australia, Australian Story.* [Online] 6 9, 2015. http://www.australia.gov.au/about-australia/australian-story/anzac-day.

17. **National Gallery of Australia.** The Aboriginal Memorial. *National Gallery of Australia.* [Online] 2016. http://www.nga.gov.au/AboriginalMemorial/home.cfm.

18. **Australian Government.** Introduction to Climate Culture. *Indigenous weather Knowledge, Bureau of Meterology, Australian Government.* [Online] 2014. http://www.bom.gov.au/iwk/climate_culture/.

19. —. The Dreaming, About Australia, Australian Stories. *Australian Government.* [Online] 3 31, 2015. http://www.australia.gov.au/about-australia/australian-story/dreaming.

20. —. Australian indigenous cultural heritage. *Australian Government.* [Online] 3 31, 2015. http://www.australia.gov.au/about-australia/australian-story/austn-indigenous-cultural-heritage.

21. —. About Australia, Australian Story, Reconciliation. *Australian Government.* [Online] 5 4, 2015. http://www.australia.gov.au/about-australia/australian-story/reconciliation.

22. **Bryson, B.** *In a Sunburned Country.* Toronto, Canada : Doubleday, 2001.

23. **Victoria State Government Australia.** Facts About Victoria. *Victoria State Government Australia.* [Online] 12 16, 2015. http://www.liveinvictoria.vic.gov.au/living-in-victoria/about-victoria/facts-about-victoria#.VyqFB4-cH4g.

24. **EPA Victoria Government.** Greenhouse Gas Emissions Reporting and Pilot Data - All facility sheet. *EPA Victoria Government.* [Online] 2005. http://www.epa.vic.gov.au/our-work/programs/past-programs/~/media/Files/greenhouse/greenhouse_pilot/docs/facility_sheet_pdf.pdf.

25. **World Nuclear Association.** Australia's Electricity. *World Nuclear Association.* [Online] 11 2015. http://www.world-nuclear.org/information-library/country-profiles/countries-a-f/appendices/australia-s-electricity.aspx.

26. **Australian Energy Market Commission.** Final Report 2014 Residential Electricity Price Trends. *Australian Energy Market Commission.* [Online] 12 5, 2014. http://www.aemc.gov.au/getattachment/ae5d0665-7300-4a0d-b3b2-bd42d82cf737/2014-Residential-Electricity-Price-Trends-report.aspx.

27. **Origin Energy.** Energy in Australia. *Origin Energy.* [Online] 1 22, 2015. https://www.originenergy.com.au/blog/about-energy/energy-in-australia.html.

28. **Flannery, T., Hueston G., and Stock, A.** Lagging Behind: Australia and the Global Response to Climate Change. *Climate Council of Australia.* [Online] 2014. http://www.climatecouncil.org.au/uploads/211ea746451b3038edfb70b49 aee9b6f.pdf.

29. **CBC News Politics.** Tony Abbott, Stephen Harper take hard line against carbon tax. *CBC News Politics.* [Online] 6 9, 2014. http://www.cbc.ca/news/politics/tony-abbott-stephen-harper-take-hard-line-against-carbon-tax-1.2669287.

30. **Australian Government.** Climate change risks to coastal buildings and infrastructure - A supplement to the first pass national assessment . *Department of Climate Change and Energy Efficiency, Department of the Environment ,Australian Government .* [Online] 2011. http://www.environment.gov.au/climate-change/adaptation/publications/climate-change-risks-coastal-buildings.

31. —. Climate change risks to Australia's coasts: a first pass national assessment. *Department of Climate Change, Department of the Environment.* [Online] 2009. http://www.environment.gov.au/climate-change/adaptation/publications/climate-change-risks-australias-coasts.

32. —. Ned Kelly. *About Australia, Australian Stories.* [Online] 03 26, 2016. http://www.australia.gov.au/about-australia/australian-story/ned-kelly.

33. **State Library Victoria.** Jerilderie Letter Ned Kelly. *State Library Victoria.* [Online] 2016. http://digital.slv.vic.gov.au/view/action/nmets.do?DOCCHOICE=282509 6.xml&dvs=1462836519894~255&locale=en_CA&search_terms=&adja cency=&VIEWER_URL=/view/action/nmets.do?&DELIVERY_RULE_ ID=4&divType=&usePid1=true&usePid2=true.

34. **Australian Government.** The Holden car in Australia. *About Australia, Australian Stories.* [Online] 12 6, 2007. http://www.australia.gov.au/about-australia/australian-story/holden-car.

35. **Holden.** Holden's Future. *Holden.* [Online] 2016. http://www.holden.com.au/about/our-company/holdens-future.

36. **Government of South Australia.** About South Australia History. *Government of South Australia.* [Online] 12 13, 2013. http://www.sa.gov.au/about-sa/history.

37. **Australian Government.** Australia's Wine Industry, Australian Story. *Australian Government.* [Online] 12 14, 2007. http://www.australia.gov.au/about-australia/australian-story/australias-wine-industry.

38. **Sydney Morning Herald.** Wallaroo. *Sydney Morning Herald.* [Online] 2 8, 2004. http://www.smh.com.au/news/south-australia/wallaroo/2005/02/17/1108500204737.html.

39. **Arrium Mining.** Arrium Mining. *Arrium Mining and Minerals.* [Online] 2015. http://www.arrium.com/our-businesses/arrium-mining.

40. **BHP Billiton.** About Us Our History. *BHP Billiton.* [Online] 2016. http://www.bhpbilliton.com/aboutus/ourcompany/ourhistory.

41. **Rio Tinto.** About Us History. *Rio Tinto.* [Online] 2016. http://www.riotinto.com/aboutus/history-4705.aspx.

42. **Government of South Australia Department of State Development.** Nephrite Jade. *Government of South Australia Department of State Development.* [Online] 2014. http://minerals.statedevelopment.sa.gov.au/geoscience/mineral_commodities/nephrite_jade.

43. **Buettener, Mason.** Stone of Heaven. *Canadian Mining and Energy.* Summer 2016.

44. **Australian Geographic.** Australia's most dangerous predators. *Australian Geographic.* [Online] 5 14, 2012. http://www.australiangeographic.com.au/outdoor/adventure/2012/05/australias-most-dangerous-predators/.

45. **Australian Bureau of Statistics.** 1301.0- Year Book of Australia, 2012 Mortality, Life Expectancy and Causes of Death . *Australian*

Bureau of Statistics. [Online] 5 24, 2012.
http://www.abs.gov.au/ausstats/abs@.nsf/Lookup/by%20Subject/1301.0
~2012~Main%20Features~Mortality,%20life%20expectancy%20and%2
0causes%20of%20death~231.

46. **Florida Museum of Natural History.** Species Implicated in Attacks,
International Shark Attack File. *Florida Museum of Natural History.*
[Online] 2016. http://www.flmnh.ufl.edu/fish/isaf/contributing-
factors/species-implicated-attacks.

47. **Australian Museum.** White Shark, Carcharodon carcharius.
Australian Museum. [Online] 2 7, 2014.
http://australianmuseum.net.au/white-shark-carcharodon-carcharias-
linnaeus-1758.

48. **Government of South Australia, Primary Industries and Regions.**
Fishing Restrictions for Sharks. *Government of South Australia, Primary
Industries and Regions.* [Online] 2016.
http://pir.sa.gov.au/fishing/fishwatch/sharks/fishing_restrictions_for_shar
ks.

49. **Fisheries Research and Development Corporation.** Status of Key
Australian Fish Stocks 2014, Reports, Sharks . *Fisheries Research and
Development Corporation.* [Online] 2014.
http://www.fish.gov.au/reports/sharks/Pages/default.aspx.

50. **Taronga Conservation Society Australia.** Australian Shark attack
File Latest Figures. *Taronga Conservation Society Australia.* [Online] 4
27, 2016. http://taronga.org.au/animals-conservation/conservation-
science/australian-shark-attack-file/latest-figures.

51. **West, John G.** Changing patterns of shark attacks in Australian
waters, Marine and Freshwater Research 62. *tarongo.org.au.* [Online]
2011.
http://taronga.org.au/sites/tarongazoo/files/downloads/changing_patterns
_of_shark_attacks_in_australian_waters.pdf.

52. **Reed, A.W.** *Aboriginal Stories of Australia.* Sydney : Reed New
Holland, 1965.

53. **Royal Flying Doctor Service.** About the RFDS. *Royal Flying Doctor Service.* [Online] 2015. https://www.flyingdoctor.org.au/about-the-rfds/.

54. **Eastern Goldfields Historical Society Inc.** Coolgardie. *Eastern Goldfields Historical Society Inc.* [Online] 2016. http://www.kalgoorliehistory.org.au/coolgardie.html.

55. **Ninti One.** Australian Feral Camel Management Project. *Ninti One, Innovation for Remote Australia.* [Online] 2015. http://nintione.com.au/our-work/natural-resource-management/australian-feral-camel-management-project.

56. **Australian Government.** Feral Animals in Australia. *Department of Environment, Australian Government.* [Online] 2015. http://www.environment.gov.au/biodiversity/invasive-species/feral-animals-australia.

57. **Surfing Atlas.** Cyclops. *Surfing Atlas.* [Online] 2008. http://www.surfingatlas.com/video/spot/3831/watch/fGPmOqQgjiI.

58. **Australian Government.** Australia's Biodiversity Conservation Strategy 2010 - 2030. *Department of the Environment, Australian Government.* [Online] 2010. http://www.environment.gov.au/system/files/resources/58321950-f8b6-4ef3-bb68-6f892420d601/files/biodiversity-strategy-2010.pdf.

59. **Western Australia Department of Environment and Conservation .** Fitzgerald Biosphere Recovery Plan. *Western Australia Department of Environment and Conservation, South Coast Region.* [Online] 2012. http://www.southcoastnrm.com.au/images/user-images/documents/completed-reports/Fitzgerald%20Biosphere%20Recovery%20Plan%202012.pdf.

60. **Parks and Wildlife Service Tasmania.** Geoheritage Continental Drift and Gondwana. *Parks and Wildlife Service Tasmania.* [Online] 7 22, 2008. http://www.parks.tas.gov.au/index.aspx?base=2889.

61. —. Geodiversity Gondwana The great supercontinent. *Parks and Wildlife Service Tasmania.* [Online] 2006. http://dpipwe.tas.gov.au/Documents/Gondwana.pdf.

62. **UNESCO.** World Heritage List Gondwana Rainforests of Australia. *UNESCO.* [Online] 2016. http://whc.unesco.org/en/list/368/.

63. **Nyoongar Tent Embassy.** Matagarup Heritage. *Nyoongar Tent Embassy.* [Online] 2015. http://www.nyoongartentembassy.com/matagarup-heritage.html.

64. **Monument Australia.org.** Catalpa Wild Geese Memorial. *Monument Australia.org.* [Online] 2016. http://monumentaustralia.org.au/themes/government/dissent/display/611 05-catalpa-wild-geese-memorial.

65. **National Museum of Australia.** 'A noble whale ship and commander' - The Catalpa rescue, april 1876. *National Museum of Australia.* [Online] 2011.

66. **Hancock Prospecting Pty Ltd.** Hancock Prospecting Pty Ltd. Home Page. *Hancock Prospecting Pty Ltd.* [Online] 2015. http://www.hancockprospecting.com.au/.

67. **Annalakshmi.** Why Annalakshmi. *Annalakshmi.* [Online] 2013. http://www.annalakshmi.com.au/mission/.

68. **Freemantle Prison.** Welcome to Freemantle Prison History. *Freemantle Prison.* [Online] 2016. http://www.fremantleprison.com/History/theconvictera/Pages/default.aspx.

69. **Ancestry.com.** Press Releases Ancestry.com Launches Largest Online Collection of Records Documenting Australia's Convicted "Founding Fathers". *Ancestry.com.* [Online] 2007. http://corporate.ancestry.com/press/press-releases/2007/07/ancestry.com-launches-largest-online-collection-of-records-documenting-australias-convicted-founding-fathers/.

70. **Australian Government.** About Australia Australian Stories Convicts and the British Colonies in Australia. *Australian Government.* [Online] 1 20, 2016. http://www.australia.gov.au/about-australia/australian-story/convicts-and-the-british-colonies.

71. —. HMAS Sydney II Commission of Inquiry Summary. *Australian Government Department of Defence.* [Online] 7 2009. http://www.defence.gov.au/sydneyii/finalreport/.

72. **Australian Museum.** Estuarine crocodile, Crocodylus porosus. *Australian Museum.* [Online] 2016. http://australianmuseum.net.au/estuarine-crocodile.

73. **Northern Territory Tourism Central.** Saltwater Crocodile. *Northern Territory Tourism Central.* [Online] 2012. http://www.nttc.com.au/saltwater-crocodile.

74. **Australian Government.** Australia's Pearling Industry. *Australian Government About Australia Australian Story* . [Online] 12 11, 2007. http://www.australia.gov.au/about-australia/australian-story/australias-pearling-industry.

75. **Department of Fisheries Western Australia.** Pearling. *Department of Fisheries Western Australia.* [Online] 2 18, 2016. http://www.fish.wa.gov.au/fishing-and-aquaculture/pearling/Pages/default.aspx.

76. **Cygnet Bay Pearls .** Home of the World's Largest Pearl. *Cygnet Bay Pearls.* [Online] 2011. http://cygnetbaypearls.com.au/pearl-farm/the-worlds-biggest-pearl/.

77. **Lake Argyle, Jewel of the Kimberly.** Ecosystem. *Lake Argyle, Jewel of the Kimberly.* [Online] 2016. http://www.lakeargyle.com/explore-and-learn/ecosystem/.

78. **Rio Tinto.** Argyle. *Rio Tinto.* [Online] 2016. http://www.riotinto.com/diamondsandminerals/argyle-4640.aspx.

79. **Northern Territory Tourism Central.** Northern Territory. *Northern Territory Tourism Central.* [Online] 2012. http://www.nttc.com.au/northern-territory.

80. **Australian Museum.** Charles Darwin on Aboriginal Australians. *Australian Museum.* [Online] 6 14, 2011. http://australianmuseum.net.au/charles-darwin-on-aboriginal-australians.

81. **Darwin, Charles.** *On the Origin of Species by Means of Natural Selection or Preservation of Favoured Races in the Struggle for Life.* London : John Murray (The Project Gutenberg Ebook#22764 Sept 25, 2007), 1860.

82. **Australian Government.** The Japanese bombing of Darwin, Broome and northern Australia. *About Australia, Australian Government.* [Online] 6 9, 2015. http://www.australia.gov.au/about-australia/australian-story/japanese-bombing-of-darwin.

83. **Battle For Australia Association.** Battle For Australia Association, The Bombing of Darwin . *Battle for Australia Association.* [Online] 2016. http://www.battleforaustralia.org.au/BABombDarwin.php.

84. **ConocoPhillips Australia.** Darwin LNG. *ConocoPhillips Australia.* [Online] 2016. http://www.conocophillips.com.au/our-business-activities/our-projects/Pages/darwin-lng.aspx.

85. **Inpex.** Ichthys in detail. *Ichthys LNG Project.* [Online] 2016. http://www.inpex.com.au/our-projects/ichthys-lng-project/ichthys-in-detail/project-overview/.

86. **Oceana.** Stolen Seafood, The Impact of Pirate Fishing on our Oceans. *Oceana.* [Online] 2013. http://oceana.org/sites/default/files/reports/Oceana_StolenSeafood.pdf.

87. **Australian Government.** Combating illegal fishing. *Australian Fisheries Management Authority, Australian Government.* [Online] 2016. http://www.afma.gov.au/monitoring-enforcement/combating-illegal-fishing-2/.

88. **Jackson, Phillip.** *The Australian Aboriginal Didgeridoo : A Comprehensive Introduction.* Australia : Phillip Jackson, 1998.

89. **Bowden, John.** *Didgeridoo, A Complete Guide to This Ancient Aboriginal Instrument, 2nd Edition.* Albany Creek, Australia : John P. Bowden, 2008.

90. **EnviroNorth.** Termites. *EnviroNorth.* [Online] 2016. http://www.environorth.org.au/windows/all/all_termites.html.

91. **Jawoyn Association Cultural Corporation.** Dreaming. *Jawoyn Association Cultural Corporation.* [Online] 2016. http://www.jawoyn.org/jawoyn-people/dreaming.

92. **The Daly Waters Pub.** History Our Story. *The Daly Waters Pub.* [Online] 2016. http://www.dalywaterspub.com/our-story.

93. **Queensland Government.** Interesting Facts About Queensland. *Queensland Government.* [Online] 1 30, 2014. https://www.qld.gov.au/about/about-queensland/statistics-facts/facts/.

94. **The Economist.** Marc Rich, King of commodities, died on June 26th, aged 78 . *The Economist.* [Online] 7 9, 2013. http://www.economist.com/news/obituary/21580438-marc-rich-king-commodities-died-june-26th-aged-78-marc-rich.

95. **Glencore.** Glencore. *Business at a Glance.* [Online] 2016. http://www.glencore.com/who-we-are/our-business-at-a-glance/.

96. **Chern'ee Sutton Contemporary Indigenous artist.** Kalkadoon History and Culture. *Chern'ee Sutton Contemporary Indigenous artist.* [Online] 2016. http://www.cherneesutton.com.au/index.php?_a=document&doc_id=8.

97. **Queensland Government.** Mount Isa. *Queensland Government.* [Online] 2016. https://www.qld.gov.au/atsi/cultural-awareness-heritage-arts/community-histories-mount-isa/index.html.

98. **Monument Australia.** Kalkadoon/Kalkatunga Memorial. *Monument Australia.* [Online] 2010.

http://monumentaustralia.org.au/themes/conflict/indigenous/display/9174
2-kalkadoon-kalkatunga-memorial.

99. **Federal Court of Australia.** Doyle on behalf of the Kalkadoon
People#4 vs Queensland (No3) 2011FCA 1466. *Federal Court of
Australia.* [Online] 1 4, 2012.
http://www.judgments.fedcourt.gov.au/judgments/Judgments/fca/single/2
011/2011fca1466.

100. —. Part 5: National Native Tribunal Report . *Federal Court of
Australia Annual Report 2013-2014.* [Online] 2015.
http://www.fedcourt.gov.au/publications/annual-reports/2013-14/part-5.

101. **State Library of Victoria.** Burke and Wills Terra Incognita. *State
Library of Victoria.* [Online] 9 10, 2004.
http://victoria.slv.vic.gov.au/burkeandwills/expedition/index.html.

102. **State Library New South Wales.** Burke and Wills. *State Library
New South Wales.* [Online] 4 5, 2011.
http://www2.sl.nsw.gov.au/archive/discover_collections/history_nation/e
xploration/burke/burke.html.

103. **Walker, Frederick.** *Journal of Expedition in Search of Burke and
Wills, The Journal of the Royal Geographical Society. Volume The Thirty
Third.* London : John Murray, (A Project Gutenberg of Australia eBook
#0600191.txt, March 2006) , 1863.

104. **Australian Government.** Great Artesian Basin Water Resource
Assessment. *Australian Government, Geoscience Australia.* [Online]
2016. http://www.ga.gov.au/scientific-topics/water/groundwater/gabwra.

105. **Great Artesian Basin Coordinating Committee.** Groundwater
Dependant Ecosystems in the Great Artesian Basin. *Great Artesian Basin
Coordinating Committee.* [Online] 2 2014.
http://www.gabcc.gov.au/system/files/resources/48e8612d-cf2b-4f9d-
b3b2-4326e58ddb26/files/groundwater-dependent-ecosystems-gab-
factsheet.pdf.

106. **Australian Government.** 4610.0 Water Account, Austalia 2013-2014. *Australian Bureau of Statisitics.* [Online] 11 26, 2015. http://www.abs.gov.au/ausstats/abs@.nsf/mf/4610.0.

107. **Australian Human Rights Commission.** eRace Archives - Australian South Sea Islanders. *Australian Human Rights Commission.* [Online] 2016. http://www.humanrights.gov.au/erace-archives-australian-south-sea-islanders.

108. **Daintree Discovery Centre.** Interpretive Guide for Visitors. Mossman, Queensland, Australia : GDG Developments Pty Ltd., 2015.

109. **Queensland Government Department of Environment and Heritage Protection.** Cassowary. *Queensland Government Department of Environment and Heritage Protectio.* [Online] 5 4, 2016. https://www.ehp.qld.gov.au/wildlife/threatened-species/endangered/endangered-animals/cassowary.html.

110. **International Coloured Gemstone Association.** Opal. *International Coloured Gemstone Association.* [Online] 2016. http://www.gemstone.org/index.php?option=com_content&view=article&id=99:sapphire&catid=1:gem-by-gem&Itemid=14.

111. **North Queensland History.** Jezzine Barracks Official Opening, 1964. *North Queensland History.* [Online] 2014. http://northqueenslandhistory.blogspot.ca/2014/04/jezzine-barracks-official-opening-1964.html.

112. **Australian War Museum.** Private James Heather Gordon. *Australian War Museum.* [Online] 2016. https://www.awm.gov.au/people/P10676327/#biography.

113. **Australian Sugar Milling Council.** Australian Sugarcane Industry Overview. *Australian Sugar Milling Council.* [Online] 2016. http://asmc.com.au/industry-overview/.

114. **Gladstone Region.** Engine Room of Industry. *Gladstone Region.* [Online] 2016. http://www.gladstoneregion.info/attractions/industrial-giants.

115. **UNHCR.** UNHCR Main Findings 2014. *UNHCR.* [Online] 2014.
http://www.unhcr.org/56655f4e0.html.

116. **U.S. Navy.** U.S. Navy Climate Change Roadmap. *U.S. Navy.*
[Online] 4 2010. http://www.navy.mil/navydata/documents/CCR.pdf.

117. **Australian Government.** Australian Mineral Commodities.
Department of Industry, Innovation and Science, Australian Government.
[Online] 2015.
http://www.industry.gov.au/resource/Mining/AustralianMineralCommod
ities/Pages/default.aspx.

118. —. Australia's wild rivers. *About Australia, Australian Government.*
[Online] 12 15, 2015. http://www.australia.gov.au/about-
australia/australian-story/australias-wild-rivers.

119. **Reed, A.W.** *Aboriginal Legends - Animal Tales.* Sydney : Reed
New Holland, 1978 .

120. **Darwin, Charles.** *A Naturalist's Voyage Round the World.*
London : John Murray (The Project Gutenberg e-book #3704 July 30,
2012), 1913.

121. **Australian Government.** Statistics. *Australian Bureau of Statistics.*
[Online] 2016. http://www.abs.gov.au/.

122. **Australian Institute of Aboriginal and Torres Strait Islander
Studies.** Aboriginal Australia map. *AIATSIS Australian Institute of
Aborignal and Torres strait Islander Studies.* [Online] 1994.
http://www.aiatsis.gov.au/explore/articles/aboriginal-australia-map.

123. **UNESCO .** Fitzgerald River, Australia Biosphere Reserve
Information. *UNESCO MAB Biosphere Reserves Directory.* [Online] 12
21, 2004.
http://www.unesco.org/mabdb/br/brdir/directory/biores.asp?code=AUL+
08&mode=all.

124. **Mount Isa Mines.** History. *Mount Isa Mines.* [Online] 2016.
http://www.mountisamines.com.au/EN/aboutXMIM/Pages/History.aspx.

125. **Peasley, W. J.** *The Last Of The Nomads.* London : Eye Books Ltd., 2004.

126. **King, Gilbert.** The Most Audacious Australian Prison Break of 1876. *Smithsonian.com History.* [Online] 3 12, 2013. http://www.smithsonianmag.com/history/the-most-audacious-australian-prison-break-of-1876-1804085/.

127. **(Umeek) Atleo, Richard E.** *Principles of Tsawalk, An Indigenous Approach to Global Crisis.* Vancouver : UBC Press, 2011.

Made in the USA
San Bernardino, CA
02 August 2018